Säbeltafche für Husaren=Ober=Officiere.

(Adjust. Vorfchrift pag. 33.)

Military
Fashion

*A comparative history of the uniforms
of the great armies from the 17th century
to the First World War*

John Mollo

Military Fashion

G.P. PUTNAM'S SONS
NEW YORK

Designed by Peter Davis
Photography by Michael Plomer
Photoset in Monophoto Apollo by
B.A.S. Printers Ltd, Wallop, Hampshire
Colour origination by
Colour Workshop Ltd. Hertford
Printed and bound in the Netherlands by
Drukkerij de Lange/van Leer & Co.
N. V. Deventer.

Library of Congress Catalog Card Number:
76-188665

Contents

List of Colour Plates

Introduction

The scientific study of military uniforms is a comparatively new subject which has become very popular in recent years as the warlike occasions of the average man have become rarer, and as the beneficiaries of the 'leisure society' have taken it up as a field for collecting. It is a new science with a very small vocabulary, although in recent years the word 'militaria' has been commonly used to describe the sectors of military collecting not already covered by the older established field of 'arms and armour'. The aim of the following chapters is to present a comparative study of the military fashions of Europe, illustrated by 'militaria' as defined above, and it would be useful to preface this with a brief introduction on the subject of military collecting.

Instruments of war, or 'weapons', have been from the earliest times amongst the most treasured possessions of man, lovingly preserved, and proudly displayed. Furthermore, they were the earliest precision instruments, in the making of which man put every ounce of his skill, for upon their efficiency depended his very existence. Victorious weapons were endowed, in the mind of primitive man, with supernatural powers, and were worshipped by him, while those of the conquered enemy were carried in triumphal processions, and then placed on permanent display in the temples of the victors as visible proof of their prowess in battle. As the decorative arts flourished, these displays of military objects, or 'trophies' became extremely popular *motifs*.

As well as arming himself, primitive man made other preparations for war. He disguised himself, for only when so disguised did man become a warrior, ready to bring fear and death to his enemy. This disguising process took many forms and involved either dressing up, or as in the case of the ancient Greeks in undressing, and gradually acquired a ritual symbolism. Thus, from the earliest times, military dress has had two distinct qualities – the functional and the symbolic – which are still discernible even in the drab uniforms of to-day.

In mediaeval times, armour came to be regarded as a work of art in its own right, and was collected and preserved as such. The coming of gunpowder, however, spelled the end of the *haute époque* of the armourers, and the introduction of regular standing armies during the seventeenth century brought in its wake the modern concept of mass-produced 'uniform' clothing, designed for a functional purpose. Nevertheless, uniforms and accoutrements continued to be collected as trophies of war. The Russians, for example, preserve to this day the standards, gorgets, cuirasses, and weapons which they took from the Swedes at Poltava in 1709. Throughout the eighteenth and nineteenth centuries, states set up arsenals where weapons were stored for use in times of emergency, and where enemy trophies were displayed. By the middle of the eighteenth century, monarchs were regarding their armies not only as fighting units, but also as theatrical groups intended to impress friend and foe alike with their ritualistic ceremonies and displays. Uniforms, once purely functional clothing, became themselves more theatrical, following, and in some cases, setting new trends in the decorative arts. Even so, they were still not regarded as works of art in their own right.

One of the first collectors of 'militaria', as distinct from 'arms and armour' was the Prince Regent, later George IV, who devoted much time and energy to the designing of new uniforms. He used as his inspiration, actual examples sent to him from all over Europe by his relatives and friends, which, when they had been examined and copied, were displayed on the walls of Windsor Castle, where they may be seen to this day.

During the Napoleonic wars, uniforms reached the climax of their development. The global nature of the conflict produced a galaxy of uniforms, which were as splendid as they could only be at a time when tactics and weapons were not yet sufficiently developed to make such splendours impracticable. Rapid changes of political fortune meant that the uniforms of the losers were often packed away while still in good condition, to be preserved and treasured by their wearers – and later by their descendants – although still for personal, family, or political reasons, rather than for any intrinsic aesthetic qualities they might have possessed.

By the end of the nineteenth century, the concept of 'scientific collecting' had become well-established. Originated by numismatists, it had been given a boost by the development of philately, where the aesthetic appearance of an object to be collected had little relevance, and all desirability centred on the collection of sets, and the identification of rarities, flaws, and misprints. This approach spread to the collection of 'military curios'. At first, helmet plates, and badges, were collected for the sake of completing sets, but gradually, as full dress gave way to drab modern fighting uniforms, military objects began to be appreciated as works of art representative of their epoch. But they retained their symbolic connotations of blood and glory – their historical significance, which was and is, a vital part of their desirability. It is perhaps in this historical desirability that 'militaria' differs most from other 'objets de vertu'.

As in other fields, the collector of 'militaria' now studies more than just the object and its historical context. He wants to know how it was made, and by whom; who was responsible for its design, and why that particular design was chosen. For this reason, there is great interest in official regulations and manufacturing specifications which often throw great light on these questions. At the same time, we now find collectors who are interested in military uniforms purely as decorative objects, and who are unmoved by their historical aspects. We even find, as in many other fields, the collector who is more interested in the object as a financial investment, than in either its appearance or history.

A point has now been reached where shortage of supply and corresponding high prices, coupled with problems of conservation and display, have made the collecting of uniforms and head-dress difficult for the average enthusiast. Collecting on a large scale is becoming more and more the prerogative of the state, and the military museum has now taken the place of the arsenal and the earlier temple. The private collector, unless he is very rich or very lucky, now has to content himself with accumulating information rather than objects. As his taste and knowledge increases, so does his capacity for information, with the result that to-day the demand for books on uniforms and other military subjects is greater than could ever have possibly been imagined as little as twenty years ago.

The early experts, enthusiastic and knowledgeable men, in many cases talented artists, accumulated the basic bedrock of our present-day knowledge, but there was little demand for their findings and the bulk of their work remains unpublished. In Great Britain the first, and only, comprehensive history of the uniforms of the British Army, by the late C. C. P. Lawson, did not start appearing until just before the second world war, and had only reached as far as 1810 when the author died in 1967. In France, there is a longer tradition of publishing uniform books, which seem generally to have been produced with more taste than in other countries, although tending to be intensely chauvinistic. The Germans, notably the Knötels, father and son, have made the best attempts so far at producing an illustrated summary of the uniforms of all the armies at all periods, although their *Uniformenkunde* does little more than scratch the surface of our ignorance. The general run of publications, nowadays, dwells closely on regulations describing particular items, on dates of introduction, and on peculiar regimental distinctions. Such works attempt the well-nigh impossible task of telling the reader exactly what a particular regiment wore at a particular time.

The intention of this book, *Military Fashion*, by dealing with objects and influences in a broad manner, was to by-pass this tangled web of detail, much of it undigested, much of it legend, and much of it pure hypothesis, to plot the key-points in the development of European military fashion, and to make a plan of the cross-influences, which the armies of Great Britain, the United States of America, France, Austria, Prussia, and Russia, who seem to me in the long run to have had the most sartorial effect, have had upon each other. It will achieve its purpose if it answers some of the questions, basic to the study of military costume, which I am frequently asked.

I would like to express my thanks to all those who have kindly allowed objects in their collections to be photographed, and those who have assisted at the subsequent sessions; Mr. A. R. Dufty, and the staff of The Armouries, H. M. Tower of London; Mr. W. Reid and the staff of the National Army Museum, whose help, given at a time when they were in the throes of moving to London, has been invaluable; Major A. J. Dickinson and Squadron-Corporal-Major C. W. Frearson, of the Household Cavalry Museum; Major Wilbur, until recently Assistant-curator of the Guards Museum; M. Jean Brunon and M. Raoul Brunon, whose magnificent collection is now part of the Musée de L'Armée; M. Lecomte and the staff of the Musée Royale de L'Armée, Brussels; Dr. Allmayer-Beck and the staff of the Heeresgeschichtliches Museum, Vienna; the Director and staff of the Smithsonian Institution, Washington D.C.; Mr. D. S. Wills for permission to photograph the cavalry buff coat and cuirass now on loan to the Tower of London; my father Eugene Mollo, and my brothers Andrew and Boris Mollo. To the last I am indebted for the great help, involving much time and energy, which he has given to me in organising the selection and photography of the objects illustrated in the book.
London, 1972   JM

I *Gott mit uns*

During the first half of the seventeenth century the continent of Europe was engulfed in an apparently endless series of wars – the culminating struggle between the Reformation and the Counter-Reformation of the previous century. In France, the great Cardinal Richelieu was steering a devious course quelling a Huguenot uprising at home, and then allying himself with the English in support of the Protestant Dutch. On the Eastern borders of Europe, from the Baltic to the Black Sea, the tide of battle ebbed and flowed as Swedes, Poles, Russians, Tartars and Turks all strove to possess themselves of their neighbours' territories. But the most savage and long drawn out of all these conflicts was the great European civil war which became known as the 'Thirty Years War'. This holocaust, so graphically recorded for us in the engravings of Jacques Callot, started in a small way, as a quarrel between a group of Protestant Bohemian nobles and the Holy Roman Emperor, Ferdinand II. But before long nearly every nationality in Europe was to be involved in a full scale war between the Catholics and Protestants, which was to bring untold misery and devastation to great tracts of Germany and to last from 1618 until the Peace of Westphalia in 1648.

In the same way that the politics of Europe were completely altered by the Thirty Years War, so the developments in military science learned by the veteran survivors changed the appearance and behaviour of armies everywhere. At first the participants relied on the methods common throughout the Middle Ages, when armies consisted of gatherings of personal body-guards and retainers, militia raised from the burghers and peasants, and hired mercenaries – the real professionals. Neither the Emperor nor his Protestant adversaries had regular armies as we now know them, and initially they were dependent on the services of free lance commanders, the last of the great *condottieri*. Both Mansfeld, who served the King of Bohemia, and Wallenstein, who organised and led the armies of the Emperor, were typical mercenaries, fighting for profit rather than conviction. Wallenstein in particular would have felt at home in any of our giant industrial concerns; playing the 'Power Game'.

HEADPIECE
Engravings by Jacques Callot, *National Army Museum*

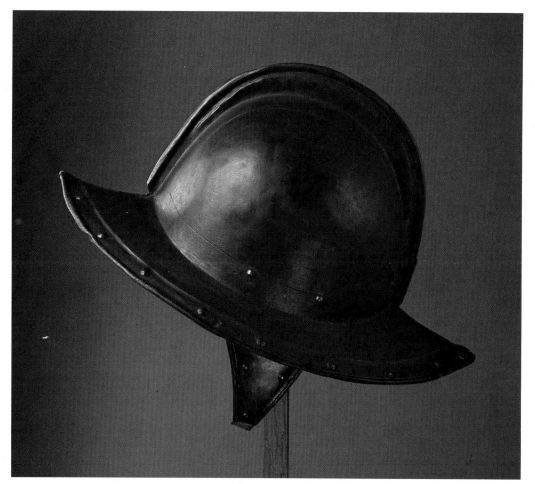

1 GREAT BRITAIN
A typical mid 17th Century pikeman's 'pot' or open-faced helmet. This type of headdress was superseded towards the end of the century by the broad-brimmed felt hat.
H.M. Tower of London

Left
2 THE LOW COUNTRIES
An elaborately etched and gilded example of the 'gorget', or throat protection, which was one of the last pieces of mediaeval armour to be retained. In its later, and smaller, form it became a symbol of rank. Mid 17th Century.
H.M. Tower of London

Right
3 GREAT BRITAIN
A trooper's 'pot', inspired by eastern models and popular until the end of the century. It reappeared again in the late 18th Century in the Austrian army. Mid 17th Century.
H.M. Tower of London

Recalled by Ferdinand in 1631, when the war was going disastrously for the Empire, Wallenstein took over the control of the Imperial war effort – on his own terms. In return for sole command – the Emperor was not even to visit the army, let alone issue orders to it – and power over all military decisions, including promotion and demotion, Wallenstein agreed to provide the necessary funds to raise the largest private army ever known. An immensely wealthy self-made man, he placed his vast resources at the disposal of the Emperor, purely as a commercial venture, from which he hoped to gain more money, more lands, more titles, and perhaps even a crown. He was a brilliant organiser, but the jealousies brought about by his arrogance and greed, led to his assassination in 1634 and on his death his great empire crashed into the dust. It is an indication of the treachery inherent in the mercenary system that two of his assassins were Irishmen and the other two Scotsmen in his service. They were richly rewarded by his enemies, two of them becoming Counts of the Holy Roman Empire. Wallenstein's 'big business' methods included the floating of loans from all the great bankers of his time, the raising of regiments under contract from wealthy nobles or merchants, and luring regiments away from his allies by the offer of higher rates of pay. His 117 North Bohemian estates – an oasis of prosperity and industry – provided grain and fodder for his army, and the factories established at Friedland and filled with German and Italian crafts-men supplied him with the necessary weapons and munitions of war.

Although mercenaries tended to serve where the pay was highest, the nationalities engaged in the Thirty Years War divided themselves pretty clearly according to their religious beliefs. Thus the English, Scots, Dutch and Scandinavians were usually to be found in the Protestant service, and the Spanish, Walloons, Flamands, Lorrainers, Croats, Poles and Ukraine Cossacks served in the Catholic cause; France, although led by a Cardinal, ended up fighting on the Protestant side. An example of the variety of service of a typical mercenary regiment may be found in the history of that commanded by the Scots soldier of fortune, Sir John Hepburn – 'one of the finest soldiers in Christendom' – which was originally raised by Sir Andrew Gray and served as part of the guard of the King of Bohemia until his defeat at the Battle of the White Mountain in 1620. Subsequently commanded by Hepburn the regiment took service with Gustavus Adolphus and formed with three other Scottish regiments the Swedish 'Green' or 'Scots' Brigade. After the death of Gustavus Adolphus, Hepburn took his regiment over to the French, where it became known as the *Régiment d'Hébron*. In 1636 Hepburn was killed before Saverne and the command passed to another Scot, Lord James Douglas, who brought it over to England in 1661. Soon afterwards the regiment returned to France where it was amalgamated with the old Scots *Gardes du Corps* of the French Kings. In 1666 after two years service in Ireland it returned to France, where it served under Turenne against the Dutch; and in 1678, now under the command of George Douglas, Earl of Dumbarton, it returned to England for the last time and was incorporated into the British Army as Dumbarton's Regiment, later the Royal Scots – the 1st Foot and the oldest regiment in the British Army.

It is hardly surprising then, with numerous regiments of such long-standing and experience serving in one European country after another, that the spread of new ideas in weapons and tactics was wide and rapid, and that a considerable uniformity in such matters existed by the end of the Thirty Years War. 'We see' wrote an English officer in 1642, in a treatise on the pike, 'the face of war and the forms of weapons alter almost daily; every nation striving to outwit each other in excellency of weapons'. By 1648 these veteran regiments were beginning to transfer their allegiance from *entrepreneurs* like Mansfeld and Wallenstein, to kings and princes. The era of the national standing army had begun.

Much of the credit for this change must go to Gustavus Adolphus, King of Sweden, who, intervening on the Protestant side, entered Germany in 1630 at the head of an army the like of which had not been seen since the passing of the Roman Legions. Small and compact – its total strength was no more than thirteen thousand, horse, foot and artillery – it was a well disciplined and highly organised body of men. Moreover, unlike its allies and adversaries – mercenaries all – it was a national army, fired by an unswerving loyalty to God and the King. *Gott Mit Uns* was its motto, and its regiments marched and fought bellowing out the solemn psalms and hymns of the Lutheran Church.

Gustavus' army was firmly based on three revolutionary principles. Firstly, the soldiers were conscripted – one man out of every ten on the parish register. Thus, as the bulk of the regiments were named after, and based on, their recruiting areas, they retained a local identity, many of the soldiers knowing their comrades from childhood. By this means a special spirit was fostered, for the men served not for monetary gain but to earn and keep the respect of their families and friends and to serve the King. Secondly, it was paid as regularly as circumstances permitted, some seventy per cent of the King's revenues being allocated to its upkeep.

In return for this – and in contrast to the mercenary, whose pay was sporadic and who was expected to implement it as best he could by living off the land – stealing and pillaging were strictly forbidden. Lastly, the high moral tone imparted to the army by the personal example of the King, and by the large numbers of army pastors, backed by a stern but just discipline, did much to keep down the time-honoured pursuits of the 'brutal and licentious soldiery'. Unfortunately the addition to the army of numerous auxiliary regiments, and the untimely death of Gustavus at Lützen in 1632, led to an adulteration of this high discipline, and by the end of the war the Swedes could pillage with the best, although the reputation for valour and discipline which they maintained for many years under Kniphausen, Torstenson, Banier, Bernard of Saxe-Weimar and others showed that he had trained his subordinates well.

Gustavus Adolphus learned his trade in Flanders under the legendary Prince Maurice of Nassau, at the end of the previous century, when his army was the school for all who wished to acquire military knowledge. Maurice himself had for many years, until his death in 1625, the unrivalled reputation of being the greatest commander in Europe, having taken over the lead in tactics and military discipline previously held by the Spaniards. The Spanish were the first to equip their infantry with fire-arms and have been credited by some authors with the invention of the 'Manual Exercise' – or, more commonly, drill. While most mercenary soldiers had to learn by bitter experience on the field of battle, the Spaniards and the Swiss concentrated on training their raw recruits to handle their arms on the parade ground, supervised by sergeant-majors who used their drill-canes abundantly and enthusiastically.

The reforms of Gustavus Adolphus were for the most part improvements on the innovations of his teacher. The infantry of the period consisted of a mixture of pikemen and musketeers armed with heavy matchlock muskets, which were fired by igniting the charge with a lighted match – a hazardous and lengthy business. Gustavus reduced the proportion of pikes to musketeers and by lightening the musket itself was able to do away with the forked rest, used when firing, which until then had been an indispensible part of the musketeer's equipment. He also developed the principle of paper cartridges containing the charge of powder and ball, which could be carried in a pouch. Formerly the musketeer carried his powder in individual containers hanging from a belt, and his bullets in a little leather pouch. This belt known in England as a 'collar of bandoliers', or more popularly as 'The Twelve Apostles' – there were usually twelve charges to each belt – was not only dangerous, being in close proximity to the musketeer's lighted match, but very noisy, and many a surprise attack was betrayed by the wind rattling the tin containers. By these means, and by concentrating on the training of the individual infantryman, Gustavus improved the fire-power of his regiments and increased their flexibility. Unlike his opponents, he could manoeuvre his infantry in lines, squares, and even triangles, if circumstances required. The Swedish infantry, formed into Brigades of about 2,000 men each, introduced the tactics of firing six ranks deep, and then charging forward with their *Schweinsfeder*, a short pike pointed at either end which served either as a weapon or as a defensive stake planted in the ground, a practice reminiscent of the Roman Legionaries and the English Archers at Agincourt. To each regiment of infantry, Gustavus allocated a light 'galloper' gun, drawn by two horses, a custom which was to be copied widely by other armies.

The Swedish cavalry was composed of regiments of horse and dragoons. During the sixteenth century cavalry had consisted of heavily armoured cuirassiers and lancers, developments of the mediaeval knight; light cavalry, armed with spears and pistols; and what the English usually referred to as 'shot on horseback' – mounted men armed with some form of carbine or short musket. The armoured German *Reiter* were for a long time the most effective cavalry in Europe, and their tactics of trotting up to enemy infantry in successive lines and blowing a hole in their serried ranks with their long horse-pistols, became the accepted practice. To counteract them Gustavus made use of 'harquebusiers' – later known simply as 'horse' – who were a mixture of cuirassiers relieved of most of their armour and armed with a short wheel-lock or flintlock carbine, a pair of pistols, a sword, and some-times a short pole-axe – and dragoons. Dragoons were a cheap form of cavalry, introduced in France about 1554, who were in reality infantry mounted on horses, as a means of transportation to the battlefield, where they dismounted and fought as musketeers. Unlike the six-deep charges 'on the trot' of the *Reiter*, Gustavus formed his horse three-deep, taught them to reserve their fire when they charged, and to charge home at a gallop using the sword. The dragoons were used as light cavalry to oppose the formidable Croats of the Imperialists, whose presence foreshadowed the appearance of various forms of light cavalry, dressed in outlandish national costumes, in the eighteenth century.

In 1642, six years before the Peace of Westphalia ended the Thirty Years War, civil war broke out in England between Charles I and his parliament. In common with other European monarchs the King had his permanent regiments of guards, both horse and foot and the balance of the armies on either side was made up of 'trained bands' of militia and of regiments raised by influential noblemen and landowners. The tactics employed on both sides were influenced by both Dutch and Swedish models; but it is not until the formation of the New Model Army by Oliver Cromwell in 1645, with its hymn-singing redcoats, that we see another body of soldiers as organised and as well disciplined as the 'Swedish brigades' of Gustavus Adolphus.

For the first fifty years of the seventeenth century the clothes worn by these polyglot bands of soldiery followed closely the cut and fashion of the civilian dress of the time, with the exception of the various royal and princely bodyguards who wore uniform clothing often of a style dating back to an

4 GREAT BRITAIN
Harquebusier's equipment
and clothing, *c*. 1640. The
buff or white coloured coat
and belts, and the cuirass
and helmet were to remain
vital elements in the dress
of German and Russian
cuirassiers until 1914.
H.M. Tower of London

earlier age. Typical of these were the English Yeomen of the Guard, in their red coats with full puffed sleeves and pleated skirts banded with blue, with the Tudor Rose and Crown embroidered in gold front and back, unchanged since the reign of Henry VII, and the Swiss Guard of the French King, in their red, yellow and blue slashed doublets and coloured codpieces. The bulk of the fighting men, however, were dressed like their more peaceful brethren in 'Suits of Cloathes' consisting of a coarse linen shirt, voluminous cloth breeches liberally adorned with buttons and gathered at the knee with ribbons, a close-fitting heavily padded doublet – an example of a civilian garment which had military origins – woollen stockings and shoes. On their heads they wore broad-brimmed hats with high crowns, and over their doublets a short cape, or *casaque*, which by an ingenious arrangement of buttons could be closed round the body to become a short 'coat'. Officers were more elaborately dressed than their men, following the latest fashions as closely as their taste or purse allowed. This difference is particularly noticeable during the 1640s when the doublet became very short and the 'petticoat breeches' very wide, leaving a wide expanse of shirt exposed in between. Both officers and men wore their hair long and usually had moustaches and beards. In this connection there was very little difference between the English 'Cavaliers' and 'Roundheads' – contrary to popular belief.

The suits of the men, being ordered and manufactured in bulk by the proprietor of a regiment, achieved a measure of uniformity, and for the sake of economy they were simply made of stout cloth dyed a fast colour like red or blue. These were by no means the only colours used, and in the opposing armies at the Battle of Edgehill in 1642 there were regiments dressed in white, green, grey, purple and orange.

Understandably enough, this kaleidoscopic range of colours, often repeated on opposing sides, led to confusion in the thick black smoke of battle, and to avoid this it became the custom throughout Europe for armies to adopt some form of identifying feature – sometimes for a whole war, sometimes for one particular operation. These 'field signs' as they came to be called usually consisted of sashes or 'Scarves', hat feathers, or arm bands of a particular colour. Thus during the Thirty Years War, of the troops on the Protestant side, the Swedes wore blue sashes, the Danes blue and orange sashes and white hat feathers – changing in 1625 to red and yellow – the Dutch orange, and the French white. On the Catholic side, the Imperial and Spanish troops wore red sashes, and the Saxons green. During the English Civil War the Royalists wore red and the Parliamentarians tawny-orange, the livery colour of the Earl of Essex. The Royalists on occasion wore crosses embroidered on the sleeves of their coats, in the same way that servants in livery often bore their master's arms on their sleeves. The more temporary sort of field signs included such things as green boughs or twigs worn in the hat, pieces of paper or handkerchiefs. Many of these signs were kept secret until the day of the action and many were last minute improvisations, as when the French on one occasion wore their shirts over their coats in an attack. The disadvantage of these signs was that they were very easy to copy or remove from a fallen enemy, and often provided a means of penetrating behind the enemy lines or of carrying out some other *ruse de guerre*. Many of the colours and emblems used for field-signs remained after the introduction of national uniform as cockades or sashes.

Apart from their clothing, soldiers carried with them their weapons and equipment, which had a certain uniformity of design and manufacture. The infantry consisted of pikemen and musketeers, but, although their days were already numbered, it was the former who were considered the superior soldiers. The 18-foot-long pike required considerable strength to handle, so the biggest recruits were chosen for this service, in much the same way that grenadiers were at a later date, while the musketeers were mostly small men. At first the pikemen had a helmet or 'combe-cap', a corselet or 'back and breast pieces' of steel, a 'gorget' to protect his throat and 'tassets' to protect his thighs. In the army of Gustavus the pikemen retained their helmets and corselets, which did not really go out of fashion until the 1650s. By 1671 an English officer could write that 'When we see batallions of pikes, we see them everywhere naked, unless it be Netherlands'. In addition to his pike, the pikeman had a sword which he carried in a leather belt over his right shoulder, and stout gauntlets to protect his hands from splinters.

Musketeers had originally worn helmets as well, but they soon abandoned them in favour of broad-brimmed civilian hats or woollen stocking caps, known in England as 'Monmouth caps'. Over their cassocks or coats they wore two leather shoulder belts – one the 'collar of bandoliers' and the other for the sword. With their matchlock muskets they carried a forked rest to support the barrel when firing, which was suspended from the wrist by a leather thong when not in use. Both musketeers and pikemen carried haversacks or 'snapsacks' for their rations and necessaries.

Of the cavalry, the harquebusiers or regiments of horse wore helmets and corselets. The helmets were of two kinds: the 'pot', or open-faced helmet, and the triple-barred, lobster-tailed helmet, copied from the Turks. The former was superseded by the latter, which was still in use at the end of the century. Back and breast plates went out gradually after 1650, for, as a contemporary observed, 'it will kill a man to serve in a whole cuirass'. Perhaps the most typical garment of horse, of whatever nationality, was the thick buff coat. These coats, which were worn under the corselet, were very expensive items, and were a much sought after form of booty. They had a curious long term effect on the dress of heavy cavalry, in the persistent use of buff as a colour for the jackets or waistcoats of cuirassiers during the eighteenth and nineteenth centuries. Horse also wore high leather boots which were made gradually heavier and stiffer as the century wore on.

Dragoons were dressed like infantry, except that they favoured the cap instead of the hat, probably because it made their muskets easier to sling when riding, and some form of boots instead of shoes. From early on, their cap seems to have been of a special pattern, based on the 'Montero' cap – a brimless cloth or velvet cap with a turned-up front which was sometimes embroidered. The exact origin of this type of cap is unknown – it may have come from Spain or perhaps Eastern Europe – but it was the forerunner of a whole range of headwear worn by dragoons and grenadiers during the seventeenth and eighteenth centuries.

Trumpeters and kettledrummers of cavalry, and drums and fifes of infantry – bands of 'Musick' had not yet made their appearance on the battlefield – wore coats or cassocks with hanging sleeves, very reminiscent of the mediaeval herald's tabard, in the livery colours, or bearing the arms of their colonel.

The first appearance of a uniform which extended beyond the bounds of a regiment came with the outbreak of the Thirty Years War, when Wallenstein clothed his army with cloth manufactured in his own mills; but the process was taken a step further by Gustavus Adolphus, who seems to have clothed each of his brigades in a different colour. The Green or Scots Brigade we have already met, but there were others as evidenced by the complaints of the citizens of Hagenau in Alsace, occupied by the Swedish army three times in eighteen months: 'We have had blue-coats, and red-coats and now come the yellow coats. God have pity on us'.

Cromwell's new model army went even further, being 'redcoats all . . . distinguished by the several facings of their coats'. Their subsequent amalgamation, after the restoration of Charles II, with his red coated guards – red and blue being the English Royal livery – established red early on as the standard colour of the British Army.

Before, however, turning to the development of regular uniformed armies during the latter part of the century we must turn our steps eastwards to examine the influence on military dress of the countries which formed the eastern frontiers of Christendom. To the east and south of the Holy Roman Empire, and allied to it through force of circumstances were the Croats and Hungarians, warlike people whose eastern and southern frontiers were under constant attack by the Turks. The Croats who served in central Europe as light cavalry in the Imperial army, and the Hungarian 'Hussars' – a form of national militia raised to defend the frontier towns – were both dressed in national costume owing much to the east. High pointed cloth caps, trimmed with fur and decorated with a feather plume, long brightly coloured *kaftans*, fastened across the front with numerous braid loops, or cords and wooden toggles, and soft leather boots, usually red or yellow, formed the basis of their dress. The light cavalry were armed with lances, curved sabres of oriental design, and pistols, while the infantry, divided into pikemen and musketeers, carried the usual equipment of the time.

To the east of the Empire the lands of the dual monarchy of Poland-Livonia – formed in 1386 to resist the onslaughts of the Teutonic Knights in the west, and the Crimean Tartars in the south – stretched from the Baltic to the Black Sea, peopled at one end by Lithuanian Tartars, and at the other by Ukraine Cossacks. The Poles were renowned for their light cavalry, the bulk of whom were dressed and armed in similar fashion to the Croats and Hungarians. They did, however, have one feature which was to be of considerable importance later on – their square-crowned fur-trimmed caps or *chapska*. Poland also retained, for much longer than anybody else, the feudal mounted man-at-arms, or *Gens d'Armes*, who went to war surrounded by a knot of his own servants. The 'Noble Comrades' (*Towarisch Hussarski*) as they were called, were clad in full armour and carried lances with banderolles, like mediaeval knights, but they had two very distinctive additional features – a pair of huge feathered wings attached to their shoulders, and leopard-skin cloaks. Their servants (*Podstowi*) were armed as lancers as well, but were less elaborately accoutred. Like the French *Gens d'Armes*, the Noble Comrades were counted up by Masters, so that a hundred Masters or lances, formed a thousand horsemen. In battle the servants formed a second rank of small squadrons, while their masters attacked in a single rank. The Ukraine, or *zaparozhe* Cossacks in Polish service, wore taller fur caps with a cloth bag, shorter *kaftans*, baggy trousers and soft boots, and were armed with lances, sabres, pistols, and carbines. Even as early as this their costume showed all the traditional elements of later Cossack uniforms.

Although the Poles were redoubtable soldiers, their intensely reactionary feudal nobility prevented the country progressing as fast as its neighbours, with the result that Poland gradually lost the opportunity of becoming one of the great European powers. By the middle of the seventeenth century she had acquired two implacable enemies in Sweden and Russia. Between 1610 and 1613 the Poles were in possession of Moscow itself; but by 1654, worsted by the Swedes and faced with open revolt on the part of the Cossacks, who offered their allegiance to Russia, her short-lived eminence came to an end. The differences between Poland and Russia were so great – one a feudal monarchy, Catholic in religion, and European in culture, and the other a despotism, fierce in the Orthodox faith, and only slightly affected by

5 THE EMPIRE
A Croatian volunteer, *c.* 1650. Eastern European folk costume of the Thirty Years War period, partly reproduced in this example, was to provide many of the elements for later hussar dress.
Heeresgeschichtliches Museum, Vienna

Western ideas – that one of them had to succumb. It was the weakness and misfortune of the Poles that smoothed the path of Russian ascendancy.

The expansion of Russia dates from the middle years of the sixteenth century, when the first *Tsar*, Ivan IV, known as 'The Terrible' defeated the Tartars on the eastern and southern borders of Muscovy. Having thus shaken off the 'Tartar Yoke', he was able to turn his attentions to the west, in an attempt to gain an outlet on the Baltic seaboard. Early on in his reign Ivan established the nucleus of a regular army by forming regiments of *Streltsy*, and in his later years, a period of the most brutal repressions, he surrounded himself with a private army of cut-throats – the *Oprichnina* – whose coal black horses, black garb, and emblem of a dog's head and broom fastened to their saddles, became a symbol of terror throughout the land.

By the middle of the seventeenth century, the bulk of the Russian army still consisted of *Streltsy*, formed into regiments, each named after its colonel, in the Western fashion. During their century of existence they had become a powerful caste, not unlike the Turkish Janissaries, able and willing to use their swords to influence political events. Each regiment was divided into *sotnias*, or hundreds, and unlike the Russian provisional levies, was armed with muskets as well as swords. Their eastern dress was similar to that of the Poles, each regiment having a set uniform. Their pointed caps were of brightly coloured cloth – cherry, pink, grey, brown or green – trimmed with fur, and their long *kaftans*, reaching almost to the ground, were lined with a contrasting colour, and trimmed with gold or silver lace for officers, and coloured braid for the men. On their feet they wore yellow, red or green boots. The *Streltsy* were armed with a sword and a matchlock, supported when firing on a rest in the form of a short pole-axe or *berdish*. Towards the end of the century these were replaced by short pikes, probably the *Schweinsfeder* of Gustavus Adolphus.

Parallel with the *Streltsy* there existed a number of regiments of 'Soldiers', officered by foreigners, and divided into pikemen and musketeers, like Western regiments. First raised during the reign of Michael the first Romanov Tsar (1613–45) there were six of these regiments by 1630, each consisting of 1,600 men divided into eight companies of 120 Musketeers and 80 Pikemen each. In 1642 two regiments of 'Elite Soldiers' were raised, officered entirely by Russians. The 'Soldiers' were dressed in western fashion with combe-cap, doublet, breeches, stockings and shoes, the pikemen wearing corselets.

Unfortunately for the *Streltsy*, the excesses committed by them immediately after the death of Tsar Theodore III, in 1682, were witnessed by the young Prince Peter, later Peter the Great, who conceived a violent hatred and distrust of them. During the Regency of his mother, Sophia, Peter retired to his estates, where he raised two 'Toy Regiments' from friends and servants, from which stemmed the nucleus of the Russian Guards and a completely modernised Russian Army.

II *The Last Word of Kings*

The Peace of Westphalia, and the end of the Thirty Years War, broke the power of the Hapsburg Emperors, and left France the supreme arbiter in Europe. Germany, whose burghers and peasants had borne the full weight of the thirty years of warfare, was reduced to a loose confederation of states only nominally under the sway of the new Emperor, Leopold I. For the time being, life in the Imperial capital was peaceful, although, after a period of comparative calm, the Turks were soon to resume their attacks on Hungary and Transylvania. In Austria, it was said, 'every day was Sunday'. Spain, proud, bigoted, and swollen out with New World riches and in the decline, was a fine prize for the greedy. The Protestant powers – England, the Dutch 'United Provinces' and Sweden – unable to equal the power of France, were for the time being prepared to be allied with her. Poland, alternating between 'vast conquests and mortal peril' was fully engaged with Russia and Sweden, and it was only in the eastern German provinces of Prussia and Pomerania that the seeds of a yet unnoticed power, alien to France, were being sown by the 'Great Elector', Frederick William of Brandenburg.

In 1659 Cardinal Mazarin died and out into the sunlight of the European scene stepped the young King of France, Louis XIV, eager to embark upon his career as an absolute monarch. By 1663, Sir William Temple could refer to him as 'that great comet which has risen rapidly – the King of France who wants not merely to be gazed at but to be admired by the whole world'.

From the first, Louis XIV directed his foreign policy towards two objectives – the restoration to France of her 'natural frontiers', and the destruction of what was left of the Hapsburg Empire. In June 1667 a French army of 30,000 men under Marshal Turenne struck at the Spanish Netherlands, crossing the Sambre and mopping up (in a series of leisurely seiges, supervised by the King and watched by an admiring court) the towns of Tournai, Douai, and Lille, all of which were retained by France in the Peace of Aix-la-Chapelle which ended the war in 1668. The Dutch Republic, however, alarmed at the growing conquests of the French, entered into a 'Triple Alliance' with England and Sweden, which affront to his ambitions so

HEADPIECE
Eighteenth century
engraving of 'The Manual
Exercise of the Foot Guards'

27

infuriated Louis that he set about planning the eventual destruction of the obstinate Dutch. He took his time however, and between 1668 and 1672 prepared his revenge with consummate skill. In the field of diplomacy, he managed not only to entice away all the allies of the Dutch, but also to sign a treaty of neutrality with his arch-enemy the Emperor, who was otherwise engaged with an uprising in Hungary. But at the same time he began improving and developing the army which he had inherited, with the aid of Vauban and Louvois, his War Minister. Under their able guidance the whole administration of the French army was overhauled. New methods of pay were devised and reserve depots of supplies, weapons, and ammunition were set up, giving the army a professional superiority it was to retain for the rest of the century. From this period date all the sophistications and refinements which were to form the basis of military science in the eighteenth century. The flat terrain of the Low Countries, and the lack of natural barriers, made the successful capture or defence of strongly fortified places a matter of first importance, and sieges became the most common of military operations. Louis was fortunate in having Vauban, the greatest military engineer of his age, at his side to direct the lengthy and complicated sieges which the King loved so much – and to reorganise the artillery and engineering branches of the army – for Louis himself was not a great innovator or practitioner in the field, and his constant presence in the field with his Court was far from helpful to his commanders. This emphasis on siege warfare brought into prominence a weapon which had in fact been in use for some time. The grenade, named after the Spanish *granada* (pomegranate) – a hollow shell filled with powder and exploded by a fuse – had been first introduced during the last years of the sixteenth century, and used intermittently since; but the frequent need for grenadiers to storm the *glâcis* and lead the assault into the breach of a besieged fortress led to a great increase in their number, and within the space of a very few years all the major armies of Europe had introduced companies of grenadiers into their ranks.

After the Thirty Years War the Swedish system of drill and tactics, perfected by Gustavus Adolphus, and the Dutch system of Maurice of Nassau, were the two main methods of training armies throughout Europe, with the Dutch system temporarily in the ascendant. Until 1662 the French seem to have paid little attention to drill and discipline, but in that year Louis XIV took into his service a certain Monsieur Martinet – a Dutchman, whose name 'is become among our military gentlemen a term of sneer and reproach' – to instruct his infantry in the Dutch manner. The Dutch style of drill, which was also used by the British and Imperial armies can be easily recognised in prints of the period as the various motions are always shown being carried out with the feet apart. This style of drill dates from a time when the matchlock and its lighted match had to be kept well away from the body for fear of an explosion. The old weapons were also very heavy and 'violent and constrained attitudes' were necessary in order to enable the soldier to perform the motions, also making it necessary for him to exercise in open order with an interval of three feet between each man. Two important developments were now to make this form of arms drill obsolete, and the French for all their military prowess were the last to realise it. The gradual introduction of the firelock or snaphaunce musket, which needed no rest, and the 'plug bayonet' which fitted into the muzzle of the musket, tended to push the pikeman into the background. The invention of the socket bayonet, which slipped over the barrel and enabled infantry to fire with the bayonet fixed – credited alternatively to Turenne and the Scots General Mackay at Killiecrankie – led eventually to faster infantry manoeuvres and volley-firing. But these were gradual changes which did not come to full flower until the

6 SWEDEN
A version of the long coat
or 'justaucorps', inspired by
the 'kaftan', showing
characteristics of 'uniform'
clothing. Second half of the
17th Century.
H.M. Tower of London

beginning of the eighteenth century. Cavalry, forgetting the example of Gustavus Adolphus, were tending to slip back into their old ways and relying on the pistol more than the sword, and made no tactical progress whatsoever for the remainder of the century.

In England, the period between 1651, when the Civil War came to an end, and 1661, when Charles II was restored to the throne, marked the beginning of British naval and colonial activity, which took the form of a sea war with the Dutch (1652–4) and the seizure of Jamaica from the Spanish by a British expeditionary force (1655). After the Restoration the control of the militia, which could only be raised for service at home, and of the military and naval forces of the country, passed to the King, and Charles found himself in possession of a small standing army. His marriage to Catherine of Braganza and the acquisitions of Tangier and Bombay as part of her dowry, turned his foreign policy more towards 'trade and plantations' than interference in the affairs of Europe, but some cunning diplomacy on the part of Louis XIV involved him in the Dutch wars of 1665–7 and 1672–4, both of which were fought mainly at sea. The bloodless revolution against his Catholic brother James II who succeeded him, led eventually to the accession to the English throne in 1688, of William of Orange, the Stadtholder of the Dutch Republic, and Louis XIV's older adversary, and almost immediately to the first appearance of the regular British army on the continent of Europe.

The era of national military uniforms was now beginning in Europe, but there was little as yet to distinguish them from civilian dress, or to connect them with a particular state, apart from the basic colours used. And here it was possible to detect something, which beginning as a coincidence, developed into a politically significant feature of uniform – the adoption of white or grey uniforms by Catholic countries, and dark blue, red or green by Protestants. Another development occurred in the wide use of national and royal badges or emblems, in addition to sashes of national colours. The emergence of national – as opposed to feudal or mercenary armies – meant that the allegiance of the troops was now owed to the state, which in the seventeenth and eighteenth centuries meant the monarch himself; and the expression of this allegiance increasingly took the form of wearing the cypher of the monarch or the various heraldic badges of his family on uniforms and equipment. Although in a sense this was a return to the feudal practice of heraldry, in effect it was for a different purpose. In earlier times, heraldry had provided a means of identification on the battlefield, which was not provided by the colour of the soldiers' coats. Now it served as a reminder to the soldier where his loyalty lay – he, his uniform, his equipment, and his weapons belonged to his monarch. The gorget, as the badge of rank of the officer, was an early vehicle for the display of the monarch's cypher and arms.

Civilian dress in the second half of the seventeenth century established a form which was to remain unchanged in its basic essentials until the French Revolution; and as in most other fields, in the world of fashion French influence was supreme. The hat, still the favourite form of wear for soldier and civilian alike, was now being worn with first one side of the brim and then the other turned up, and it only required the third side to be turned up for it to become the three-cornered hat or *tricorne* of the eighteenth century. Military hats were usually bound with coloured or white tape, and had a cord encircling their low crowns. When the hat was turned up, the brim was held in place by some form of tie, and this soon became another suitable place for the display of national cockades – the remnants of the old field signs. Officers' hats were usually liberally decorated with feathers and ribbons which offered the same scope for national display. The hair was worn long, and, in the case of officers, had developed by 1700 into the long full-bottomed wig. One of the earliest references to the pigtail occurs in 1684 when James Douglas, Colonel of the Scots Regiment of Foot Guards, ordered the men to 'tye the hair back with a ribbon' to keep it from blowing in their eyes when firing.

The biggest change was the substitution of the long coat and waistcoat for the old suit of coat and doublet. The long coat first appeared about 1660, and was originally a very simple garment with open skirts stitched at the waist, collarless, and with short sleeves turned back to form wide cuffs, revealing the shirt gathered at the wrist. A scarf or neck cloth, which developed into the cravat – copied from and named after the Croat soldiers of the Emperor – was worn round the neck, and here again an opportunity was taken for displaying regimental differences by having them made of coloured cloths, a tradition which was kept on in the Prussian Army with the use of coloured stocks, and by American-influenced armies of the present day who wear coloured silk scarves when on parade.

By 1680 the coat had become more elegant in cut; by 1700 it had acquired voluminous skirts, gathered in pleats on the hips, and was much shorter, just reaching to the knee. The 'vest' or waistcoat, was of similar length and cut as the coat and sometimes had long sleeves which appeared below the coat cuffs. The coat or justaucorps, as it was called in France, was obviously derived from the eastern *kaftan*, already described as being the normal dress of the Hungarians, Croats, Poles, Russians and other eastern peoples, and the fact that it was sometimes known in France as the coat '*à la Polaque*' suggests that its origin was recognised at the time. The English diarist, John Evelyn, writing in 1666, describes the King putting on his 'Eastern dress . . . a comely vest after the Persian mode'.

The coats of the nobility and gentry – amongst whom we should include military officers – were elaborately trimmed with gold or silver lace, or with froggings or *Brandenbourgs*, also derived from the *kaftan*. The coats of the poorer classes, which provided the basic pattern of the soldiers' coat, had a single row of closely spaced buttons down the front, and horizontally placed pocket flaps low down on each front skirt. By 1700, breeches had become very plain but full, and continued to be worn gathered at the knee, together with coarse shoes and stockings. On campaign the soldier usually wore a second pair of stockings to protect his breeches from the mud, but after 1700 gaiters or 'spatterdashes' came into use.

Helmets and corselets for infantry were gradually being discarded so that by the 1670s the only difference between pikemen and musketeers, apart from their weapons, were the bandoliers of the latter. The gradual introduction of the firelock did away with the bandolier in favour of the *cartouche* box, and the wide use of the bayonet led to the adoption of a waistbelt, which by drawing in the waist of the rather shapeless coat contributed even further to the eighteenth century silhouette.

Officers carried 'espontoons', and their rich clothing was given some semblance of uniform by the sash and gorget, the last remnant of armour which was now becoming a means of distinguishing rank. Sergeants carried halberts, useful for dressing the lines in action or on parade, and their coats were made different to the men's by the addition of gold or silver lace on the back seams, cuffs and pockets. Cavalry, during the second half of the seventeenth century, wore much the same basic clothing as the infantry. The regiments of horse, in addition to their hats, coats, breeches and stockings, usually wore back and breast plates, a buff coat, boots and sometimes a helmet, while dragoons wore caps of various shapes and leggings, and were generally armed and equipped as infantry even down to the musicians who carried side-drums and *hautbois*.

Following the principle of 'Without uniform no order; without order, no army', Louvois set about giving France an army worthy of her, and one of his first reforms was to make the state responsible for the clothing of the army, as opposed to the Colonel-Proprietors of regiments. From 1668 some regiments had worn uniform, and Louvois held these up as an example to the others, but no pressure was used – for obvious economic reasons, regiments were not asked to change all their clothing at one fell swoop – and it was only gradually during the ten years between 1670 and 1680 that uniform came into general use.

Louvois was very insistent that all unnecessary luxury should be avoided, and he often had to remonstrate with colonels of regiments on the subject of useless lace and trimmings. All he was concerned about was that the uniform of the soldier should be of good French cloth, and as alike as possible to the recruit's own clothing, to avoid problems of cut and fit. In October 1672, Louvois informed colonels that the King would distribute a *justau-corps* – presumably of good grey drugget – to each soldier and the first major step had been taken.

Slowly the grey-white coat became general for infantry, the colour of the cuffs and linings being the only difference between regiments. A few foreign regiments kept their old colours – the Swiss and the Irish had always worn red – and the *Maison du Roi* who had been the first to be completely clothed by the State, kept the red, white and blue royal livery of France. In 1670 the thirty 'old Corps' of French Infantry were each given a grenadier company, dressed in fur-trimmed cloth caps similar to those worn by the Poles.

As in other European armies, the French cavalry consisted of horse and dragoons. In 1676 the dragoons were given red or blue coats and the *bonnet à flamme* – or fur-trimmed cap with a hanging cloth bag, similar to the early grenadier cap; and in 1690 the horse were given uniform clothing, blue with red facings for royal or princely regiments, and grey with red or blue facings for the remainder.

The development of military uniform in England and Scotland followed closely the fashions being set across the Channel. The remnants of the Parliamentary army, and the Royalist regiments which had accompanied Charles II in his exile, were amalgamated to form a standing army clothed generally in red, an exception being the Royal Horse Guards clothed in the blue livery of the Earl of Oxford. A painting of Charles II leaving for England shows what is probably Lord Wentworth's foot guards wearing buff coats over their short red coats, and helmets. By 1670 the short coat and the fall-down linen collar, so typical of the Civil War period, had given way to the long *justaucorps* and waistcoat worn with a neck cloth. At first pikemen kept their corselets and helmets, and occasionally they wore coats of the reverse colours of the musketeers, but by 1672 they were dressed exactly like the musketeers in hats and coats, although they sometimes wore a sash as a distinguishing mark.

With the addition of Tangier to the possessions of the British Crown, regiments of both cavalry and infantry were raised for garrison duties. The numerous paintings of this period provide much useful evidence about their dress and depict amongst other things early attempts at a special hot-weather clothing. As on the mainland of Europe, the firelock was slowly superseding the matchlock, although it was not until the reign of William III that the proportion of firelocks was as much as half. Plug bayonets seem to have come into use in the British Army about 1662.

In 1678, eight years after France and fourteen years after Austria, grenadier companies were added to infantry regiments, and for the first time the braid loops which were to become so typical a feature of British infantry uniforms made their appearance. The 'looped clothes' of the grenadiers were again directly influenced by the *kaftan*, and this eastern appearance was accentuated in the deliberate attempts to make grenadiers look as outlandish and terrifying as possible. 'Now were brought into service a new sort of soldier called Grenadiers' wrote John Evelyn after seeing some exercising at Hounslow in 1678, 'who were dexterous in flinging hand grenades. Everyone having a pouch full. They had furred caps with coped crowns like Janizaries which made them look very fierce, and some had long hoods hanging down behind as we picture fools. The clothing being likewise piebald, yellow and red. . . .' At first these grenadier caps were very low with a cloth crown and fur trimming, but by the time of James II they had become cloth caps with a stiffened cloth front – either square or mitre-shaped, reminiscent of the descriptions of the old 'Montero cap'.

Charles II's brother, James Duke of York, who had served under Turenne and was a keen observer of the reforms which Louvois had introduced into the French army, came to the throne in 1684, and during his short reign as James II, brought the British army up to a very high standard, taking great pride in the formation of 'the best paid, the best equipped, and the most sightly troops of any in Europe'. The description of the coronation of James II by Sandford gives a very good description of the appearance of a British private soldier of the period:

'. . . The Private Soldiers (of the First Regiment of Foot Guards) were all new clothed in coats of broad cloth lined and faced with blew. Their hats were black laced about with silver, turned up and garnished with blew ribands. Their breeches were blew broadcloth, and their stockings of blew worsted. . . .'

'The Musketeers were armed with snaphaunce muskets with sanguine barrels, 3 foot 8 inches in length, good swords in waist belts and collars of bandoliers and the Pikemen pikes 16 foot long each headed with a three square point of steel, good swords in broad shoulder belts also about their waists sashes or scarfs of white worsted fringed with blew.

'The Grenadiers cloathed as the Musketeers but distinguished by caps of red cloth lined with blew shalloon and laced with silver galoon about the edges and on the frontlets of the said caps (which were very large and high) was embroidered the Kings cypher and crown.

'Each of these Grenadiers was armed with a long carbine strapt the barrel three foot 2 inches in length and a cartouch box bionet grenado pouch and a hammer hatchet.'

The officers of the same regiment wore elaborate suits in a wide variety of rich materials, their rank being indicated by their 'corselets' or gorgets. Those of the captains were gilt; the lieutenants had 'steel polished and sanguined and studded with nails of gold', and the ensigns silver plate.

The nucleus of the British Cavalry was formed by the Troops of Life Guards formed in 1660, and the Royal Horse Guards who were added to the establishment in 1661. Later, various regiments of horse clothed in crimson, as opposed to red, were raised – the regiment raised for service in Tangier subsequently becoming the 1st or Royal Dragoons. In 1681 a second regiment of Dragoons, the Scots Greys, was formed in Scotland; until 1687, when they changed to red coats faced with blue, they wore grey coats.

The horse wore hats and crimson coats. The buff coats of the earlier part of the reign of Charles II gradually developed into a buff waistcoat or 'vest' worn under the coat. The triple barred helmet seems to have been retained until 1677 – in Tangier at least – and after that cavalrymen usually wore a steel skull cap or 'pot' under their hats, while the back and breast plates were kept in store and only handed out when required. At the beginning of the reign, horse were armed with a pair of pistols and a sword carried in a shoulder belt, but after 1677 they were issued with carbines.

In 1673 a troop of dragoons, or 'Horse Grenadiers' – enlisted men not gentlemen – was added to the Troops of Life Guards. The observant Mr Evelyn was a bit late spotting them this time, and it is not until December 1683 that he writes, 'The King had now augmented his Guards with a new sort of Dragoons, who carried also grenadoes and were habited after the Polish manner, with long peaked caps very fierce and fantastical'. Like the Infantry Grenadiers, the coats of the Horse Grenadiers were looped down the front, on the cuffs, and on the pocket flaps.

The Dragoons wore red coats – except for the Royals, who kept their original crimson – hats, or fur trimmed caps – the *bonnet à flamme* of the French dragoons. As most of the men – except the horseholders – fought on foot, they probably wore something similar to the leather leggings, laced or buckled down the sides and with stiff tops, worn by the French dragoons. In 1672 their weapons consisted of a halberd and pair of pistols each for the N.C.O.s and twelve other men, and matchlocks, bayonets and swords for the remainder. In 1687, they had 'strapt' snaphaunce muskets, cartouche boxes, bayonets, grenado pouches and hammer hatchets; between 1695 and 1697 they were no longer issued with pistols and grenado pouches.

In 1671 Louis XIV had completed his warlike preparations, and in May 1672, having passed in review his army of over 100,000 men – probably the largest army yet seen in the western world – he marched against the Dutch without declaring war. In the six years of fighting which followed his victorious army established France's supremacy in Europe. By the Peace of Nijmegen, which ended the war in 1678, Louis had not only made territorial gains at the expense of the Emperor, but had also considerably strengthened France's vulnerable northern frontier. The war had heralded the arrival of two newcomers to the field of European politics, the Elector of Brandenburg and the King of Sweden, the first as the only ally of the Dutch and the second as an ally of Louis XIV. Although both rulers ended the war on the same side – against the French – they had in fact met in battle in 1675 when the Swedes were defeated by the Prussians at Fehrbellin.

The 'Great Elector' Frederick William of Brandenburg, the creator of the Prussian army, had concerned himself ever since his accession in 1640 with the reoganisation and enlargement of his territories. After the Peace of Westphalia he played a cunning game between the Swedes and the Poles which resulted in both kingdoms recognising him as sovereign Duke of Prussia. During the latter part of the century he followed a course of political expediency, sometimes siding with Louis XIV and sometimes with the Emperor, at the same time gradually building up the Brandenburg-Prussian army, until it emerged at Fehrbellin as a formidable instrument – over 45,000 strong. This army, which first saw action against the Poles in 1656, was largely officered by Swedes – veterans of the campaigns of Gustavus Adolphus – and from them it inherited his traditions of strict discipline and unswerving loyalty as well as his motto, 'Gott mit Uns'. In the Great Northern War of 1655–60 and in subsequent wars including the War of the Spanish Succession, the rude soldiers of the Elector gave a good account of themselves, but a final polish was added to their initial toughness when many notable French Huguenots, including the redoubtable Schomberg, joined their ranks after Louis XIV rashly expelled them from France in 1685.

7 AUSTRIA
An officer of cuirassiers, *c.* 1700. A fine example showing how the practical dress of the Thirty Years War period was retained by heavy cavalry. *Heeresgeschichtliches Museum, Vienna*

The Prussian army had no dress regulations until 1685, when dark blue became the predominant national colour. A Gobelins tapestry shows infantry and cavalry in about 1688, the year of the Great Elector's death. Musketeers are shown wearing black hats decorated with a red ribbon, dark blue coats with white buttons, lining and deep turned back cuffs and stockings, and blue cloaks lined with white. Their arms are a matchlock and a *Schweinsfeder*, a sword in a buff leather waistbelt, and a cartouche box and powder horn attached to a buff leather shoulder belt. The sergeants are dressed in red coats with blue cuffs and carry halberds, the officers in grey with crimson facings, and the drummers in light blue coats with hanging sleeves, heavily laced in silver and with red neck cloths, sashes, and stockings. Drawings of a slightly later period (1698–1700) show an officer and private of the Garde-Grenadière. The private has the usual blue and white coat, a red neck cloth and a blue waistcoat. His grenadier cap is of crimson cloth with white front and back flaps embroidered with crimson grenades; the front bears the eagle and the cypher of the Elector Frederick III, which also appear on the white grenade pouch; and he is armed with a strapped snaphaunce, socket bayonet and a sword. The officer, armed with a 'fusée', or small firelock, has a crimson and gold grenadier cap, shoulder belt and pouch, a scarlet and gold coat, and black breeches and stockings.

The cavalry shown in the tapestry are curiously old-fashioned in their appearance. On their heads they have brown three-cornered hats with crimson ribbons. Their coats are buff with white laced sleeves and blue turned-back cuffs, the sleeves probably being part of the vest worn under the buff coat. Brown breeches, high brown boots, a black neck cloth fringed with white, and a grey sash complete this rather subdued costume. The equipment and weapons consist of a sword worn in a brown shoulder belt and a snaphaunce carbine suspended from a blue and white belt.

Although her army had been beaten at Fehrbellin, in 1675 Sweden was still the greatest northern power. Charles XI reigned over Sweden, Finland, Ingermanland – the site of the future St. Petersburg – Estonia, Livonia, and West Pomerania. In 1697 he died and was succeeded by his young son Charles XII, and Sweden's envious neighbours, thinking that the time was ripe to recoup some of their losses, formed a league against him comprising Russia, Saxony and Denmark. Peter I, who had become Tsar in 1689, had already shown some military prowess in his expeditions against the Turks in Azov in 1695–6. In the summer of 1698, while on a protracted tour of Western Europe, he learned that the *Streltsy* had risen up. Returning home rapidly, he crushed the rebellion with the aid of his 'toy' Preobrajenski and Semenovski regiments, now fully paid regular regiments, and massacred the *Streltsy* with appalling brutality. In 1699, Peter's antiquated army was defeated by the young Charles XII – who had turned out to be a brilliant general – all but the two 'Guards' regiments fleeing from the field. Peter was forced to set about the creation of a new Russian army as quickly as possible, abolishing the *kaftan* and other oriental forms at the very moment that the other armies of Europe were adopting them.

In the East, the power of Turkey, after a long decline, once more became formidable and by 1661 Transylvania had become a Turkish fief. However, the defeat of the Turks at St. Gothard in 1664 by the Imperial troops under Montecuculi, brought a period of peace lasting until 1678, when the dangerous revolt of the Hungarians under Count Tököli – encouraged by Louis XIV – tempted the Turks once again to attempt the conquest of Hungary. The Emperor Leopold, fearful for the safety of Vienna, allied himself with the Poles, and gave the command of his armies to Prince Charles of Lorraine. The war started with Vienna besieged by the Turks, but its relief in September 1683 by Sobieski put an end to the Turkish domination of Hungary. There was spasmodic warfare for some years, however, and it was not until Prince Eugene of Savoy routed the Turks at Zenta in 1697 that the Emperor regained most of the territory of Hungary.

The army of the Emperor developed along much the same lines as those of the other European powers, but dress regulations were not issued until 1708. By 1680, however, the Austrian infantry were uniformly dressed in black hats, white neck cloths, and pearl grey coats with cuffs and linings of a regimental colour; the breeches were of the same regimental colour and the stockings grey. The six Dutch (Walloon) regiments were dressed in green with crimson facings. The Austrian army had grenadiers rather earlier than the others – 1664 – with fur trimmed caps with a hanging bag, and by 1670 the flintlock musket was in general use, and with it brown leather waistbelts and cartouche boxes.

With its close proximity to the Croats, Hungarians, and Turks, various national costume features appeared in the Austrian army. Thus the artillery, who were mainly recruited in Bohemia, wore with their grey coats a fur cap with hanging fox tails, which was to reappear in North America as the celebrated 'Davy Crockett' cap.

The two regiments of Austrian dragoons were dressed in blue coats with red cuffs and shoulder knots, brown equipment, big boots, and black hats bound with white tape and decorated with a red and blue striped band.

Between the Peace of Nijmegen in 1679 and the outbreak of the War of the Palatinate in 1688, Louis XIV, by a policy which can best be described as diplomatic blackmail, forced the German states to ally themselves with Austria, Spain, and Sweden. But no sooner had the war started than Louis XIV's smooth path of aggression was interrupted by the bloodless accession of his arch-enemy, William of Orange, to the English throne, and the subsequent entry of both England and Holland into the war against him. Although the French army fought with distinction throughout the war, suffering only one reverse at the hands of William III in the loss of Namur in 1695, the length of the war and the need for a friendly Europe in the forthcoming problem of the Spanish Succession persuaded Louis XIV to make peace. This was finally concluded by the Treaty of Rhyswick in September 1698, and Europe settled down to two years of uneasy peace before the dawn of the eighteenth century.

III *Rex versus Rex*

By the beginning of the eighteenth century, the new creeds of 'Absolutism' and 'Nationalism' were well established and the era of ferocious religious strife gave way to one of dynastic struggles, limited in scope, and comparatively peaceful compared with the horrors of the Thirty Years War. The wars of the first six decades of the eighteenth century all followed the same pattern. The Great Northern War (1700–21), the Wars of the Spanish (1702–15), Polish (1733–5) and Austrian (1740–8) Successions and the Seven Years War of 1756–63, were concerned entirely with rival claims to the great thrones of Europe and with the maintenance of a delicate balance of power. The alliances and groupings were often different but the basic causes were always the same. Furthermore, although there were many bloody and celebrated battles – Poltava, Blenheim, Fontenoy, Mollwitz and Minden, to select but a few – and equally famous commanders, none of the wars ended in the total defeat of any of the participants, but in nicely calculated political settlements. The regular armies of the eighteenth century were too valuable to be thrown away carelessly, for the men were highly skilled professionals who took much time and money to train. This husbanding of armies led to a situation where both sides performed equally well, and neither had a clear advantage. Wars ended not because one side won a crushing victory but because it rated success too costly or too remote to be worth the effort. As a result wars were shorter and less destructive to the civilian population, while at the same time, improvements in weapons and the techniques of handling them led to even bloodier battles and to commanders considering the preservation of their own armies of more importance than the destruction of the enemy. The eighteenth century was the 'Age of Reason', and logic and order were two of the most admired virtues. In the management of armies, as in the other arts, symmetry and regularity replaced the religious fervour of the seventeenth century, and warfare became less of a crusade and more of a pursuit for gentlemen – to be conducted in as much comfort as possible, and in accordance with strict rules. Between 1700 and 1763 the monarchs of Europe marched their armies to and fro across its wide terrain with the

HEADPIECE
'Exercice' from *Art Militaire*, France, eighteenth century, *Mollo Collection*

8 PRUSSIA
An officer of the *Bataillon Grenadier-Garde v. Retzow, Nr. 6, c.* 1750. The combination of simple lines and complicated *rococo* detailing is typically Prussian. Facsimile copy of the lithograph by Adolph Menzel, 1851.
Mollo Collection

deliberation and precision of chess-players.

Armies in the eighteenth century were large and cumbersome. Between 1713 and 1786 the Prussian army increased from some 38,000 men to 200,000, and the Russian army from 130,000 to over 450,000. The bulk of the officers came from the nobility and considered it their right to go to war accompanied by a retinue of servants and fleets of baggage-waggons, which, together with the general mass of camp-followers, made movement a slow and tedious business. When halted, armies camped in long lines by battalions and squadrons as if on the parade ground and the routine of the day was punctuated with *reveille*, guard mounting parades, and the ceremonious beating of Retreat. When it finally came to fighting, victory lay entirely in the fire-power of the infantry. The general acceptance of the flintlock and bayonet by the beginning of the century led to increasing reliance on mass of fire in place of the manoeuvre common during the latter part of the seventeenth century. The long jointless lines of men discharging ponderous showers of lead at each other at fifty paces distance, made the use of cavalry impossible; and the victors were usually those who could fire the largest number of volleys in the shortest time. The precision and ceremonial which accompanied these tactics have been immortalised in the 'heroic chaff' of Fontenoy, when verbal exchanges between the British and French Guards, accompanied by the bowing and removal of hats in the 'Salute', were the prelude to a hail of lead delivered at thirty paces. In the matter of strict discipline and drill the Germans, by nature of their national character, were far superior to the French, and in the eighteenth century French influence in military matters was rapidly overtaken by that of Prussia.

Prussian drill, as opposed to the then universal Dutch drill, was the invention of Frederick William I, who came to the throne as 'King in Prussia' in 1713. This extraordinary monarch – the personification of a drill-sergeant in appearance and behaviour – was to provide a model for all military-minded royalty for the next century and a half. The stories of his eccentricities are numerous. He is said to have exchanged his father's priceless collection of Chinese porcelain with the Elector of Saxony for a fully equipped regiment of dragoons, and his passion for tall men – preferably with broad faces – led him to despatch agents throughout the length and breadth of Europe; seeking out and kidnapping suitable recruits for his 'regiment of useless giants'. During his reign Prussia became one great garrison, where every man who had a 'Fine person' was compelled to serve, and where even little children were enlisted from birth.

Together with his drill-master, Prince Leopold of Anhalt-Dessau, Frederick William I set out to achieve nothing less than perfection in the exercising of his infantry. The old showy and useless motions of the Dutch exercise, which harked back to the days of the matchlock, were altered, and performed close to the body so that the troops could perform them in close order, as they would on the battlefield. The rate of fire was increased, partly through continual practice and partly through the introduction of the iron ramrod, from one shot per minute to an unheard-of five or six.

At the same time, methods of marching were improved, the pace and direction being finely adjusted by pendulum, pace-stick and drum-tap, so that wheelings and evolutions could be performed with speed and accuracy. The King and the 'Old Dessauer' managed between them to produce an infantryman who would react to orders promptly and accurately, and who could be relied on to advance on the enemy without losing the all-important dressing, loading and firing whilst on the move. Nevertheless, Frederick William's army was a plaything, not for use but for amusement and show, for 'his whole pleasure and employment was . . . the exercising and reviewing

them; he never chose to expose them to the dangers and fatigues of war. . .'.
The serious business was left to his son, Frederick the Great, who took full
advantage of the discipline to which his army had been trained and used it
in the field with strategic and tactical genius. When he came to the throne it
was the custom for commanders to form their line of battle, before recon-
noitring the enemy. Frederick, however, reintroduced manoeuvre by developing a method of moving rapidly from column into line, and by mounting
mass attacks on the defenceless flanks of his opponents. For the execution of
these attacks he relied mainly on his cavalry, who were brilliantly led by
Seydlitz and Zeithen who had both been trained in the light cavalry duties of
hussars.

The Great Elector first established the machinery of the Prussian military
system, which was to be served with devoted loyalty by generation after
generation of the impoverished noble families of East Prussia. Frederick
William I, for all his grotesque absurdities, built on that system and laid the
foundation of the excellence of the Prussian army, which was used to full
advantage by his son.

The next development of note was the rise to prominence of the new
Russian army which combined in its organisation, drill and weapons the best
of the new western ideas and the oldest traditions of Muscovy. Like the
Prussian army, part of its inspiration was Swedish, for, after the defeat of
Charles XII at Poltava in 1709, the Baltic German nobles who traditionally
formed the backbone of the Swedish army were permitted to keep their
lands provided they continued to serve Peter I in a military capacity. Unlike other European armies the Russian army was based on the feudal
obligation of the nobility to provide serfs as soldiers. These peasant recruits
were in effect sentenced to the army for life, at least until 1795, when a
twenty-five years period of service was introduced. Removed from their
villages with the 'Mass for the Dead' ringing in their ears, they became
members of a special caste set somewhere between the noble and the serf.
'The title of soldier is the most noble in the Empire' proclaimed Peter I, but
it is doubtful if the young villager would have agreed as his beard was cut
off and he was crammed into tight outlandish clothing. In one way, however, he might have felt at home in the army, for it was run on very much
the same lines as a large country estate. The officers were the noble landowners, the non-commissioned officers the bailiffs, and there were plenty of
priests on hand to say Mass before battle, or to accompany the troops into
action carrying their portable Communion-tables.

In spite of defeats at the hands of the Turks in 1711, the new Russian
army soon became a body to be reckoned with. Even the incompetence of
Peter the Great's successors did little to halt its progress, for its traditional
enemies – Sweden, Poland and Turkey – were all in decline. During the
Seven Years War, Russia was opposed to Prussia, but the accession to the
throne of Peter III – formerly Duke of Schleswig-Holstein – saw the introduction of the Prussian system into the Russian army. The reign of Peter III was
short-lived and the Prussian trend was halted by his successor, Catherine II
and her native Russian generals, only to be restored by Paul I in 1796 with
even greater enthusiasm.

After a hundred years of continuous warfare, the power of the Austrian
Empire was considerably diminished by the beginning of the eighteenth
century and was to be further weakened by problems of the succession and
the growing antagonism of Prussia. The regular army, composed of German,
Dutch and Hungarian regiments, was trained in the Franco-Dutch school.
During the reign of Maria-Theresa it underwent considerable reorganisation,
and after the Seven Years War it took part in a series of wars against Turkey,

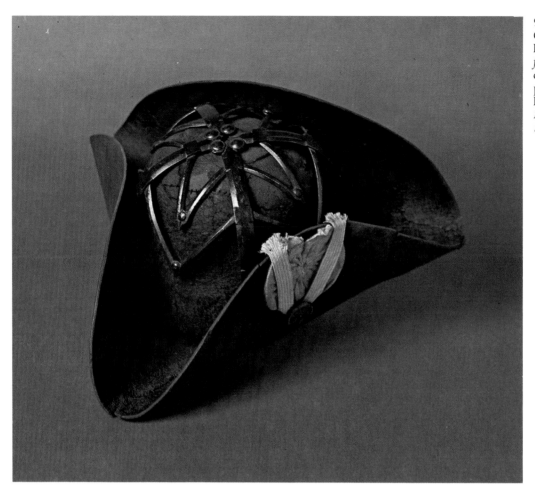

9 FRANCE
Cavalry soldier's *tricorne* hat, *c.* 1760. The *calotte de fer* or 'skull' worn as an outer protection, has been photographed outside the hat.
Musée de l'Empéri, Salon-de-Provence

10 PRUSSIA
Officer's *tricorne* hat, *c.* 1770. Note that in this later example the front point is 'cocked' higher.
Musée de l'Empéri, Salon-de-Provence

fighting side by side with the Russian army. At this period it developed along very practical lines, and the technical troops, in particular those concerned with bridge construction, were of a very high standard. Of even greater importance to the development of both tactics and uniform were the Austrian auxiliary troops – Croats, Pandours, Tolpatches and others – who were originally raised to colonise and defend the outlying parts of the Empire, and who were found to be invaluable for reconnaissance screens and ambuscades when recruited for service with the regular army.

In spite of some notable successes whilst under the command of the Marshal de Saxe during the war of the Austrian Succession, the French army had gradually lost the pre-eminence it had enjoyed under Louis XIV, and during the Seven Years War it received a severe shaking which had done nothing for its morale. With a very high proportion of its officers – one in fifteen – recruited from the ranks of a small and exclusive nobility, the army was beginning to suffer from the combined effects of their arrogance, incompetence, and cupidity, until the situation was to some extent saved by the appointment of the Duc de Choiseul as Secretary for War in 1761. He immediately embarked on a programme of reforms, which, although they were too late to have much effect on the efficiency of the French army during the war years, were to produce dividends during the American Revolution of 1776–83.

Under his guidance the prerogatives of regimental colonels – one of the worst causes of financial abuse – were reduced, and the system of obtaining recruits removed from their control. A start was made on a system of military education which was to bear fruit rather sooner than anyone might have expected, with the entry of one Napoleon Buonaparte into the Military School at Brienne in 1779. At the same time, improvements made in the French artillery service by Gribeauval, and the introduction of a whole range of lighter, more mobile field-pieces, were to give France a lead in such matters until 1870. In the field of drill and tactics Choiseul, like many other military thinkers of his day, adopted the system which had served the Prussians so well, to such an extent that by the time of the French Revolution French barracks were equipped with clockwork pendulums and had geometrical scales carved into the pavement of the parade ground.

But at the same time there were other reformers trying to seek out a system which would get away from the inflexible and formal line. As early as the War of the Austrian Succession, Marshal Saxe had been proposing the attack in column supported by skirmishers, which was later adopted by the French army, although he never had the opportunity to test his theories in action. During the Seven Years War the army of the Duc de Broglie was divided into separate units which suggested the divisional system of the Napoleonic wars. All these new ideas had to contend with the apathy of the nobility who held all the key positions; but with all its imperfections the French army by 1789 was probably the best in Europe.

Under the great Duke of Marlborough, the British army became, for the first time, a force to be reckoned with in Europe. During the War of the Spanish Succession British infantry established the ability to maintain a steady and regular fire which was to become their hall-mark up till 1914. The flintlock and socket bayonet were in general use by 1706, and the discipline of the British and the superior quality of their weapons made their fire far more effective than that of their opponents. The secret of their success lay partly in the fact that the British fired by platoons instead of by successive ranks, and partly in the excellence of their drill insisted on by the Duke, who occasionally put the whole army through the 'Platoon Exercise' under his personal direction, signalling the time by flag and drum.

Marlborough also improved the performance of the British cavalry, often charging in person at their head. The French, who still kept to the old-fashioned tactics of firing from the saddle at the halt, were time and time again bowled over by the shock tactics of the British, who were limited to only three rounds per man, for the whole campaign, and were thus forced to rely on their swords.

On the administrative side, Marlborough took great pains to see that his men were adequately clothed and fed – on the march to the Danube before Blenheim, stocks of boots were arranged beforehand at points along the route – and his vast train of excellent British wheeled transport was one of the wonders of the age.

Until the beginning of the eighteenth century military costume was little more than civilian clothing adapted to the rigours and necessities of war, but now their paths began to diverge. The minute attention which the King of Prussia paid to the dress of his men and the extraordinary style which he developed for them are described in *A Plan of Discipline for the use of the Norfolk Militia*, published in London in 1759:

'in order, therefore, that his soldiers might appear to the utmost advantage, . . . and not without a view to economy; he caused their coats to be made so very short, that they barely reached halfway down their thighs; and so scanty in the body and sleeves, that they could scarce put them on; their breeches reached scarcely down to their knees; and their hats were so small, as hardly to cover their heads; so that they were forced to have a contrivance to pin them on, for fear of their falling off when they were exercising. Their hair was queued back and powdered, with only one or two small curls on each side of the face; to this was added square toed shoes, with high heels; a long sword, with a broad blade, worn very high upon the hip; and white gaiters, which as well as waistcoat and breeches, (that were generally white also), were continually chalked to keep them clean; for the least speck of dirt on any of them was punished with the utmost ferocity. This appeared the more extraordinary, as, at the time, the prevailing fashion of dress was every-where totally different, and being added to a sort of uprightness and stiffness in their air and motions, that was peculiar to themselves, made them really have very much the appearance of puppets.'

However strange they may have looked at first, it was not long before their success in battle led other countries to ape their powder and pigtails, and even civilian fashions were influenced by them. As Fortescue points out, 'not wholly with a light heart', Frederick William I was the first great military tailor ever to sit on a throne, and he was certainly not the last.

Throughout the eighteenth century the largest part of any army was the infantry, divided into battalions, each battalion having a Grenadier company. During the War of the Austrian Succession and the Seven Years War a start was made on the introduction of 'Light Infantry' but it was not until the end of the century that the principles of light infantry tactics were properly established. Of the infantry certain regiments in every army were designated as 'Guards' regiments and dressed in a correspondingly richer fashion, than the 'Line regiments'. In general the national characteristics of each army were expressed in the colour of their uniforms rather than in their shape or decoration, which remained much the same in every country for the first half of the century. At the beginning of the century there were still armies not entirely uniformed. The Russian army, raised afresh between 1700 and 1709, had regiments of line infantry, the cut of whose clothing was fixed, but not the colour, while the officers wore very much what they liked until about 1730. By the middle of the century the Russian army was dressed in green except for the artillery who wore red, the Prussian army in dark blue, the Austrians and French in grey-white natural wool, and the British in red.

The bulk of soldiery still wore the hat, which by the beginning of the century was already 'three-cornered' with the side immediately over the left eye held up by a button and loop behind which there was usually a ribbon cockade in national colours. In addition the hat was usually laced round the brim with gold or silver lace for the officers and yellow or white tape for the men. By 1756 the brim of the hat had become smaller, and the term 'cocked' was coming into use, the officers of the British Royal Artillery being desired 'not to appear upon the Parade for the future with hats cocked otherwise than in the Cumberland manner'. Captain Cutherbertson of the 5th Foot laid down that

> 'The cocking of a Soldier's hat in a becoming manner, being a principal ornament of his appearance, should be very much attended to; the short smart cock is certainly most adapted to a military man, as it gives a sort of Martial Air, adds to his height, and always sets firm on the head: four inches and a half are enough for the breadth of the leaves (brims), as anything above that size, drowns the face, unless it be remarkably full and broad; . . .'

By the late 1750s the hat was being worn at an angle, set low over the right brow, and tipped up on the left. The chief Prussian contribution to the hat was the use of feather plumes and woollen *pom-poms* of different colours for the easier identification of battalions and companies. Eventually the hat became *bicorne* in character, and by the time of the French Revolutionary Wars could be worn either across the head – 'athwartships' – in the old-fashioned manner, or with the points front and back – known in the British service as 'fore and aft' – which apart from being easier to keep on when riding was considered much more fashionable and dashing. The large cocked hat worn across the head was retained by reactionary senior officers in several countries as late as the 1820s.

Apart from the hat, there were the various forms of cap, of which the grenadier cap was developing in various distinct ways. The most unusual perhaps was the type introduced by Peter the Great for his guards. This consisted of a leather skull cap with a brass plate in the front bearing the doubleheaded eagle emblem of the Russian Empire, and a low neck flap. Above this last was a small brass plate with the cypher of the Tsar which served as a socket for a tall red and white plume. This exotic confection is an early example of the influence of baroque art on military dress, and is very reminiscent of the type of bogus classical helmet worn by the heroes of the operas so frequently performed at Versailles.

The more common type of grenadier cap was the stiffened conical cloth cap with a tassel at the top, and small turnbacks, front and rear, embroidered with various devices. The English pattern had a tall mitre-shaped cloth front, while the Prussian pattern, introduced by Frederick William I and later copied by the Russians, had a stamped white or yellow plate, suitably embellished. The third main type was to be seen in the Austrian army by 1748 and was a development of the fur-trimmed cap of the Hungarians and Poles. This consisted of a tall pointed fur cap, with a hanging cloth bag and tassel at the back and a metal plate at the front. By the 1760s both the French and British armies had adopted grenadier caps of this type.

Far left
11 PRUSSIA
Officer's grenadier cap,
Füsilier Regiment Nr. 32,
c. 1760.
Musée Royal de l'Armée,
Brussels

Left
12 SCHLESWIG-HOLSTEIN
Officer's grenadier cap,
Leib-dragoner Regiment.
One of the regiments taken
to Russia by the Duke when
he became Tsar Peter III,
1762.
Mollo Collection

Below left
13 GREAT BRITAIN
Left Officer's grenadier
'mitre' cap, 3rd Foot,
c. 1750.
Right Officer's grenadier
cap, Honourable Artillery
Company, *c.* 1710.
National Army Museum

Right
14 RUSSIA
Soldier's grenadier cap,
c. 1760.
Musée Royal de l'Armée
Brussels

15 AUSTRIA
Soldier's grenadier cap,
1740–64. An example of
the fur grenadier cap
favoured by Catholic
countries.
Heeresgeschichtliches
Museum, Vienna

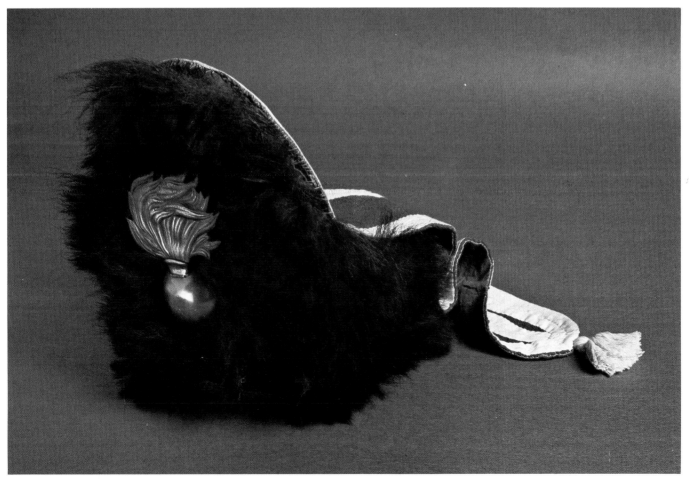

47

Another curious form of cap was the Russian *polakem* – presumably copied from the Lithuanian Tartars – a cloth or felt cap with flaps which could be turned down to protect the ears and neck from the cold. This was worn by Russian line infantry and dragoon regiments until 1720, and although short-lived is interesting in as much as it seems to be the original for the caps worn by the Red Army.

The Prussian army had another version of the genadier cap, which originated in the artillery about 1740 and was later adopted for the Field Fusilier regiments. This was a black oilcloth skull cap with an ornamented brass plate slightly lower than that of the Grenadiers.

By the middle of the eighteenth century, the use of royal arms, cyphers, and the insignia of orders of chivalry had become general for the embellishment of grenadier caps, gorgets and cartouche boxes. The Prussian army used the cypher of the King, the national emblem of the black eagle with outstretched wings, and the star of the Order of the Black Eagle founded by Frederick I in 1701. The Russian army used the cypher of the reigning monarch and the double-headed eagle. The guards regiments also used the star of the Order of St. Andrew founded by Peter the Great in 1698. The French and Austrian armies tended to use cyphers and national emblems – the *Fleur-de-Lis* of France and the double-headed eagle of the Holy Roman Empire – rather than insignia of orders. In England, however, the star of the Order of the Garter was much in evidence embroidered on the fronts of the grenadier caps of the guards, while all grenadiers had the white horse of Hanover embroidered on the small front turn-up of their caps.

Turning to the soldier's coat, the gradual widening of the skirts at the beginning of the eighteenth century had resulted in the formation of pleats which fanned out over the hips, just below the waist. Gradually the hang and the shape of the coat was altered by inserting further pleats at the back. After 1745 the coat became more elegant, the main alterations consisting of moving the side seams round to the back, dropping the shoulder seams, reducing the fullness of the skirts, and curving the fronts away to the sides. By 1770 the narrow back, sloping fronts, tight cuffs and high stand and fall collar marked the transition of the coat from the practical garment of the seventeenth century, to the dress coat of the nineteenth century.

As the ordinary coat became more and more elegant, a coat for everyday or outdoor wear was gradually developed. Double-breasted, with a turn-down collar and looser in fit, the 'frock', as it was called, was becoming fashionable by 1730. Military coats of the period were versions of the 'frock' in that they were often double-breasted, although the two lapels were usually worn buttoned back. At the beginning of the century military coats were still ample in cut and single-breasted with full skirts. Gradually, how-ever, it became the custom to turn the skirts of the coat back and hook them together to keep them out of the way when on the march, which had the effect of making the low placed pockets inaccessible. The first major develop-ment in the coat came from Prussia, where the poorness of the country and the rapid increase in the size of the army made strict economy vital and the amount of cloth in the uniforms of the army was cut to a minimum. By 1729 the Prussian infantry were wearing coats, the skirts of which hardly reached down to the knee, with narrow turnbacks and lapels in the regimental facing colour. By 1760 the skirts were even shorter, and small upstanding collars, closed at the front, were being worn.

One of the features peculiar to Prussian uniforms at this time was the use of tasselled loops on the coat, apparently derived from the *Branden-bourgs* on the *kaftan*. The men had them in worsted braid, and the officers in gold or silver wire embroidery. The designs of the officers' loops varied considerably and were one of the first applications of *rococo* – a style much beloved by the King of Prussia – in the manufacture of military uniforms.

The accession of George II to the throne of Great Britain led to a gradual adoption of Prussian ideas, and a corresponding attention to matters of dress. The King had only been on the throne four months when he announced his intention of giving the army fixed clothing. In 1742 the *Representation of the Cloathing of His Majesty's Household, and of all the Forces upon the Establishments of Great Britain and Ireland* – the first book to give illustrations of every regiment in the army – was published, and soon after the Duke of Cumberland commissioned the Swiss painter, David Morier, to portray the soldiers of the various regiments that had served under him in the war. One of the most characteristic features of English uniform, indicative of the amount of money colonels were prepared to lavish on their regiments, was the generous use of worsted braid – usually white, woven with coloured stripes or other motifs – for edging lapels, cuffs and waistcoats, and for forming loops where the button-holes occurred. By 1776 the skirts of the coat reached to within six inches of the ground when the soldier was kneeling, for 'long skirts, besides being inconvenient, drown the size and take from the soldier's appearance that smartness which is admired'. The skirts were to be tacked back permanently and closed with a lace loop or other ornament.

In both France and Austria, the coat remained very simple, being, with the exception of the French guards and certain foreign regiments, grey-white natural wool with coloured cuffs and facings. After the Seven Years War both armies adopted the shorter Prussian style of coat. In 1759 French officers, whose distinguishing mark was the gorget, were ordered to wear 'epaulettes' on their shoulders. This innovation, introduced by Choiseul, was very unpopular at first, and the epaulette was commonly referred to as the *Guenille à Choiseul* (the Choiseul Rag).

The origin of epaulettes lies in the bunches of ribbons worn on the shoulders of the *justaucorps* at the end of the seventeenth century, which were partly decorative and partly practical in that they could be used to prevent the shoulder belt from slipping. The design of the epaulette comes from the custom of tying these ribbons into a bow or knot, and leaving the fringed ends hanging free. The shoulder cords or 'aiguillettes' worn by certain officers, non-commissioned officers, and men, developed through the same need to secure the shoulder belt, but from the boot-lace-like 'points' which were used to secure the sleeves of the buff leather coat to the body. In the French and British armies the epaulette replaced the older shoulder cords, while in the Prussian and Russian armies shoulder cords were retained by the bulk of officers until a much later date.

By the middle of the eighteenth century the white stock, a development of the white neck cloth of the previous century, had given way to the black stock made of horsehair or velvet; in the Prussian service, stocks of regimental colour were often worn.

In the first years of the century, the waistcoat was worn open to the waist revealing a quantity of shirt; and the breeches, being covered to a large extent by the ample skirts of the coat and waistcoat, were cut more for comfort than elegance. As the coat and waistcoat became smaller and neater, and more of the breeches were shown, they became gradually tighter over thighs and knees. About 1750 the centre fly opening was replaced by the flap opening. At first military breeches had been of a dark colour – either the same as the coat or the facings of the coat – but gradually it was found extremely difficult to keep them clean, and white cloth or linen breeches came into use. These could be washed and restored to their pristine bright-

16 FRANCE
Military accoutrements
showing the use of the
arms of France.
Top Officer's grenadier cap
plate, 1774–93.
Centre Officer's pouch,
*Grenadiers à Cheval de la
Maison du Roi, c.* 1760, said
to have been worn by
Louis XV.
Below Officer's pouch,
Guard and line grenadier
regiments, *c.* 1760.
*Musée de l'Empéri,
Salon-de-Provence*

Right
17 GREAT BRITAIN
Officer's coat, Colonel St.
George's Regiment, later the
Lancashire Fusiliers, *c.* 1737.
The embroidery, which is
civilian in character,
probably follows the owner's
taste rather than a regi-
mental pattern.
National Army Museum

ness by colouring with bran and whitening. By the 1770s white waistcoats and breeches were the general rule.

Foot soldiers wore shoes which were the same for both feet and which were changed around daily 'to prevent them running crooked'. Strong linen gaiters were worn with the shoes – white for dress occasions and black for normal wear. By the 1770s short gaiters reaching up to the swell of the calf were becoming popular, as they were cooler and more comfortable to wear on the march.

The following passage from the *New Regulations for the Prussian Infantry*, published in London in 1757, illustrates the lengths to which 'spit and polish' were taken in the Prussian service:

'One of the essential parts of the *Prussian* service is that Regularity which is so carefully attended to from the highest Officer down to the private Man; the Soldier being obliged to hold himself in continual Readiness to parade, is by that means kept constantly employed in preserving his Arms, Clothes, Accoutrements and Person in proper Order.'

'Recruits are not only taught to walk, stand, and exercise, but also to dress. In the Evening every Soldier must curl up his hair in Papers, and in case he is not able to dress it properly himself against the Parade-time in the Morning, he must have it done at the Captain's Quarters by the *Friseur* of the Company, where the Non-commission Officers are to take care that the Men are powdered, brushed, and properly dressed, when-ever they go upon Guard, or the Company is to be reviewed.'

'That there may be an uniformity in the Appearance of the Hair, all the Men are to have it dressed in the same Manner. The Grenadiers are to wear Whiskers, which they are to tie up at Night, that they may lose no time in dressing them in the Morning. The Whiskers are to be raised with black Wax, to keep them stiff and smooth.'

'All Soldiers and non-commissioned Officers, are to put on their Gaiters before they are dressed; and that there may be no Wrinkles in them, a false Calf is fixed, so as to fill up the Hollow between the inside of the Knee and the Calf of the Leg.'

'When a Soldier is to appear on parade, or to Mount Guard, the Buttons of his Gaiters and every thing of Brass about him must be perfectly bright. Every Year in the month of *May* the whole Army is new clothed from Head to Foot, and the old Cloathes the Soldiers are allowed to sell, the Facings and Collars being first cut off, that the Peasants may not appear in the Uniforms of Soldiers.'

'A Soldier who has been on Furlough, must at his return to the Company, bring with him a tanned Calf's-Skin, (which are very cheap in Prussia) and three Ells of coarse Linen, and deliver them to the Captain at Arms, who deposits them in the Company's Store-Room in order to be returned to the Soldier, when he shall want Shoes, Gaiters, or Pieces of Linen for mending the Lining of his Clothes.'

'All the Arms, Halberds, and Espontons are well polished:and that the Arms may continue so, every Soldier has a thick piece of Buck-Skin in his Pouch, with which he is to rub the Barrel of his Piece very well as soon as he is relieved from his Post, as Sentry; or comes off Guard: By the frequent Repetition of this, the Polish becomes so lasting, as at length not to be spotted even by Rain; besides, the Arms are burnished by the Regimental Gunsmith with seed Oil, Emery, Starch-Powder, and the Steel-Polisher. The Stock of the Firelock is rubbed over with a brown Paste, and afterwards, very hard with Oil and Wax, which give it a Gloss'.

'The Slings are varnished with red; the Paste both hardens the Stock and secures it from Worms; and the red Varnish is also a good Preservative to the Leather'.

'The Pouches are of the thickest tanned Leather, and to be kept glossy, by being frequently rubbed with black Wax, that the Cartridge-Box may not contract any Damp, or the Rain penetrate into it. Every Soldier has sixty Cartridges in his Box, which are tied up close in a leather Bag; and on all Parties detached against the Enemy, are carefully examined'.

'The Cartridge-Boxes, Slings, Waistcoats, Hat-Laces, Stocking, Facings and Collars for every Company are coloured together, in the Quarters of the Captain at Arms that there may be no Difference between them, which would sometimes be the case, especially in the Yellows'.

'A Comb, Brush, Looking-glass, Wax, for the Shoes and Whiskers, a piece of Buff-Leather, a wooden Polisher, a Screw-Driver, a Set of Gaiter Buttons, a Hook for buttoning the Gaiters, and a Worm, are little Articles which no soldier is to be without'.

The dress of the cavalry, which at the beginning of the century, consisted of regiments of horse and dragoons, was basically the same as the infantry. Hats, coats, waistcoats, breeches, big boots and stout gauntlets were the main items of clothing. During the War of the Spanish Succession, Marlborough's cavalry were issued with cuirasses which, like the French, they wore under their coats. Vestiges of the buff coat worn by seventeenth century horsemen remained in the use of buff or buff-coloured cloth waistcoats by the British and French horse. The coats of the Prussian cuirassiers remained buff until the 1730s when they were changed for coats of straw-coloured kerseymere. These coats were cleaned with a special mixture of coloured whitening but, as there was considerable difficulty in obtaining a uniform colour, it was later ordered that white pipeclay only should be used.

About 1780 short coats which were very simple in design with 'gauntlet' cuffs and a border of lace down the front of the jacket were introduced, made of white cloth instead of leather. These short *Kollette* as they were to be called later were of very similar design in the Prussian, Russian and Austrian armies. Dragoons of all armies being mounted infantry retained the infantry style coat with lapels.

The line infantry, the horse, or cuirassiers, and the dragoons formed the backbone of every army and were to continue to do so for a considerable time longer. However, during the first half of the century they were joined by a new species of 'Light' troops, both cavalry and infantry, who, apart from the effect they were to have on tactics and training, were largely responsible for the introduction of a wider variety of military clothing, some of it of a very elaborate and fanciful nature. The role of light cavalry was fulfilled by the 'Hussar'.

Hungarian hussars began to appear in central Europe soon after the defeat of the Turks at the gates of Vienna in 1683. As the pressure on the borders of the Empire was lessened, the hussars were formed into regular regiments, under the command of hereditary chieftans, for service with the Austrian army. A trickle of deserters from the Imperial army, regarded at first as curiosities, were employed as servants by the officers of the armies of Louis XIV; and later a corps of Royal Hussars – consisting of Croats, Poles and Turks – was formed, but it was disbanded by Louvois after a short career, when its Colonel lost it at cards.

The first regular regiment of French hussars, later called 'Bercheny' was formed in 1701 and existed as the 1st Hussars up to and during the French Revolution. By 1752 there were seven regiments, and Hungarians were being replaced by Germans from Alsace-Lorraine. As these would only enlist in

54

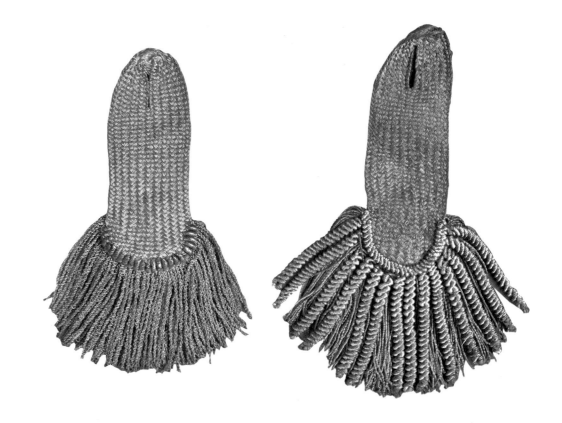

18 FRANCE
Above left Junior Officer's epaulette, *c.* 1760.
Right Senior officer's epaulette, *c.* 1760.
Musée de l'Empéri, Salon-de-Provence

Left
19 GREAT BRITAIN
Dress coat, of regimental pattern, worn by Captain the Hon. Thomas Needham, 3rd Regiment of Foot Guards, later the Scots Guards, *c.* 1768.
The Guards Museum

Right
20 GREAT BRITAIN
Officer's helmet, 15th Light Dragoons, 1763–84. The British version of the French classical helmet.
National Army Museum

regiments where their own language was spoken, commands in French hussar regiments continued to be given in German until after the Revolution.

Hussars were first taken into Prussian service about 1721, and by 1745 there were eight regiments. The Russian army raised five regiments of hussars in 1741, recruited from Serbians, Hungarians and Georgians, the number of regiments increasing to fifteen under Catherine II.

The British did not introduce hussar regiments until the early years of the nineteenth century, but they were none the less very conscious of their usefulness, for in the War of the Austrian Succession (1740–8) both sides were subjected to the constant depredations of each other's hussars. Sam Davies, Footboy to Major Honeywood of the King's Regiment of Dragoons, has left us a vivid description of the French hussars at the time of the Battle of Dettingen, 16th June, 1743:

'. . . . . . First there Cap, which is made of hareskin, they ware no Cote but a Westcote, which is very tite upon them. There briches and their Stockins are all of a peace, the stockins lace down behind, the Boots are like your Haf Boots. They have a skin which they hang on one side which side the weather comes. They carry a small Carbine slung over there Shoulder, so when they fire them they put it under there arm, so look over there Shoulder. They have 2 Pr of Pistolles and a Simmeter but when the Queen's Hussars come, thay will soon put an End to those Gentle-men . . . . . .'

Hussars proper first appeared in the British Isles during the '45 Rebellion, in the service of Prince Charles. James Ray, a 'Volunteer under His Royal Highness the Duke of Cumberland', says of them that 'Their Hussars were most of them young men dress'd in close plaid-waistcoats and large fur caps but having very bad horses . . .' At the same period, the increasing popu-larity of Germans, in particular Hanoverians, as horse masters, led to the employment of several in the suites of such people as the Duke of Cumber-land, very often dressed in full hussar dress.

In 1759, as the result of experience gained during the Seven Years War, the first regiment of 'Light Dragoons' was formed in the British Army; but although their tactics were essentially those of hussars, no attempt was made to clothe them in the Hungarian fashion. The Prussian General Warnery, in his *Remarks on Cavalry*, published in England in 1798, has the following to say about light cavalry:

'The advantage of having Hussars with an army, being generally allowed, each Sovereign was desirous of having some squadrons of them in his service; at first none were admitted but Hungarians, deserters, or others, but afterwards, Germans were received, and in course of time, Poles; and when those corps were successively augmented, no preference was given to Hungarians, experience having proved that it was not necessary to be born in Hungary to become a good Hussar. I am of the opinion, however, that light dragoons would render the same service, in effect to what purpose to masquerade the natives of a country, by giving them Foreign dress that is more expensive, and at the same time, the most inconvenient that can be imagined . . .'

However inconvenient it may have seemed to foreigners, the hussar uniform, which was essentially the same in every army, was a development of Hungarian national dress. The original hussars with their shaggy caps and cloaks, their high cheek bones and turned-down Mongol moustaches, mounted on small Tartar bred horses, and armed with curved scimitars, were a grim and undisciplined host, but all the features of future hussar elegance were already present in one form or another. The fur busby or *kalpak*, worn during the first part of the eighteenth century by Austrian hussars, was gradually replaced by a tall cylindrical felt cap, called a *haiduk* – from the Turkish *haidud*, meaning a 'marauder'. In 1752, the uniforms of the seven French hussar regiments were changed, the busby being replaced by the *mirliton* – an elaborated version of the haiduk – a tall black felt cap with a long cloth *flamme*, or tail, black on one side and coloured on the other, which could be wound round the cap or left hanging. By the middle of the century, hussars were powdering their hair and blackening their eye brows and moustaches. Austrian and French hussars wore their hair divided into two plaits, one over each ear, weighted down with lead, which provided rudimentary protection against sword-cuts. These plaits were also worn by Austrian grenadiers.

The jacket or *dolman* – originally a short *kaftan* fastened at the front by means of cords and wooden toggles – became gradually a closely braided shell jacket; and the slung *pelisse* – originally a piece of sheepskin – became a replica of the jacket, braided and lined with fur or wool. In 1756 the Prussian Hussars adopted the *mirliton* or *Flügelmütze*, although they retained the fur cap for wear in the winter. The Prussians and Russians both wore leather breeches and short boots, with a pair of close-fitting trouser legs worn over them, which were known as *esquavar*, *schalavery*, or *charivari*. Two other features of hussar dress deserve mention – the barrel sash, consisting of cords passing through a series of woven tubes, and then tied round the waist – originally a picketing rope and the *sabretache*, originally a sack carried from the sword belt which contained necessaries and plunder. This gradually became a very decorative item, being embroidered with cyphers and other emblems, like the front of the grenadier cap. It was gradually adopted by other types of cavalry, the first being the Prussian cuirassier regiments about 1762.

A second sort of light cavalry were the Polish Uhlans. Not so common as hussars, they were almost entirely Poles in the service of Saxony 'unless you assimilate them with the pretended Prussian Bosniacks' according to General Warnery, who also says that they should be 'all Tartars of Lithuania, brave, faithful and steady, and by no means drunkards'. The *Voluntaires de Saxe*, formed in 1743 for French service, consisted of six squadrons of 160 men each, of whom 80 were dragoons and 80 uhlans armed with lances. Their costume, which was to provide the inspiration for the uniforms of lancer regiments everywhere, was based on Polish national dress and consisted of a fur-trimmed cap with a square crown instead of a conical bag, known as a *chapska*, from the Turkish word for a cap; and a long sleeveless coat known as a *kountouch*. The uhlans of the *Voluntaires de Saxe* wore a curious helmet with a neo-classical crest and a long horse-hair tail, green coat and baggy trousers, and boots *à la Hongroise*. Their arms were a lance with pennon, a curved sabre, and a pistol stuck in their waist-belt.

The Marshal De Saxe was the natural son of the Elector of Saxony, who was later King of Poland, and when he first came to Paris, after the War of the Spanish Succession, he was accompanied by his own regiment of uhlans. Apart from being perhaps the greatest soldier of his age, he was a notorious rake with a particular penchant for actresses. It is possible that his close connection with things theatrical provided the inspiration for the neo-classical helmets worn by his *Voluntaires*, which was one of the first consciously designed pieces of military uniform.

Apart from hussars and uhlans, there were Cossacks, by now mainly in

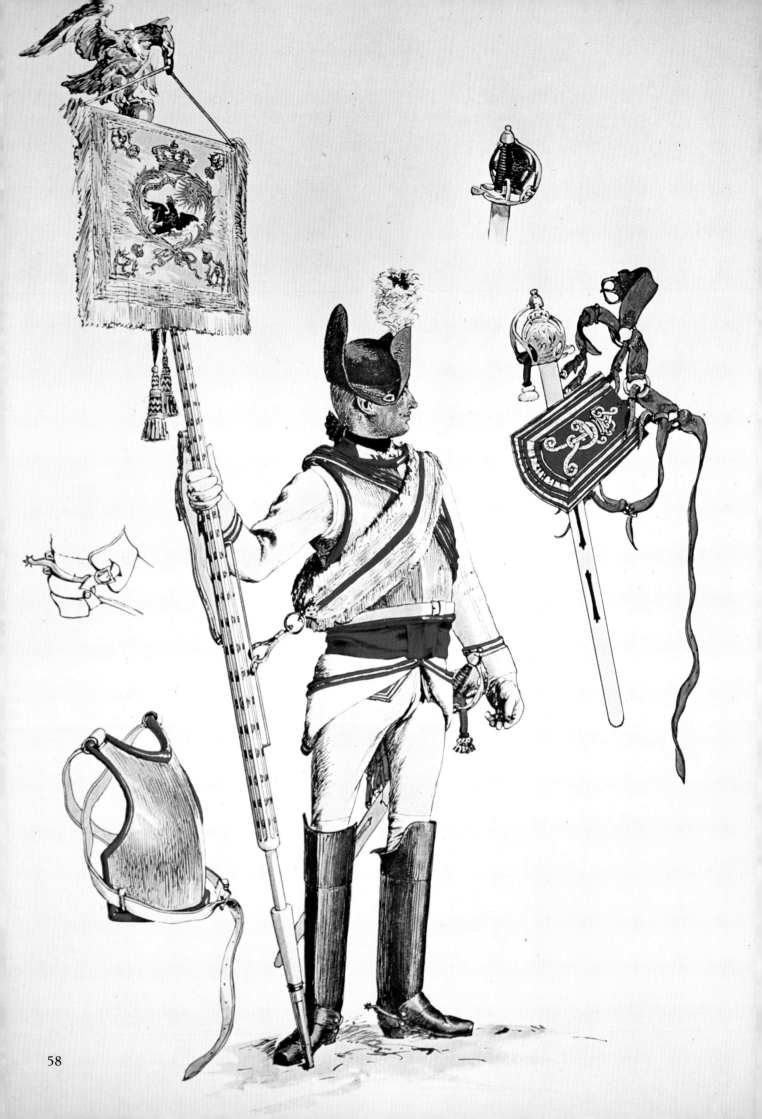

21 FRANCE
Soldier's *'mirliton'* or
'bonnet', *2me Hussards*,
1785.
Musée de l'Empéri,
Salon-de-Provence

Left
22 PRUSSIA
Standartenjunker, Garde du
Corps, c. 1760. The buff
coat of the Thirty Years
War period has now been
replaced by a white or
straw coloured cloth
Kollett. Facsimile copy of
the lithograph by Adolph
Menzel, 1851.
Mollo Collection

Right
23 FRANCE
Officer's helmet, dragoon
regiments, 1785. A later
version of the neo-classical
helmet introduced to France
by the *Voluntaires de Saxe*
in 1743.
Musée de l'Empéri,
Salon-de-Provence

Russian service. Under Peter I these consisted of the Cossacks of the Don, the Cossacks of Little Russia, and the zaparozhe Cossacks. The Cossacks of Little Russia were irregular Cossacks, as opposed to the Ukraine Cossacks who occupied the same areas but who by 1700 had their own military system whereby a certain number were 'registered', a custom introduced during the period of Polish domination in order to control their numbers and reduce their potential. The zaparozhe Cossacks were those living *za porogami* or below the rapids of the Dnieper river, where for a long time they formed an independent military community, intrenched in the islands of the river, and making constant war on the Turks and Crimean Tartars.

Cossacks, apart from those of the Ukraine who wore a semblance of uniform, were dressed in variations of their native dress. The Don Cossacks wore *kaftans* and *demi-kaftans*, with or without buttons and loops, silk Turkish sashes, red or yellow boots, and fur-trimmed caps with velvet crowns. They were armed with a variety of Russian, Turkish Persian or Crimean Tartar weapons. The 'regular' Ukraine Cossacks wore different costumes according to their rank. Thus, the Colonel wore a blue cap bordered with fur, a long Damask *kountouch*, a green pelisse with hanging sleeves, and red boots. He was armed with a curved sabre, and carried his mace of office. The *Sotnik* or leader of the *Sotnia*, had a red cap, a blue *kaftan* with red collar, cuffs and linings, red boots and a curved sabre. The Cossack soldiers had low red caps edged with fur, a *joupan* – shorter than a *kaftan* – of blue cloth lined with red, baggy white trousers, and black boots. Their arms were a short sabre and a musket, the ammunition for which was carried in a black pouch worn on a shoulder belt. The auxiliary Cossacks of Little Russia, who went to war armed and equipped by several neighbouring families, wore low white fur-trimmed caps, long white *svitkas*, over a yellow *Kountouch*, and black boots. They were armed with short sabres, muskets, pouches and belts like the regular Cossacks. The zaparozhe Cossacks wore varied clothing, slightly different from that of their neighbours, the Cossacks of Little Russia. In general it consisted of a fur cap with a red cloth bag, a red or blue *kaftan* with hanging sleeves, over which was sometimes worn a *svitka* with open sleeves knotted behind underneath a hood. They were armed with a curved sabre, a dagger, a lance, two pistols, and a musket. The zaparozhe Cossacks shaved their heads, retaining only a long tuft, the end of which was rolled round the left ear; they also wore very long drooping moustaches.

The proliferation of all types of irregular eventually brought about certain changes in the appearance of regular cavalry. The first was the adoption in 1762 of a crested helmet by French dragoon regiments. This helmet, which marked the beginning of a specifically French style of uniform recognisable until 1914, first appears being worn by the dragoons and uhlans of the *Voluntaires de Saxe* in 1743. The uhlan helmet has already been described; the dragoon helmet was slighly different, and consisted of a brass skull, surmounted with a neo-classical brass crest, fluted at the sides. From the top of the crest a mane of horse-hair flowed down behind the wearer, affording him some protection from sword cuts. The lower part of the skull was surrounded with a band of sealskin, and on each side there was a brass rosette. The regulation helmet of 1762 was essentially the same, except that the large Medusa's head on the front of the early helmet was changed for a smaller one on the fore-part of the crest. The horse-hair mane was black, except for the Colonel's Company who had white horse-hair, and were mounted on grey horses.

The introduction of Light Dragoons into the British Army was a development in the same tradition. Apart from the short-lived regiment, formed in 1745 as the Duke of Kingston's Light Horse, which took part in the Battle of Culloden, little was done to form proper light cavalry until 1755, when Light Troops were added to eleven British cavalry regiments. These troops wore the usual uniforms of their regiments, except that their carbine belts were altered to permit them firing their carbines on horseback, and they were given classical helmets evidently inspired by those of the French dragoons. The English version consisted of a boiled leather skull reinforced with brass sidebars, and with a leather neck flap which could be rolled down in bad weather. There was a small crest with a horsehair tail, which, according to the regulations, was to be half red and half the colour of the regimental facings. In addition there was a small turned-up flap in front, usually of pierced brass, bearing the royal cypher surmounted by a crown. The Light Troops were disbanded in 1763; but in 1759 the first regiments of Light Dragoons were raised, wearing similar helmets to those of the Light Troops, except that instead of the neck flap, they had a turban which was intended to fulfil the same function. The helmets varied very much between regiments, some having brass skulls and others japanned copper, and the front plates came in all shapes and sizes, some being plain metal while others were of red cloth trimmed with fur.

In 1740, Frederick the Great formed a body of mounted *Jäger* intended for scouting and courier duties. Recruited mainly from officials of the forestry service, they wore hats, green coats, and green *charivari* over leather breeches, and were armed with rifled carbines.

In 1769, Austrian *Chevaux-légers* regiments were given the ingenious *Kaskett* – said to have been of Spanish origin – which consisted of a low cylindrical crown with a flat top. In front, and attached to the crown by a leather toggle and loop, was a leather flap with a rounded top, slightly higher than the cap, edged all round with braid. Round the side of the cap was a cloth flap which could be pulled down and tied underneath the chin. On the front flap was a large brass plate with an irregular rococo border, which, from 1770 to 1790, bore the Imperial cypher, and after that date the Austrian double-headed eagle.

With all these different types of irregular or light cavalry, came a corresponding array of light infantry. They were first used by the Austrians during the War of the Austrian Succession, when the Queen of Hungary raised bands of Croats and Pandours to protect the encampments of the Austrian army. Their effectiveness was soon noted by Marshal Saxe, who formed his own irregular troops, including *Mons. Grassin's Regiment des Arquebusiers* who were raised in 1744 at his suggestion and were the first rifle corps in the French army. The first light troops in British service were the four companies of Highlanders raised in 1725 to police the Highlands, who later became the Black Watch.

On the outbreak of the Seven Years War the Austrians again raised many light troops including the Tyrolean *Jäger* who were celebrated for their marksmanship. At Kolin in 1756 they inflicted a sharp reverse on Frederick the Great, as a result of which he increased the one company of *Jäger* in the Prussian army to a battalion. At the same time the Duc de Broglie formed a special Corps of *Chasseurs* and gave a company of light infantry to each battalion in his army. During the war, several irregular units, known as Freikorps, were raised by both the Prussians and Austrians, one of the largest of which was the Prussian Freikorps *v. Kleist*. This consisted of *Jäger*, infantry, dragoons and hussars all dressed in dark green, except the hussars who had red dolmans and dark green pelisses. The Austrian *Jäger* regiments wore the *Kaskett* and grey uniforms.

The Pandours and Croats, regardless of which country they served, wore variations of their national dress, of which certain features were to become important in the development of military uniform. Their headdress was usually the plain cylindrical *mirliton*, their short-skirted jackets and waist-coats were braided in hussar fashion and their legs were encased in tight breeches and *charivari*.

By the end of the Seven Years War the various European armies had reached a simultaneous stage in their development. The main body of the infantry consisted of battalions of musketeers or fusiliers as they were now sometimes called – each with its Grenadier company – supported by skirmishers and irregular infantry. The cavalry, consisting of cuirassiers or horse and dragoons, had its attendant light cavalry in the form of hussars, uhlans and light dragoons. But although there were signs that the linear tactics of Frederick the Great could be countered by the intelligent use of light infantry, warfare in Europe, where the flat terrain allowed the manoeuvring of large formal armies, remained practically unchanged. It was the armies of those countries who had colonial possessions who were suddenly to encounter a very different state of affairs.

IV *Forest and Steppe*

From the middle of the seventeenth century onwards, the colonial aspirations of the maritime nations of Europe became increasingly identified with the maintenance of the 'Balance of Power' in Europe, with the result that warfare was carried beyond the limits set by the familiar battle-grounds of Germany and Flanders, into distant and unknown territories. The next stage in the development of military dress was to take place, far from the eagle eye of Frederick the Great, in the trackless Indian-infested forests of North America and the wide steppes of Southern Russia; and to bring with it a rejection of the powder and pipeclay of the 'civilised' European army.

By 1690, only Britain and France remained as rivals for the possession of the heartlands of the North American continent. At first the distances between the scattered settlements had prevented any great contact between the two nations, but as the parent countries embarked on the long series of wars in Europe the colonists of the New World were gradually involved. Each of the great European wars had its American counterpart. Thus in 1690 there was 'King William's War', followed by 'Queen Anne's War', 'King George's War', and finally the 'French and Indian War' of 1754–63 in which France forever lost her hold on North America, and in which Britain trained the very same colonial soldiers who were to drive her out of the Thirteen Colonies.

The numerical superiority of the British settlers did not prevent the French at first gaining the upper hand in the succession of bloody raids and counter raids which took place during King William's War. In the first place the French possessed far more soldierly qualities and were backed up by a large regular force, while the British settlers had to rely on a virtually untrained militia and a few 'Independent Companies' of regulars. Secondly, the French tried to convert the Indians, and treated them far more kindly than the British who were mainly interested in acquiring and settling on their lands. The Iroquois, the Lords of the Wilderness, took full advantage of the situation, however, and became skilled at playing the British and the French off against each other.

HEADPIECE
Light Infantry from *Manual of Exercise according to the late regulation by the Duke of York*, 1795

The capture of Port Royal in Acadia, in King William's War, by a hastily gathered force of provincials led to British supremacy at the very threshold of Canada. By the Treaty of Utrecht in 1713, Great Britain retained Hudson Bay, Newfoundland, and Acadia, but the French were left in possession of the vital Cape Breton Island. Here, between 1721 and 1740, the French constructed the fortress town of Louisburg to designs by Vauban, and filled it with 4,000 rowdy Swiss mercenaries, fishermen and smugglers. On the outbreak of 'King George's War' in 1744, Governor Shirley of Massachusetts conceived the madcap plan of capturing Louisburg without the aid of regular troops. After initial scepticism, he managed to whip up enough enthusiasm to turn the venture into a Protestant crusade against the Roman Catholics, and a small force of untrained militiamen was despatched to Cape Breton Island under the command of one William Pepperrell, who was as inexperienced as his men. Incredibly the expedition succeeded, and on June 15th Louisberg surrendered to the New Englanders. When under the provisions of the Peace of Aix-la-Chapelle it was handed back to France in return for Madras, the colonists began to suspect that the interests of England did not necessarily coincide with their own. Although the British and the French were now nominally at peace, the situation in North America was far from resolved, and another outbreak was inevitable. The French, incensed by the British colonisation of Nova Scotia by 4,000 ex-soldiers and their families, turned their attention to the Ohio country, and in order to keep English settlers out started to build a chain of forts stretching from Quebec to New Orleans. In 1753 the young George Washington was sent by Governor Dinwiddie to order the French out of the territory allegedly belonging to Virginia, and at the same time to report on French activity in the area. The following year he led an expedition to the vital 'Forks of the Ohio', the site of the newly-built Fort Duquesne, and was involved in a skirmish in which he and his Indians dealt with a small party of French. The results were momentous – 'A volley fired by a young Virginian in the backwoods of America that set the world on fire. French reinforcements were despatched to Quebec, Louisburg was strengthened, and in May 1756, Great Britain and France declared war after a whole year of campaigning had taken place.

In January 1755, the first two regular British regiments ever to be stationed in North America were despatched to Virginia to form the nucleus of an expedition against Fort Duquesne; and to command them the Duke of Cumberland sent the sixty year old General Braddock, formerly of the Coldstream Guards. Cumberland considered Braddock to be the best exponent of large formal movements like that which had almost defeated the French at Fontenoy, but neither realised what was in store for veterans of Flanders when faced by impenetrable forest and an enemy who ignored all the precepts of Turenne and Frederick the Great. The result was disaster. On the evening of July 7th, 1755, Braddock and his 1,400 men, nearly half of whom were Provincials, were set upon by Indians led by the French captain Hyacinth de Beaujeu – stripped to the waist but still wearing his silver gorget – when only ten miles from their objective. In the ensuing shambles, Washington tried to persuade Braddock to let the men fight in Indian fashion, but he obstinately refused to let them break ranks and take cover. Of the 1,459 British troops engaged nearly 1,000 were casualties, shot down on the forest track by an unseen foe; the best of the officers were dead and wounded, and Braddock himself was buried in the middle of the trail so that the column would obliterate his grave and protect it from desecration by the redskins. 'It may truly be said' says Fortescue, 'that over the bones of Braddock the British advanced again to the conquest of Canada'. History has been unfair to Braddock in accusing him of being too proud and rigid to

24 UNITED STATES OF
AMERICA
A *tricorne* hat typical of the
rough clothing worn by the
early American
revolutionary soldier, 1775.
Smithsonian Institution

25 GREAT BRITAIN
Officer's helmet, 9th Light
Dragoons, 1784–1812. A
late version of the so-called
'Tarleton' helmet, which
first made its appearance in
North America at the time
of the revolution.
National Army Museum

appreciate the problems of this new kind of fighting, for there is plenty of evidence, in his orders, that he tried to lighten his men as much as possible and to drill them to fight in file instead of in line. His defeat was crushing, but the French were not in the least surprised, for it had long been their rule never to expose regular troops in the forest without a sufficient force of Indians and irregulars to cover them. The Virginian Provincials came out of the debâcle well, showing that there was an abundance of good irregulars to be found in America.

On September 8th 1755, after an action known as the 'Bloody Morning Scout', Sir William Johnson and a body of Provincials avenged Braddock when they repelled and put to flight a French regular column under the command of Count Dieskau, on the shores of Lake George. After the battle Johnson's Mohawks deserted him and left him without any scouts. He at once began to fill their place by recruiting a body of 'Rangers' from the New Hampshire frontiersmen led by one Robert Rogers. Originally the 'Ranging Company of Colonel Blanchard's New Hampshire Provincial Regiment', Rogers' Rangers were taken into royal pay becoming 'His Majesty's Independent Companies of American Rangers'. Recruited from trappers and frontiersmen whose mode of life was the same as the Indians', they were experts in woodcraft, and were accustomed to carry out long-distance raids to obtain information or cut off the enemy's supplies. They were the only troops to operate during the winter;' . . . in the tomblike silence of the winter forest, the breath frozen on his beard, the ranger strode on snowshoes over the spotless drifts; like Dürer's Knight, a ghastly death stalked ever at his side'.

In 1757 William Pitt became Prime Minister and immediately launched his 'Grand Strategy', which included attacks on the three gateways to Canada – Louisberg, Fort Ticonderoga, and Fort Duquesne. The task of capturing the first was given to Amherst with 12,000 men and a somewhat larger naval force under Admiral Boscawen and was successfully completed in July 1758. The attack on Fort Ticonderoga was embarked upon by Abercrombie – known as 'Aunt Abby' to his officers – with 15,000 men. This expedition was repulsed in a regular Flanders-type battle before Ticonderoga, the British losing Lord Howe – 'The best soldier in the British Army'. The expedition to Fort Duquesne was given to the colonists who eventually entered it, abandoned and destroyed, as were the dreams of French conquest in the Ohio country.

Abercrombie was recalled and Amherst was left to plan the campaign for 1759. In July the French blew up Ticonderoga and Crown Point in the face of an attack by Amherst and the southern route to Canada was open. In September, Major-General James Wolfe made his celebrated ascent of the Heights of Abraham and wrested Quebec from the French, both he and the French Commander, Montcalm, dying in the action. The power of France in the New World was broken. Never again would the Indians hold the balance of power, and the long nightmare of ambush and attack was over for the colonist. At this moment of victory there was no sign of the gathering storm clouds over England's American possession. In the universal rejoicing it was not apparent that within ten years the mother country would become the wicked step-mother and the redcoat a symbol of tyranny and oppression.

In these closing years of the French and Indian war, Amherst, Wolfe and Howe headed the revolt of practical men against the retention of powder and pipeclay for forest fighting. In emulation of the successes of Rogers' Rangers and other similar companies, Wolfe started to form a rudimentary light infantry from his regular regiments. He ordered the formation of a body of 'Light Infantry from the different corps to act as irregulars; the regiments that have been any time in America are to furnish such as have been most accustomed to the woods and are good marksmen and those from Europe are to furnish active marchers and men that are expert at firing ball and all in general must be alert spirited soldiers able to endure fatigue'.

Lord Howe went even further than Wolfe. When he arrived in America with the 55th Foot in 1757, he attached himself to Rogers' Rangers, adopted their rough dress and joined their scouting parties. On his return he proceeded to impart his newly acquired knowledge to the men under his command; and it is probably due to him that the 80th or Gage's Light Infantry, the first light infantry regiment in the British Army, was formed in 1758. Howe's drastic reforms were not accepted without demur. Officers used to campaigning in luxury in Flanders did not take kindly to having to do their own washing or carry their own eating utensils.

Up until the period of the French and Indian War, the dress of the military in North America closely followed European fashion, if we allow for the time lag in the transmission of changes caused by distance. The provincial militia were supplied with weapons and equipment only. The men wore their own clothes and only the officers had any semblance of uniform. Regiments raised for service were sometimes clothed in a uniform manner, two regiments raised for the attack on Port Royal in 1707 being dressed in red and blue. Later a uniform coat was sometimes supplied but not the nether garments. The Connecticut regiment stationed at Fort Edward in 1757 were ordered 'always to appear with their hats Cok'd., and with shoes and stockings on, before they march to ye grand parade'. After 1739 certain regular British regiments were raised in America and the cloth for their uniforms was sent direct from England together with pattern coats as samples. Where uniforms were issued they were usually red, blue or green, and occasionally, in the northern provinces, 'drab' or brown.

The main change in American uniform came from copying the Red Indians who dressed themselves in the skins of the animals they hunted. The French trappers – the *coureurs du bois* – early on adopted the Indian dress of fringed buckskin shirts, leggings and moccasins, and gradually the English copied them. When Washington, who was a great dandy, was commissioned in 1755, he ordered a 'proper suit of regimentals', specifying that as he did not much like gaiety in dress his coat should have a 'neat embroidered button hole' instead of lace. The officers of his Virginia regiment were smartly turned out in blue with red facings, laced waistcoats and hats, but according to an eye-witness '. . . the ordinary soldiers have no uniforms nor do they affect any regularity'. When Washington went off with Braddock, his officers wore native buckskin shirts instead of their regimentals. Braddock himself did at least make some attempt to rationalise the dress of his regulars. Officers were ordered to carry fusils instead of their espontoons, and to leave off their gorgets and sashes. Sergeants were to carry firelocks like the men; and the men were to put thin bladders between the lining and the crowns of their hats to ward off the sun. The regimental colours were taken into the field but the equipment of the men was lightened as much as possible so that they could carry more food.

It was the influence of the Rangers and their effect on soldiers like Howe and Wolfe which introduced a measure of practicality into British uniforms. The Rangers at first wore a mixture of their provincial uniforms and Indian clothing. They put the sleeves of their coats on their waistcoats, and wore their shortened coats over them. With them they wore a skirt or petticoats rather like those of sailors of the period, and buttoned leggings. On their heads they wore bonnets similar to those worn by Scottish Highlanders or a small 'flap hat' which consisted of the crown of the normal cocked hat with all but a small piece of the brim in front cut off, the remaining part being turned up to form a flap. Their arms usually consisted of a firelock, toma-hawk and scalping knife. The officers affected Indian beadwork round their hats and on the cross-belt from which they hung their powder horn and bullet bag.

Wolfe's light infantry copied the Rangers in cutting down the size of hats and coats. In his orders the new dress is described in detail:

'. . . the sleeves of the coat are put on the waistcoat, and instead of coat sleeves he has two wings like the Grenadiers, but fuller; and a round slope reaching about half-way down his arm; which makes his coat of no incumbrance to him, but can be slipt off with pleasure; he has no lace, but the lapels remain; besides the usual pockets, he has two not quite so high on his breast, made of leather, for ball and flints; and a flap of red cloth on the inside, which secures the ball from rolling out, if he should fall. His knapsack is carried very high between his shoulders, and is fastened with a strap of web over his shoulder, as the Indians carry their pack. His cartouch box hangs under his arm on the left side, slung with a leathern strap; and his horn under the other arm on the right, hanging by a narrower web than that used for his knapsack; his canteen down his back, under his knapsack, and covered with cloth, he has a rough case for his tomahawk with a button, and it hangs in a leathern sling down his side, like a hanger, between his coat and waistcoat, no bayonet, his leggings have leathern straps under his shoes, like spatterdashes; his hat is made into a cap with a flap and a button and with as much black cloth added as will come under his chin and keep him warm when he lies down; it hooks in the front, and is made like the old velvet caps in England.'

An account of light troops at the reduction of Louisburg describes them as having 'The beard of their upper lips, some grown into whiskers, others not so but well smutted on that part. . . .'. Howe instituted similar changes in dress with the troops under his command. The '80th Light-Armed Regiment of Foot' otherwise known as 'Gage's Rangers', raised in 1758, were dressed in short reversible coats, red on one side and brown on the other, with black buttons, and carried no colours.

In 1755 at the instigation of the Duke of Cumberland, the 62nd or Royal American Regiment – renumbered in 1757 as the 60th – was raised as a special corps combining the advantages of both regulars and rangers. By Christmas Day 1755, 4,400 men had been raised – largely from German settlers in Pennsylvania – and been divided into two battalions. The 1st was commanded by the Swiss, Henri Bouquet, who set about training his men to be specialists in forest fighting. In a submission to the Duke of Cumberland dated 12th May 1757 regarding the dress of his regiment, amongst other suggestions, he mentions long loose trousers reinforced with leather below the knee, and 'un bonnet à l'Almande' with a skull of boiled leather and a neck flap.

In the 60s, various other 'Light-Armed Regiments' were raised in the British Army including the short-lived (1761–2) 119th or Princess' Own Regiment, who wore short jackets and a curious peaked helmet based on the light dragoon pattern. After the Seven Years War, light companies in the British Army were severely reduced. The disciples of the Great Frederick were in the ascendant, and many colonels, feeling that the peculiar dress of the Light Infantry spoilt the uniform appearance of their battalions when on parade, abandoned them completely, and relied on merely cropping their hats and coats should an emergency arise.

The emergency came in 1776 when the Thirteen Colonies declared

26 UNITED STATES OF
AMERICA
Coat worn by Peter
Gansevoort as Colonel of
the New York Volunteers,
1776.
Smithsonian Institution

themselves independent and entered into armed conflict with Great Britain. In April 1775, after mounting tension, General Gage despatched the flank companies of the Boston garrison, to Concord, twenty miles away to seize the military stores gathered there by the provincial Congress. After a brush with the local militia at Lexington on the way out, the British returned to encounter the fire of a hastily assembled force of provincials. In spite of the fact that a large proportion of the British force consisted of light infantry, they were severely mauled by their assailants hidden behind walls and houses. Two months later, at the Battle of Bunker Hill, General Gage mounted a direct frontal assault against a position held by well-concealed marksmen. In spite of heavy casualties his beautifully dressed lines gained the crest and the rebels withdrew, having gained a moral victory. Both actions showed how much had been forgotten in the short time since Howe, Wolfe and Amherst.

The war started by the incident at Lexington was to last until 1781. In that year, the Americans, although on the point of collapse, managed with French assistance to bottle up part of the British army in Yorktown and force it to surrender.

The armies of the American revolutionaries consisted mainly of militia, and most of the regular fighting was done by their French allies. The British Army, on the other hand, having been drastically reduced after the Seven Years War relied largely on hired German auxiliaries and on loyal provincial regiments. The American War brought about another revolution in tactics, for the British Army now encountered an untaught civilian army. Gradually, Washington created the 'Continental Army' consisting of regular regiments; but in the few battles where drill and manoeuvring were required his men were usually outfought by the British. Once again it was the irregular soldier who was found to be of most use in the wild and thinly populated countryside, and the British formed special corps to meet the American rifleman with his own weapons. The regulars too were loosened out; the number of ranks was reduced from three to two, the files opened up, and all movements carried out loosely with a considerable amount of independent action allowed in their execution. This loose order was possible partly because there was little fear of cavalry attacks – the bulk of regular cavalry being used as mounted infantry. On their return to England, British officers were convinced that the musket was of more importance than the bayonet and that the longer the front of fire the better.

In the opposing army, the transition was from looseness to stiffness. At the beginning of the war, American units were trained on a variety of textbooks including the 'Norfolk Discipline' and the British manual published in 1764, and there was little uniformity in their drill. Eventually they came under the hand of a half-pay German captain who called himself 'Baron von Steuben'. He prepared a book of his own, based on English, French, and German sources, which became the standard manual for the Continental army, and was to remain so for over a quarter of a century. Steuben simplified the words of command, and also used the two-ranks system. Under him the army of the United States changed from a rabble of citizens with muskets into a semblance of a disciplined European army.

The attempts of the officers of the Continental army to improve themselves did not escape the notice of Captain Ewald of the Hesse Cassel *Jäger*, trained marksmen, recruited from huntsmen and gamekeepers, and armed with the rifle. 'When American baggage fell into our hands . . . every wretched knapsack, in which were only a few shirts and a pair of torn breeches, would be filled up with military works such as "The Instructions of the King of Prussia to his Generals",' unlike the British officer, 'whose portmanteaux was rather filled with bags of hair powder, boxes of sweet-smelling pomatum, cards (instead of maps) and then often on top of all, novels or stage plays.'

In 1785, two years after the war came to an end, Cornwallis, fresh from America, watched the last manoeuvres directed by Frederick the Great 'such as the worst general in England would be hooted at for practising; two lines coming up within six yards of one another and firing until they had no ammunition left; nothing could be more ridiculous'. The wheel had come full circle, however, because also watching was a staff officer by the name of Dundas who in 1788 published an elaborate work extolling the Prussian system, which was eventually adapted for the use of the British army in 1792. Dundas' 'Eighteen manoeuvres' re-introduced close order and three ranks, and the march by plummet and pace-stick and in some ways put the clock back, but on the other hand it was beneficial in that it abolished the custom of colonels employing their own particular systems in their regiments.

The tactics of the American rebels at the outbreak of the war re-awakened interest in the dormant light companies, and these went to war dressed in accordance with the report of the Board of General Officers dated 4th March 1771. The most common type of cap consisted of a black leather skull rein-forced with three bands of chain and a plate on top, with a front plate bearing the number of the regiment surmounted by a crown with G.R. on each side. The short jacket had wings on the shoulder and was worn over a sleeved red waistcoat; the breeches were white and worn with calf length gaiters. As the war progressed, dress became more varied. Contemporary watercolours show British infantry in wide brimmed slouch hats with feather, short single-breasted jackets – probably the waistcoat – and 'overalls' consisting of breeches and gaiters in one piece. The remainder of the infantry wore the uniforms laid down in the 1768 Warrant but there was a tendency to simplify. The officers and sergeants of the Foot Guards serving in America were ordered to make up their coats with white instead of gold lace, and officers of other regiments removed the lace from their coats completely, which were now often worn buttoned up. Gorgets and espontoons were dis-carded in favour of firearms. In the winter, special clothing was issued; blanket-coats and leggings, woollen or fur caps and long knitted hoods, and fur mittens. In the summer, overalls of white or striped canvas were general wear. The British had only two regular cavalry regiments in America, the 16th and 17th Light Dragoons; they were dressed in their normal uniforms, but each troop was issued with four rifled carbines.

It is sometimes forgotten that the American revolution was also a civil war and that the colonists were divided about 60 per cent to 40 per cent in favour of remaining under British rule; in fact it was the stupidity of the British, rather than the power of the rebels, that lost them the colonies. The supporters of the Crown were hated by the rebels, and were known by them as 'Tories'. In fact a very large army could have been raised from the Tories, but the apathetic British government made no effort to do so. Once regiments were formed they were neglected, supplied and clothed with British cast-offs and generally distrusted. Instead the British government preferred to pay out good money for the services of German mercenaries, who did more harm than good to their cause.

Most of the Loyalist regiments were clothed in green in 1776, but two years later, much to their disgust – for they had no desire to be taken for British regulars – they were ordered to wear red. In the early years they were divided into battalions with the normal grenadier and light companies.

By 1780 only five of the original twenty-seven regiments remained but they were larger and more varied in organisation. The Queen's Rangers first commanded by Rogers, and then by Simcoe, had eight companies of riflemen,

27 UNITED STATES OF
        AMERICA
Officer's coat, Washington's
Continental Army, 1776.
Blue and buff were very
popular colours for
'gentlemen's' clothes of the
period.
Smithsonian Institution

one of grenadiers, one of light infantry, one of highlanders, and one of hussars, which was later augmented by three troop of light dragoons and a three-pounder cannon. The Queen's Rangers were generally dressed in dark green and bore on their caps a silver crescent badge.

The other famous Loyalist corps was Butler's Rangers, who wore dark green faced with red, and a leather cap with a low brass plate, reminiscent of those worn by Prussian Fusiliers.

There were several cavalry corps, notably the King's American Dragoons who were dressed in red like British regular cavalry, and Tarleton's Legion who wore green. The portrait of Tarleton by Sir Joshua Reynolds shows him wearing a peaked leather helmet with a bearskin crest passing over it from front to rear. This headdress, which was to become very popular in the British and French armies, has been claimed by American writers as their only contribution to military dress, but when the French adopted it in 1791, it was known as a *Casque à la Tarleton*.

In addition to the regulars and the provincials, or 'Tories', the British enjoyed the services of various German corps. Between 1776 and 1780 contingents from Hesse Cassel, Hesse Hanau, Brunswick, Anspach, Bayreuth and Anhalt Zerbst arrived in America. In general they were infantry and artillery units dressed in dark blue after the Prussian manner with hats, grenadier caps, and fusilier caps. The exceptions were the Hesse Cassel and Brunswick Jägers, who wore dark green, with brown leather equipment and leggings; and the Anhalt Zerbst Regiment who wore white with red facings and a felt cap *à la Hussard*. The Brunswick Dragoons wore light blue coats with yellow facings, buff waistcoats and breeches and hats, while the Würtemburg Hussars, according to the Chelmsford Chronicle of April 5th 1776, made 'an appearance singularly formidable, with their tall fur caps, their long stiffened moustaches, plaits, green uniforms and yellow boots'. On service, most of the German infantry wore striped ticking overalls.

The American revolutionary soldier generally wore whatever he could lay his hands on. The first uniform regulations appeared in 1779, but even after that the problem of supplying new clothing in a country of vast distances and hardly any communications kept their appearance fairly ragged. The articles of clothing issued were those common to most European armies with one or two exceptions, which were developments of the American tradition of forest fighting. The most typical and common garment was the fringed hunting shirt so much beloved by Washington. Made of linen or homespun, it was loose and comfortable and could be dyed regimentally if required. Originally worn by riflemen, these shirts or 'frocks' became general wear for most of the army. The regimentals of the Continental army when issued were of basic blue, although shortages of that colour and the latitude allowed to regimental commanders to decide on their own led to a variety of colours being used. White waistcoats and breeches were generally preferred and after 1778 one-piece overalls, woollen for winter and linen for summer, were adopted by most regiments.

The cavalry consisting of four regiments of light dragoons were dressed in helmets and coats of various colours, the 4th wearing British scarlet coats captured from the 8th and 24th Regiments of Foot. There were also several partisans corps dressed in a wide variety of colours and styles.

In 1780, the general and staff officers of the Continental army were given a uniform blue coat, with buff facings and linings. When Washington took command of the Continental army before Boston in July 1775, general officers were ordered to wear ribbons similar to those of orders of chivalry, over their waistcoats and under their coats. The commander-in-chief wore a light blue ribbon, major-generals purple, brigadiers pink, and brigade-majors and A.D.C.'s green. Regimental field officers were to wear red or pink cockades in their hats, captains yellow and subalterns green. Sergeants were to have red epaulettes or strips of cloth on the right shoulder, and corporals green.

In 1780, new regulations for the distinguishing of rank were introduced. Major-generals were to have two silver stars on their epaulettes and a black and white hat plume, and brigadiers one star and a white plume. Field officers were to wear two epaulettes – silver in the cavalry and infantry and gold for the artillery – and company officers one only – captains on the right shoulder, and subalterns on the left. Different staff officers wore different coloured feathers in their hats to indicate their duties or appointments. Non-commissioned officers were distinguished by woollen epaulettes, white for infantry, yellow for artillery and blue for cavalry, sergeants to have two, corporals only one on the right shoulder. Where epaulettes were unobtainable, strips of cloth were used in their place.

In May 1780 a large French army under Rochambeau arrived at Newport. The French contingent was dressed in its regular European uniform and does not seem to have altered its dress in any way to suit local conditions, other than adopting a black and white cockade in courtesy to Washington whose officers wore the black cockade. In return the Americans adopted the black and white 'Union cockade' as a symbol of the expected unity of the French and Continental armies.

With the end of the Seven Years War, and the beginning of a period of comparative peace in central Europe, Russia was free to embark on a policy of expansion in the south-east in an attempt to secure her 'natural frontiers' along the coast of the Black Sea. Under Catherine the Great, who speedily ousted Peter III, the Russian army continued to develop into a disciplined Western style army. During her reign there emerged a group of native-born Russian generals – 'Catherine's Eagles' – who were to have an important effect on this development. The most celebrated of these was Suvorov, who composed a series of maxims aimed at improving the morale and striking power of the Russian soldier. In his campaigns against Polish insurgents in 1794 and against the Turks, and other Eastern hordes, he never lost a battle but was always opposed to irregular forces. In his Turkish campaigns, in particular, he was assisted by the Austrians, who preferred to help Russia than to allow the Turks to regain the frontier provinces of the Empire. The Austrian army provided most of the technical services of the Russian army and a proportion of other troops, sometimes as high as fifty per cent. The terrain over which Suvorov fought was wide and open, and his opponents undisciplined, so that although changes from normal methods of warfare were found to be necessary they were of a different kind from those prevalent in North America. Catherine's lover, Prince Potemkin, a brilliant administrator, was made Viceroy of the newly conquered territories, known as 'New Russia', and it was he that brought about the various reforms in the clothing and equipment of the Russian army led by Suvorov and Rumiantsev. These reforms have usually been hailed as a purely Russian invention, but in fact they represent a form of rationalisation common among military thinkers of the time and contained many features of Polish and Austrian origin.

At the beginning of the reign of Catherine II, the innovations of Peter III were promptly discarded, and the uniforms of the Russian army reverted to those of the time of Elizabeth. The composition of the Guard, with the exception of the cavalry, remained unchanged. The *Chevaliers-Gardes* became a permanent body, for guards of honour only, with a pantomimic court dress strongly reminiscent of the mock classical armour worn in eighteenth century operas; and a squadron of hussars and two *sotnias* of Cossacks were formed for escort duties with the title of 'Hussars and Cossacks of the Imperial Court'. The infantry of the line, considerably augmented, lost the distinctive facing colours which had previously been left to the choice of colonels. Grenadiers retained their caps, now ornamented with the cypher of Catherine II, while the remainder continued to wear the hat. In 1763 this had a brim three inches wide, but by 1780 it was much higher and shorn of its braid border. The coat, which was either double or single-breasted, was worn hooked up in summer, and buttoned over, in the case of the former, in winter. The skirts of the officers' coats were worn loose, and those of the rank and file hooked up. In the regiments of the Guard the coat became tighter and the collar higher after 1786, when the rest of the army received the 'Potemkin uniform'. Waistcoats were also single or double-breasted, those of the officers being laced according to rank. The waistcoats of the men had sleeves and were worn in summer months without the coat, together with white linen trousers.

Up until 1786 both officers and men powdered their hair and wore it tied in a queue, the knot of which was at the height of the collar and the end in line with the waist. After 1786 the chasseurs of the Guard and the troops of the line wore their hair short and unpowdered, while officers of the Guard and line and the rank and file of the remaining units of the Guard retained their powder and pigtails.

In 1770 companies of *Chasseurs à Pied* were attached to each battalion of infantry; later they were formed into a corps of chasseurs four battalions strong. The chasseur companies of the three regiments of the Guard wore uniforms based on those of the Pandours. Their round black caps had a peak front and rear, and were worn with braided green jackets and tight pantaloons. The chasseurs of the line wore similar caps, green sleeved waistcoats, and pantaloons like the Guards.

The cavalry of the line underwent several drastic alterations. Regiments of carabiniers were raised to take their place alongside the cuirassiers and dragoons. In 1786, as part of the general rationalisation programme, hussars and lancers were converted to *chevaux-légers*, and were later augmented with a light troop of *chasseurs à cheval*; these in turn were formed into complete regiments. Perhaps the most interesting, if shortlived, experiment was the formation between 1769 and 1775 of so-called 'Legions' – powerful mixed units of all three arms, reminiscent of the modern 'Combat Group'.

In 1786, at the instigation of Prince Potemkin, the uniforms of the line were completely changed for the eminently practical but ugly 'Potemkin uniform'. The hair of the men was cut short and left unpowdered and all regiments of line infantry, chasseurs, cuirassiers, dragoons, cheveaux-légers, artillery and engineers received a version of the new uniform.

The hat was replaced by a helmet consisting of a black felt skull, with a small peak edged with black leather. At the front there was a metal plate, and at the back a band of coloured cloth – the colour varying with units – from the upper edge of which hung two cloth flaps, which could be used in winter to protect the ears and neck by crossing them underneath the chin and fastening them to the top button of the lapel. Regiments and arms were further differentiated by a coloured woollen crest placed transversely across the helmet.

Instead of the coat or *Kollett*, all arms now wore the *kurtka*, a short jacket of Polish origin, which above the waist resembled the ordinary coat except that the collar was higher. Below the waist it had short tails edged with a broad coloured band which was left loose in winter, to form a kind of tunic, and hooked back in the summer. The *kurtka* was considerably in advance of its time, and was the prototype of what was to become the universal jacket of the Napoleonic wars. The trousers were loose and had a broad band of coloured cloth cut with an ornamental edge down the outer seams. Below the knee, from mid-calf downwards, they were reinforced with black leather and there was an opening on the outside which closed with seven buttons. In summer months, waistcoats and trousers of white linen were worn. The sleeved waistcoat was cut like the *kurtka* but had wooden buttons covered in white linen, and the trousers were the same as the cloth ones except that they had no leather reinforcement. The equipment worn with the new uniform consisted of a black or white leather waist-belt which supported the cartouche pouch, a black leather pack and a metal water-bottle. There were considerable regimental variations in the colours of the various parts of the uniform; the infantry of the line and the dragoons having red and yellow cloth bands and yellow crests to their helmets, green *kurtkas* with red facings, and red trousers. The cuirassiers had straw coloured *kurtkas*, and the carabiniers blue. The regiments of *chasseurs à cheval,* and the four regiments of hussars raised in 1788, wore the *mirliton.* After 1786 the chasseurs of the Guard wore a variation of the 'Potemkin uniform', in that they wore *kurtkas,* although their caps were of a special regimental pattern.

The 'Potemkin uniform' was principally intended for the rank and file, although, in the army commanded by Potemkin himself, officers wore a version of it for active service and guard duties. However, while all these new ideas were being tested on the frontiers of the Russian Empire, the heir-apparent, Paul Petrovitch – the future Paul I – was busily turning the clock back to the days of his father Peter III. Around his country estate at Gatchina there were stationed a number of regiments which he dressed and drilled according to his own whim – that is to say in strict accordance with the worst excesses of Frederick William I. While the quantity of troops was not large, the changes which he made in their dress are interesting as they foreshadow the complete rejection of Potemkin's principles which was to take place when he came to the throne.

The oft-repeated statement that Catherine the Great restored to the Russian army its truly national character, in place of the Prussianism of Peter III, is not strictly true. In the temporary rejection of powder and pipe-clay, Russian leaders like Suvorov and Potemkin were expressing the general swing away from formalism characterised by the end of the eighteenth century. We have seen, in the case of the British Army, that while this was admirable for irregular warfare, the order and discipline of the Prussian system was still necessary when regular armies met in battle. The great Suvorov's victories were small in size and won against either insurgents or native irregulars; and it is doubtful if the Russian army could ever have defeated Napoleon without the solid foundation of order and discipline built up by Paul I and his successor Alexander I.

In 1786 Frederick the Great died. In October of the same year, an unknown Corsican was commissioned into a French artillery regiment, to embark upon a military career which was for a time to shatter all the previously held tenets of warfare. All the theories and experiments of the eighteenth century would combine to defeat those armies which still clung to the Prussian system; but finally it would be the discipline and fire-power perfected by Frederick the Great that would defeat the new Alexander.

v *Liberty or Death*

On August 10th 1792 the scum of Paris, reinforced by five-hundred ruffianly *Marseillaises*, stormed the Tuileries Palace. As the infuriated mob hurled themselves at the stolid red-coated Swiss Guards on duty in the forecourt, they were watched with mounting disgust by a sallow-faced lieutenant of artillery recently arrived in Paris. The ensuing massacre – in which 1,200 of the insurgents and some 800 of the 900 Swiss were killed – was the turning point in the French Revolution which had started in 1789. Louis XVI and Marie Antoinette fled to the hall where the National Assembly met, and shut themselves up in the tiny reporters' box. By the evening the power of the monarchy had been finally broken, and the National Convention was in charge of the destiny of France. But even at this moment of victory the seeds of the downfall of the Convention were already being sown. On April 20th Louis XVI had declared war on his wife's nephew, the Emperor Francis II of Austria, and at this very moment the armies of Austria and Prussia were moving towards the frontiers of France, bent on punishing this insult to Absolutism. At the same time the young Napoleon Buonaparte, shocked at seeing soldiers threatened by civilians, was watching and waiting 'at the disposal of Providence'.

The Revolution which had started off so hopefully in the summer of 1789, welcomed as the dawning of a new age by all liberal men, had come about through the gradual collapse of the monarchy as a form of government. The worsening economic situation, the splendid isolation of the 25,000 noble families from the everyday running of the country, the dissemination of new ideas and philosophies concerning the nature of man and his rights, and the ever present example of a successful revolution in North America all contributed to the outbreak. Unfortunately, the moderates were gradually ousted by the fanatics, the days of glory turned into the 'terror', and by 1792 Republican France stood alone facing the united monarchies of Europe, who viewed her liberal ideas with fear and distrust and the resulting blood bath with loathing.

In July, as Austria and Prussia declared war and advanced towards the

HEADPIECE
From *Manual of Exercise according to the late regulation of the Duke of York,* 1795

French frontier, every able-bodied Frenchman was called upon to fight for his country. The outcome of the impending battle seemed certain; the untrained rabble of *sansculottes*, could be no match for the disciplined veterans of the enemy. On September 20th 1792, the Allied commander-in-chief, the Duke of Brunswick, inexplicably turned away after a brief artillery duel at Valmy. The impossible had happened; the citizen-army had beaten the regulars. 'From this day and this hour', wrote Goethe, 'dates a new epoch in the history of the world'.

In the 'Revolutionary Wars' which followed, and which lasted until the Peace of Amiens in 1802, France was opposed to Britain, Austria, Prussia, the Netherlands, Spain, Portugal, and the various states of Italy and Germany – even Turkey – with various degrees of success. In the initial flush of self-confidence after Valmy, the French army defeated the Austrian army at Jemappes and occupied Brussels, but their success was short-lived and in the following year, in face of numerous setbacks, a *levée en masse* was ordered, and France became one large armed camp; warfare was suddenly no longer a sport for kings, but once again, as it had been during the Thirty Years War, a matter of belief involving the whole of the population. There was resistance, though, and in the same year the Royalist citizens of Toulon opened their gates to the British. The convention ordered the town to be retaken and it was here in December of the same year that Buonaparte first came to prominence with his brilliant handling of the Republican artillery.

The French royal army, already in a state of disintegration, was completely shattered during the Terror. In the disorders of July 1789 five out of the six battalions of the *Gardes Françaises*, the heroes of Fontenoy and the pride of the Maison du Roi, deserted to the mob and took an active part in the capture of the Bastille. The King, in a vain attempt to prevent bloodshed, ordered the army to retire from Paris, leaving the defence of the capital to 12,000 hastily formed National Guards. The Comte d'Artois, brother of the King, the Prince de Condé, and numerous other generals and officers fled from the prospect of the guillotine. The bulk of the army stood by in the provinces waiting for orders that never came, to be gradually taken over by the primitive and turbulent militia which sprang into existence throughout the country.

The final blow was struck in a series of military reforms promulgated by the National Convention in the early part of 1791. The whole of the Household troops, with the exception of the Swiss Guard, was disbanded; the remaining cavalry and infantry regiments, including the foreign regiments, were stripped of their princely and territorial titles and given numbers instead. New regulations introducing promotion on an elective basis reduced military discipline to an impossibility. To become an officer the candidate had either to rise through the ranks or pass an examination; but a quarter of the vacancies for a sub-lieutenancy was reserved for non-commissioned officers, to be filled either by seniority or election. In a similar manner one-third of the field-officers, and half of the generals, were appointed by election. Finally, after Louis XVI's unsuccessful flight to Varenne, all ranks of the army were required to swear a new oath of allegiance from which the King's name was omitted. The officers, with generations of hereditary service to the monarchy behind them, felt unable to serve now that the King was no longer head of the army, and thousands of them resigned. By September 1791 two-thirds of all French officers had left to join their *émigré* relatives across the frontier. The Republicans were not sorry to see them go. France had renounced the lust for conquest, and had no need of a tyrant's army. If she were attacked, a people in arms, led by their own elected officers, would be more than a match for the 'mercenaries' of the enemy.

Decrees of February 21st and August 12th 1793 established a Republican Army. The infantry regiments were formed into *Demi-Brigades* consisting of one former royal battalion and two new volunteer battalions, a system which led to both old and new battalions acquiring each others bad habits. Former light infantry battalions were formed into *Demi-Brigades Légères*. The cavalry, on the whole, were left to themselves because of the difficulty of raising and mounting new volunteer regiments at short notice. Regiments like the 1st or Berchény Hussars, still composed of Germans, carried on as though nothing had happened at all, retaining their old drill and customs, and maintaining their fine discipline.

When war came, the sudden need to defend the country from the onslaught of the Austrians and Prussians left no time for the training of the new citizen army in the refinements of linear tactics. All that there was time to do was to devise a method of getting the large bodies of volunteers as near to the enemy as possible before their enthusiasm waned. The answer lay in the combination of trained skirmishers, taken from the light companies of the regular regiments, and massed columns of attack as already suggested by Saxe and his disciples. The skirmishers, used to operating on their own, would advance and fire on the enemy while the main column awaited the result. If the enemy wavered, the column could usually be urged upon to advance and close with the bayonet. The surprisingly half-hearted opposition offered by the allies during the opening stages of the war increased the confidence of the raw Republicans to such an extent that the onslaught of their columns, accompanied by the shouting of political slogans and the singing of revolutionary airs like *La Marseillaise* and *Ça Ira*, became irresistible. All the carefully worked out systems of the eighteenth century were swept away by what one historian has called 'novel forces of overwhelming strength'.

Under the various revolutionary governments human life was cheap and the gaps left by heavy casualties were soon filled by conscription. Poverty at home meant that the army could no longer afford a large baggage-train and it had to live off the land, which meant keeping on the move in order to survive. Political commissioners attached to the various armies, and the constant threat of the guillotine, kept generals active and energetic; indeed Buonaparte's victories in Italy in 1796 were not so much the result of his own innovations as of energy taking over from inertia. His expedition to Egypt resulted in the loss of his entire army and in a less politically disturbed period he would probably have been court-martialled and shot; but as it turned out, he was able to turn the political situation to his own advantage.

Turmoil in politics and the arts of war was accompanied by corresponding changes in military dress. The distinction maintained in every European army between the regular regiments, in their neat modified civilian dress, and the irregular regiments, dressed partly in practical clothing and partly in outlandish national dress, was ignored in the new French army. Powder was done away with as symbolic of tyranny, and the long-haired unkempt look was all the rage. The officers put in charge of the ragged ill-shod troops either paid no regard to the matter of clothing at all or affected an outrageous dandyism, in imitation of the *Incroyables* who infested the Palais Royal gardens. With the whole-hearted delight of savages presented with beads and trinkets, the elected officers of the Republic festooned themselves with feathers, flowing cravats, extravagantly cut coats encrusted with gold embroidery, voluminous tricolour sashes, pelisses, sabretaches, and anything else which caught their ill-educated fancies. In time, Napoleon was to master the worst sartorial excesses, but from now onwards the French army was to retain its own peculiar style of dress bred from the early days of the Revolution.

28 FRANCE
Marine's 'round' or
top-hat, c. 1800.
*Musée Royale de l'Armée,
Brussels*

Right
29 AUSTRIA
Dragoon wearing the 17th
Century style helmet which
was taken into use again
during the Turkish war of
1788–9.
*Heeresgeschichtliches
Museum, Vienna*

Left
30 AUSTRIA
Soldier's cap, or '*Kaskett*',
infantry regiments, 1769–98.
Perhaps the source of
inspiration for the British
'Waterloo' shako introduced
in 1812.
*Heeresgeschichtliches
Museum, Vienna*

On the outbreak of the Revolution the regular regiments retained the major part of their old uniform, which in the last years of the *ancien régime* had been growing gradually stiffer and more Prussian in style. The volunteers who fought side by side with them wore whatever they could lay their hands on. The red woollen 'Cap of Liberty' – copied from the Americans – and the Phrygian cap – the symbol of the great classical democracies whose heir the Convention claimed to be – could be seen in the ranks side by side with the smartly cocked *bicorne*. Red, white and blue striped linen trousers, loose, ample, and plentifully patched, peasant clogs, and the sleeveless *carmagnole* jacket of the worker, were worn with parts of the new blue uniform of the National Guard. The rivalry between the *blancs* of the older army and the *bleus* of the new was intense until they shook down together under active service conditions. The former called themselves 'soldiers of porcelain' because they had received their baptism of fire, their less fortunate compatriots were mere 'soldiers of pottery'.

The regulation headdress of both infantry and cavalry was the cocked hat, now bicorne rather than tricorne in shape, and adorned with the red, white and blue cockade of the Republic. Grenadiers wore the old fur cap, with a metal front plate, reintroduced in 1789 after thirteen years of disuse. After a few years of campaigning the state of these caps became so bad that grenadiers tended to wear the ordinary hat with a red woollen tuft or horse-hair plume. Many soldiers wore the cloth *bonnet de police* or forage cap – a descendant of the old dragoon *bonnet à flamme* – with its long falling tail ending in a tassel. The dragoons continued to wear their classical brass helmets, introduced in 1762, but they now had leather peaks attached to the front. The hussars retained their *mirlitons* sometimes seen with peaks as well. In 1791, a version of the 'Tarleton' helmet was introduced for the *demi-brigades*, and in the following year it was adopted by the *chasseurs à cheval*. This helmet was made of black felt, or leather with brass reinforcing bars, with a leopardskin turban and a black woollen crest, but the manufacture was generally so poor that many regiments sent them back to store. The 46th Regiment received their helmets in 1793, but by 1796 they were so un-comfortable and smelly that they threw them into the river at Strasbourg on their way back from exercise at the Citadel, the grenadiers starting the demonstration. The regiment was charged five francs per man for the hats which were given out as replacements, but they appeared quite satisfied with their deal. Other regiments, like the 9th *Demi-Brigade*, retained their helmets as late as 1798. An order of September 7th 1793 ordered the battalions of light infantry to wear helmets of varnished leather of a green colour. When the helmet went out of use, however, instead of returning to the hat, they adopted a peaked shako similar to that worn by the light cavalry. This alteration was regularised in October 1801, when the shako was specified in detail. The body, which was slightly wider at the top than at the bottom, was black with a peak, a lozenge shaped metal plate in front with the national cockade over it, and a button and lace loop on the left side from which sprang a tall feather plume. This was the first appearance of the infantry shako which was to become standard throughout the French infantry, and its derivation from the Hungarian or Croat *mirliton* is clear, as some regiments had bags or *flammes* around these shakos as late as 1810.

The manner in which the hat was to be worn in the cavalry was described in an order of June 7th 1801:

'The cavalry will wear the hat with front point in the direction of the left eye, the right eyebrow almost covered, the left uncovered by an inch. The officers and non-commissioned officers should set an example to the men so that they became accustomed to this manner of wearing their hats, and that the hats themselves acquire the right shape.'

Occasionally the commander of a regiment might give the order for the hats to be worn *en colonne*, or fore and aft. In 1798 Generals Kellerman and Bourcier submitted a project for the reorganisation of the cavalry including the suggestion that all the cavalry should be given metal helmets similar to those of the dragoons. In 1801 the 8th Cavalry-Cuirassiers adopted the helmet in accordance with these proposals.

The coats, waistcoats and breeches of the Infantry were white with cuffs and lapels of regimental colour. The white of these uniforms, being natural wool, had a grey-beige tinge to it and showed up slightly differently to the white of the turnbacks. The coat had a small upright collar closed in front, as did the waistcoat, which also had long sleeves with coloured cuffs. Officers wore similar uniforms but with a gilt or silver gorget, and epaulettes indicating their rank of either gold or silver lace. The blue coats of the national guard were similar in cut, but had red collars and cuffs and white lapels and turnbacks. By 1801 the cut of the coat had changed slightly. The collar became higher and the lapels were so cut that they could be hooked up close across the breast for the first few inches, then falling away at an angle towards the skirts. This very typical French arrangement, known as the *habit-veste*, was the most common form of uniform coat as late as 1812, and was retained by Guards units right up until the end of the Empire.

The cavalry wore blue coats of a similar cut with blue collars and shoulder straps, and lapels, cuffs and turnbacks of the facing colour. Their waistcoats and breeches were buff coloured, the former made of cloth and the latter of leather. The only change during the revolution was the substitution of the tricolour for the white cockade. The cuirasses worn by the Cuirassiers du Roi, later the 8th Cuirassiers-Cavalry, consisted of both front and back pieces of steel attached at the shoulders with brass scales, and at the waist by a narrow leather strap. The lining of the cuirass, which was of cloth, extended beyond all the edges and was slightly gathered. This basic pattern of cuirass became standard throughout the French army and exists until the present day.

The dragoons wore green coats of similar cut to the cavalry, but dark green with different regimental facings. Their waistcoats were buff cloth and their breeches buff leather. The *chasseurs à cheval* and the hussars retained their former uniforms: the chasseurs in dark green dolmans and tight breeches, and the hussars in all their former glory of red, blue, light blue, pearl grey, brown and green.

After the death of Frederick the Great in 1786, the Austrian army emerged as the most important and effective in Europe. In the period between the end of the Seven Years War and the French Revolution when the Austrian army took part in the wars against the Turks, in company with Russia, various attempts were made to rationalise the uniforms of the army, which were in any case comparatively simple. At the outbreak of the Revolutionary Wars the uniforms in use were a modified version of those introduced in 1769, but in 1798 new regulations introduced an even simpler style of dress. The presence of Austrian units in the low countries, in the early years of the war, gave both their allies and their opponents a chance to see how functional or otherwise their uniforms were and they were freely copied by all the participants.

Austrian influence turned out to be greatest in the matter of a suitable headwear. From 1769 the headdress of the infantry and *chevaux-légers* was the *Kaskett*, while the grenadiers continued to wear their fur caps with a

Officer's jacket, 16th or the
Queen's Light Dragoons,
1796–1812. Worn with the
'Tarleton' helmet and a
pelisse, the British Light
Dragoon uniform was the
equivalent of the continental
hussar's dress. This
particular jacket was worn
by Cornet Polhill *c.* 1812.
National Army Museum

Left
32 AUSTRIA
Soldier of the
*Husarenregiments Dragobert
Sigmund Graf Wurmser,*
c. 1800.
*Heeresgeschichtliches
Museum, Vienna*

large and highly ornamented brass front plate. The cloth bag at the back was folded up and attached to the body of the cap by means of a yellow and black woollen cockade on the right side. Until the outbreak of the war, infantry officers had continued to wear the cocked hat, but gradually officers on active service adopted the same headwear as their men so as to offer a less obvious target. In 1798 the *Kaskett* was done away with and the entire army with the exception of hussars, uhlans, and grenz (frontier) infantry, was issued with a variant of the classical helmet. The Austrian version had a boiled leather skull with front and back peaks. A leather and brass crest supported a *chenille* of yellow and black wool. On the front there was a brass plate with the Imperial cypher. This helmet was copied in a variety of designs by the Russians, Prussians, and British.

Cuirassier and dragoon regiments continued to wear the cocked hat except for a short period during the Turkish war of 1788–9, when they appeared in the old open cavalry helmet with the lobster tail so common during the seventeenth century. This helmet appears to have been known at the time as a *Pickelhaube*, thus providing a direct link between the Thirty Years War and the 1914–18 war. After 1798 both cuirassiers and dragoons adopted a helmet of slightly different shape from the infantry, although a drawing by J. B. Seele in the Royal collection, dated 1799, shows a party of Austrian dragoons wearing a variation of the *Kaskett* with a plume on the left side, a leather crest on top of the cap and a peak in front.

The hussars and some of the grenz infantry regiments wore a peakless cylindrical cap with a lace loop and rosette in front, which, in a few years, was to become the standard headdress for all hussars. After 1798 this cap was worn with a peak, giving it an even more modern appearance and turning it into a proper *shako*. Other grenz infantry regiments wore a plain felt cap, obviously based on the *mirliton* and *haiduk*; this also was given a peak in 1798, and was probably the model for the so-called 'stovepipe' shako later adopted by the British. Although the Austrians had been experimenting with the formation of regiments of Polish uhlans since 1781, it was not until ten years later that the first regular 'lancer' regiment was formed. The traditional Polish fur cap, with the squared off and padded crown, was worn by this regiment with a black and yellow plume. When a peak was added, in 1798, the rudiments of the lancer's *chapska*, which was later to reach such magnificence, could already be seen.

The basic colour of the uniforms of the infantry and cavalry was to remain white as a result of an unsuccessful series of experiments with a grey cloth in 1775. The cut of the coat was short and loose with distinguishing regimental colours. The infantry had a broad turned-down collar, a shoulder strap on the left shoulder, large round cuffs, and broad turnbacks, all in the facing colour. The cuirassiers and dragoons had a low stand-up white collar with regimental patches on the fronts, small round cuffs, and white turnbacks edged with regimental coloured braid. Both infantry and cavalry coats were single-breasted, buttoning up the whole way from waist to neck. Artillery and grenz regiments wore the infantry coat in brown *Jäger* and engineers in grey, and *chevaux-légers* in green.

Austrian infantry regiments were divided into German and Hungarian, a distinction which was only noticeable below the waist. The former wore white cloth waistcoats and breeches, with black knee-length gaiters, and the latter tight blue breeches, piped and decorated with Hungarian knots in black and yellow worsted cord. This fashion was retained with the new 1798 uniform which gave the infantry a short single-breasted white jacket with a high collar, small neat cuffs, and short turnbacks in regimental colours. The new cavalry jacket adapted the old pattern to the new shape, retaining the collar patch and the laced turnbacks. With the new uniforms officers started to wear the short black *Kaputfrock*. This is the first appearance of the knee-length double-breasted frock coat. With its yellow collar and black and yellow tasselled sash it was a particularly elegant and effective uniform.

The newly-formed lancers wore green coats with red collars, lapels, cuffs, and turnbacks with green waistcoats and white breeches. Hussars continued to wear their garishly coloured national uniforms, but by 1770 they had started to wear overalls which buttoned all the way down the sides and were held down by a strap under the instep. An interesting fact about the Austrian lancer formations is that, on the regimental payrolls, the ancient distinction between the *Towarisch* and the *Podstowi* was retained. The former was no longer a noble but a volunteer, and the latter no longer a servant but an enlisted man.

Alongside the Austrian army in the early years of the long conflict against the French stood the Prussian army, recently bereaved of its great leader. His successor, Frederick William II, tried in a rather half-hearted way to put a stop to its apparent decline by means of a series of reforms of organisation and uniform, but the problem was too deep-rooted to allow an easy solution. The advanced age of the bulk of the senior officers, and their complete reliance on the leadership of Frederick the Great, led to a complete lack of initiative in the high command, and the custom of exempting persons of ability from military service on economic grounds led to a corresponding lack of quality amongst the lower ranks. Frederick William II tried to cure all this, but the performance of the allied commander-in-chief at Valmy showed that he had not succeeded.

When Frederick the Great died in 1786, the Prussian army had only one regiment of foot *Jäger* and three regiments of light infantry. Frederick William II tried to strengthen this arm of the service by amalgamating various units to form twenty 'Fusilier' battalions who, in spite of their name, were in fact light infantry. The remainder of the infantry – 141 regiments in all – were reorganised to consist of one battalion of grenadiers and two of musketeers, each company having ten riflemen who could be assembled in battalion groups under an officer. Finally, in 1787 steps were taken to form a corps of horse artillery. In 1797, Frederick William II died, to be succeeded by Frederick William III in whose reign the Prussian army continued on its downward path until it was crushed at Jena.

As in the French and Austrian armies, the Prussian infantryman was relieved of his hat, but only for the time being, as it was restored to him in 1798 after the death of Frederick William II. Instead, he was issued with yet another variant of the *Kaskett* – this time a low-crowned cap with a high front and back flap, edged with regimental lace. In the centre of the front flap there was a large metal emblem; a grenade for the grenadiers, the royal cypher for musketeers, and the Prussian eagle for fusiliers. The hat was, however, retained by infantry officers, and for cavalry – cuirassiers and dragoons. In 1798 the foot guard grenadiers were issued with a new pattern grenadier cap, which was given to the line grenadiers in the following year. This new cap was a mixture of the Austrian *Kaskett*, the old mitre-cap, and the Russian helmet worn by Potemkin's army. Basically it consisted of a low flat-topped felt cap with a cloth neck flap in the regimental facing colour, and a front peak. Attached to the front of the cap was a high leather plate edged all round with black wool and embellished with a large metal grenade. Below this was a second metal front plate stamped with a black painted Prussian eagle.

The coats of the infantry were at first made looser than they had been in the previous reign, and the broad lapels were made so that they could be

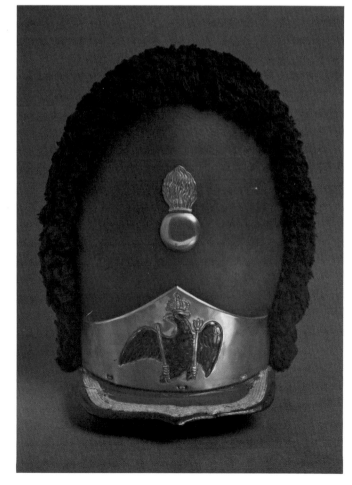

37 GREAT BRITAIN
Soldier's coat, Battalion
Company, 2nd, or
Coldstream Regiment of
Foot Guards, *c.* 1793. Coats
of the 'Flank Companies' –
Grenadier Company and
Light Company – had
'wings' on the shoulders.
The Guards Museum

Page 88
Above left
33 AUSTRIA
Soldier's shako, Hussar
regiments, 1800. The version
of the traditional headdress
of the *haiduk*, which was
the forerunner of the *shako*.
Heeresgeschichtliches
Museum, Vienna

Below left
34 AUSTRIA
Officer's helmet, Infantry
regiments, 1798–1809.
Heeresgeschichtliches
Museum, Vienna

Above Right
35 PRUSSIA.
Officer's gorget, guard
infantry regiments,
1786–97.
Mollo Collection.

Below Right
36 PRUSSIA.
Soldier's grenadier cap, line
grenadier regiments,
1798–1809. The Prussian
version of the Austrian
kaskett.
Musée Royal de l'Armée
Brussels

buttoned over. The turnbacks were red for every regiment; but the collars, which became gradually higher, the lapels, and the cuffs, were in regimental colours. The fusiliers – as light infantry – wore green with variously coloured facings. After 1798 there was a return to the earlier more impracticable style of dress, with the coat, now more properly a jacket, becoming tighter. Ostensibly for reasons of economy, the lapels, which were now hooked all the way down, were sewn down, and the waistcoat was reduced to a false bottom sewn to the underside of the jacket. In 1794 the white breeches and gaiters, introduced in 1787, were protected by wearing loose canvas trousers over them. These were grey when new but constant washing turned them white after a time.

The Prussian cuirassiers now abandoned their black cuirasses, retaining the short *Kollett* – the last relic of the old buff coat – which was white for all regiments except the 2nd, who clad their bulky forms in a delicate shade of lemon yellow. The *Kollett* now had a high collar of the regimental colour with a patch of the coat colour at the front. The cuffs, of a shape generally known as 'gauntlet', were of the facing colour edged with broad regimental braid, also used down the two front edges of the *Kollett* which were closed with hooks. Two shoulder straps of regimental colour and coloured braid round the two short tails completed the *Kollett* which was worn with a waistcoat, which showed very slightly below it. A coloured waist girdle, leather breeches, jacked boots, leather gauntlets, a pouch and belt, a broad braided carbine belt, and an embroidered sabretache worn high on the hip completed what was one of the most elegant uniforms of the period. The dragoons wore a blue uniform similar to that of the infantry. The collars, lapels, cuffs, and braid trimming to the small skirts were in the regimental colour. Waistcoats were white cloth and breeches whitened buff leather. The equipment consisted of a pouch and belt, a carbine belt, and a waist belt for the broadsword, or pallasch, and bayonet. The Prussian hussar regiments altered their uniforms very little during this period, except that like the Austrians they adopted buttoned overalls when on service.

With the accession of Paul I to the Imperial throne, in 1796, the Russian army went through a smartening-up process to remove any traces of the laxness of the Potemkin era. Under his petulant eye, Prussianism returned to the Russian army; but how far this process extended to areas free from his personal interference is not clear. The stiff pipe-clayed infantrymen illustrated by the nineteenth century historian Viskovatov, with their glazed expressions and their hair painfully scraped back into the fiercest of pigtails, are very different from the musketeers seen in Switzerland in 1799 by the German artist Kobell. These have unpowdered hair, plain double-breasted green coats, pantaloons and calf-length boots. With their canvas haversacks over the right shoulder, and their fur packs on their backs, they present a very business-like appearance.

Under Paul I the bulk of the infantry, the cuirassiers and the dragoons wore the cocked hat. Grenadiers wore the metal-fronted mitre-cap, and fusiliers the slightly smaller version, both exactly like the Prussian model. Hussars wore the *mirliton*, and a regiment of Poles, dressed very similarly to those in Austrian service, wore a completely cylindrical *chapska*, stitched into vertical flutings, with a cloth band round the lower half.

The green infantry coat was worn hooked together in front, although it appears to have been double-breasted. The collar, cuffs and turnbacks were different colours in accordance with a complicated system of 'Inspection' areas introduced first by Peter III and again by Paul I. White waistcoats and breeches were worn with the old-fashioned high gaiters – white for the Guards and black for the Line. After 1800 the coats had fall-down collars, decorated in the Guards with lace loops. The officers retained spontoons, and wore gorgets and sashes. The Guards regiments each developed their own pattern of embroidered loops for the collar and cuffs, after the Prussian style.

The cuirassier regiments wore white, like the Austrians and Prussians, with leather breeches and jacked boots. The collar of the *Kollett* was still the fall-down pattern, but otherwise the uniform was identical to that of the Prussians, complete with braided carbine belt, girdle, and sabretache. Like the Austrians, however, cuirassiers retained the front piece of the cuirass, enamelled black and attached by a system of white buff straps round the wearer's back. The *chevaliers-garde* squadron, later enlarged to a regiment, wore an elaborate *super-veste* over their *Kollette* instead of cuirasses — a relic of their operatic Court dress of Catherine's time. After 1800, when Paul I accepted the Grand Mastership of the Order of St. John of Jerusalem, the *super-veste*, together with many other items worn by Guards regiments, was embellished with a white Maltese Cross. Dragoons were dressed in exactly the same fashion as the Prussians except that their coats were green.

Before leaving the Russian army, it is necessary to remark on a curious uniform worn by Russian hussar officers in undress. With their hair strictly tied and powdered, and their black moustaches, their appearance was strange enough to begin with, but the addition of a huge cocked hat, and a long braided *kaftan* reaching almost to the ground, gave them an extraordinary appearance; but it was not many years before British hussar officers were sporting the long *kaftan*, now in the guise of the long pelisse coat, greatcoat, or redingote.

By 1800 Cossacks seem to have been dressed in a more regular fashion, with fur caps rather like those worn by hussars, and short jackets and baggy trousers.

The French royal officers — and in some cases men — who fled their home-land, assembled across the German frontier and in 1797 formed themselves into three main divisions. As a general rule, the regiments they formed clothed and armed themselves at their own expense, but relied on their Prussian and Austrian allies to provide them with food and lodging. Under-standably there was very little system or order in their dress, and features from Austrian and Prussian uniforms were thoroughly mixed up with those of the *ancien régime*. The history of the *émigré* regiments is a sad one. Rather like the loyalists in America, they were neglected and, instead of being built into a powerful weapon with which to restore the monarchy to France, were so starved of provisions and money that they had to be disbanded. Of the three 'Armies' — they were little more than 5,000 strong — those of the Princes of Bourbon were disbanded after the disastrous campaign of 1792. The third, which was a much more serious organisation formed at Worms in the summer of 1791, was commanded by the Prince de Condé. It survived the 1792 campaign and in the following year, on receipt of the news of the execution of Louis XVI, it was taken into Austrian service. When Austria made peace with France in 1797, it was taken over by the Russians. In 1801 it was disbanded, and those who wished to continue serving against the French were transferred to British service and formed into the *Chasseurs Britanniques*. The Army of Condé tried very hard to preserve its French identity. The whole army wore the white cockade in their hats, and a white armband decorated with fleur-de-lis; moreover they were only allowed to accept and wear royalist French decorations. Otherwise, like the other two armies, their uniforms were a very mixed bag, changing constantly as they passed from the service of one country to that of another. Other isolated units of *émigrés* were to be found in the armies of Austria, Sardinia, Spain,

Sweden, and Great Britain, who also took into her pay the Swiss regiments who, faithful to the French monarchy for over a century, had resigned in disgust after the massacre of their compatriots at the doors of the Tuileries. The *émigrés* are of importance in that in exactly the same way that the roving mercenaries of the Thirty Years War were the carriers of new ideas in tactics, so the variety and outlandishness of their dress was to serve as a model to their more conservative allies, the British.

In 1793, a British expeditionary force under the command of the young Duke of York was despatched to Holland. After a series of minor but hard-fought actions in support of the Austrians, the British army was compelled to re-embark for England in 1795, in which year the Prussians, Dutch, and Spanish all made terms with France.

1796 saw the rise of Buonaparte to real power, with his appointment as Commander-in-Chief of the army confronting the Austrians in Italy. When he took it over, this army was little more than a rabble of starving unpaid men. Through sheer force of personality he managed to improve it sufficiently in a few weeks to beat the Austrians at Lodi and Arcoli, and at Rivoli in the following year. The war with Austria ended with the Treaty of Campoformio, and France was left with only one enemy still in the field – Great Britain.

Europe was now quiet, so in an attempt to strike at British possessions in India *via* Persia and the Middle East, Buonaparte set off on an expedition to Egypt, accompanied by a large train of *savants*, archaeologists, mathematicians, zoologists, artists and others. Arriving in Egypt on June 30th, Buonaparte soon defeated the disorganised hordes of Mameluke cavalry and Janissary infantry, and occupied Alexandria. On August 1st he suffered a severe blow when his entire fleet was destroyed in Aboukir Bay by Horatio Nelson, as a result of which he was trapped in Egypt with his whole army. An attempt to make his way back to Europe through Syria and Asia Minor was baulked by the obstinate defence of the small town of Acre by the Turks, aided by Captain Sir William Sydney Smith, Louis de Phelypeaux (a royalist French officer who had been a fellow-pupil with Buonaparte at Brienne), and the companies of two British warships. In October 1799, Buonaparte left his army, returned to France and almost immediately took over the government as First Consul.

In 1799 Great Britain, still determined to be the undoing of the 'Corsican Ogre', formed a second Coalition in which Russia, Austria, Portugal and Turkey were her main allies. The British despatched two expeditionary forces overseas; the first to Holland, again commanded by the Duke of York. Allied with a Russian force, the British made little headway against the French and, in spite of a victory at Egmont-op-Zee in October 1799, finally evacuated Holland, not to return for ten years.

The second British force, commanded by the best and most experienced British general of the time, Sir Ralph Abercrombie, was despatched to Egypt in 1801 to 'try conclusions' with the French army left behind by Buonaparte. At the bloody and dearly-won battle of Alexandria, Abercrombie defeated Menou, the French commander, and captured Cairo.

In May 1800, Buonaparte turned his attention once again to the Austrians in Northern Italy. Crossing the Alps by the St. Bernard Pass with his whole army, he fell on the rear of the Austrians and defeated them at the Battle of Marengo on June 14th. The Austrians under the Archduke John suffered a further crushing defeat at the hands of Buonaparte's only serious rival in the French service, General Moreau, some months later at Hohenlinden.

On February 9th 1801, the Austrians and French signed the Treaty of Luneville. The King of Naples, part of the coalition, added his signature on

93

March 29th. Paul I of Russia had already retired from the struggle; the Coalition was at an end. Exactly a year later, in March 1802, England signed the Peace of Amiens, and France was left the victor in Europe, with her boundaries stretching to the banks of the Rhine, and a group of satellite republics fashioned in her image. In the same year, Buonaparte was made Consul for life.

By 1793, whatever George III and the Royal Dukes may have had to say on the subject, the British army was in a deplorable condition. As is usually the case at the outbreak of war, it was sadly reduced in numbers, smartness and efficiency. Apart from the Foot Guards and a few other regiments, the force sent to Holland under the Duke of York was little more than a hastily impressed rabble, dirty and badly dressed, many of the recruits having 'slop' clothing only – canvas jackets and trousers. By the end of the war, however, things were somewhat better. The reforms of Dundas regularised the drill and smartened the men; those of the Duke of York made certain long overdue improvements in their general lot while Sir John Moore and his disciples were setting into motion a continuation of the type of training started by Wolfe and Howe.

In 1793 the infantry and the heavy cavalry – Household Cavalry, Dragoon Guards and Dragoons – wore the cocked hat. The grenadier companies kept their fur caps for peace-time duties but tended to wear hats when on active service. The light companies wore a whole gallery of hats and caps, based on the round or top hat; sometimes the crown was square-topped, sometimes round like a bowler hat, sometimes with a turban round it and sometimes with a fur crest like the Tarleton helmet, which was also the regulation headdress of the light dragoons.

Gradually as the war proceeded and the British came into contact with foreign troops they adopted many of their fashions, which in their turn were regularised to become part of official uniform. Thus by 1800 the Infantry were wearing the 'stove-pipe' shako with a peak and an ornamental brass front plate, a sort of cross between the Austrian *kaskett* and the hussar *mirliton*. Woollen tufts on the front indicated the company – white for the right flank or grenadier company – white with a red base for the centre or battalion companies – and green for the left flank or light company.

The basic red coat of the British infantryman also went through some drastic changes during this period. In 1796 the custom of turning up the collar, which had been creeping in for some years in imitation of civilian fashion, was officially sanctioned. In 1797 the coats were ordered to be buttoned up in front. Soon after lapels were done away with and the coat became a short, single-breasted, jacket with small cutaway skirts. Regimental differences, which were rife in the British army owing to the fact that colonels still contracted for their regiment's clothing, consisted in different coloured collars and cuffs and in a bewildering variety of regimental worsted laces which were used for trimming the jacket. Grenadiers and light companies wore 'wings' on their shoulders, and battalion companies shoulder straps with woollen tufts.

At the outbreak of the war, the infantry wore either white breeches with black knee-length gaiters or white pantaloons with black calf-length gaiters; but in some places, particularly in hot climates, all-in-one white canvas overalls were worn. In the Egyptian expedition of 1801, the British infantry wore plain round hats and loose white trousers.

Up to 1796 the heavy cavalry were dressed in long red coats, those of the dragoon guards being double-breasted with lapels, and the dragoons single-breasted with laced buttonholes. After 1796, both had short single-breasted jackets laced across the front in a variety of ways. By the end of the period the cocked hat was going out of use in favour of various different patterns of 'watering caps' which were really shakos. The biggest change in British cavalry uniforms at this time was the adoption of blue 'shell' jackets and sleeved underwaistcoats by light dragoons in 1784. In 1796 these were changed for short laced *dolmans* of completely hussar appearance. From about 1790, officers of some regiments had started wearing pelisses, quite unofficially; and although there were still no hussar regiments in the British army by name, the light dragoons fulfilled their function quite adequately. But perhaps not sufficiently for the Prince of Wales, who now emerges not only as the arbiter of elegance in the heartlands of St. James's – known popularly as 'the four corners of the World' – but also as a military enthusiast in the tradition of Frederick William I. In 1791 the Dukes of York and Cumberland paid a visit to Berlin, and while they were there they were bombarded with requests from the Prince to send him samples of Prussian uniforms. In particular he wanted 'the complete uniform, accoutrements, saddle, bridle, etc., of one of Zeithin's Hussars . . . as one day they may give us some little ideas for our own. . . .'.

At the beginning of the Revolutionary Wars, there were still no official hussar regiments in the British army, other than those formed from *émigrés* and other foreigners. At one time the 25th Light Dragoons were known as 'Gwynn's Hussars' or the 'British Hussars', but this title seems to have been self-awarded. A description of the regiment at Southampton in 1796 is hardly flattering:

'They were dressed in dirty grey jackets, leather helmet caps, fearfully heelballed, white leather breeches, shoes and long black gaiters. They wore white feathers thrust into the side of their helmets and sabretaches tucked up so as to descend no lower than their hips. . . .'

The grey jackets were issued to light dragoon regiments for service in India, where the regiment subsequently served. The *émigré* hussar regiments remained a sufficient time in the British Isles before being shipped off to end their days in the West Indies, to create a considerable amount of interest amongst the military and to gladden the heart of the Prince of Wales, whose father obstinately refused to let him serve abroad. After inspecting the Hompesch Hussars in 1796, he was so impressed with their appearance that he gave them the title of the 'Prince of Wales's (Hompesch) Hussars'. By 1800 the light dragoons were wearing *mirlitons* now called 'flugel caps' in England, sabretaches, tight breeches and Hussar boots.

In 1792 the *Rules and Regulations for the formations, Field exercise and Movements of His Majesty's Forces'* was published with the blessing of the Duke of York in his capacity of Commander-in-Chief. Its real author was the pedantic and schoolmasterish Scotsman Sir David Dundas, and it was a compilation of the Prussian system, destined to serve the British army as its basic drill-manual until 1870. Dundas could not abide the irregular formations which had been creeping in ever since the American War. Whenever light companies assembled in battalion strength they used a drill of their own invention and their rapid movements found no favour with 'Old Pivot', as he was irreverently named. In his opinion light infantry,

'. . . instead of being considered as an accessory to the battalion, . . . have become the principle feature of our army, and have almost put grenadiers out of fashion. The showy exercise, the airy dress, the independent modes which they have adopted, have caught the minds of young officers, and made them imagine that these ought to be general and exclusive . . .'

But in spite of his fumings, developments in the field of skirmishing continued apace with the absorption into the 5th Battalion of the 60th Regiment of the *émigré* and other foreign chasseurs and *Jäger* sent to the West Indies. Furthermore, in 1800 an experimental corps of riflemen was formed which subsequently became the famous 95th or Rifle Brigade. Both the 5th and 6th Battalions of the 60th and the 95th were dressed in green – the former with red and the latter with black facings. The officers wore light dragoon dress complete with Tarleton helmets and sabretaches, while the men wore stovepipe shakos and black equipment. The orders of these regiments, as was the case with the European *Jäger* regiments, were given by bugle-horn and whistle.

Dundas' remarks about the airs and graces of young officers bring us to the difference between the French Revolutionary and preceding periods. Until the middle of the eighteenth century, clothes had been purely and simply garments to cover and protect the body, subject, of course, to fashion and the wealth of the wearer but developing slowly along a narrow path. The eighteenth century passion for travel and classical antiquities, and the increase in political theorising, led to clothes being worn to express a particular idea or attitude to life. The 'Romantic' movement in the arts, which dates from the great cataclysm of 1789, was already being expressed in England some years earlier with the emergence of the 'Dandy' or 'Macaroni'; and with the custom of wearing fancy dress clothes, either Eastern or of an earlier period like the 'Van Dyck' suits in which the sitters of Gainsborough and others liked to be portrayed. The healthy no-nonsense outdoor life of the English country gentleman, and his love of hunting and racing led to a special English style of dress, careless, and simple yet extremely elegant. Starched neckcloths, sombre blue or brown coats with big brass buttons, immaculate leather 'smallclothse' and hunting boots with leather tops were avidly copied abroad, in reaction to the stiff dress clothes of the tyrants and their courts. The French, furthermore, in adopting as their ideal the democracies of the Ancient World, also adopted their fashion. The gauzy dresses – and the morals – of the Roman courtesans uncovered on the walls of Pompeii and Herculaneum became all the rage in the 'permissive society' let loose by the Revolution. The *Merveilleuses* and their male counterparts, with their high waists and padded bosoms, were faithfully imitated by younger officers of any army which would allow them to get away with it – mainly the British and the French. The swing away from the standards of the *ancien régime* is also illustrated by the specifically British habit of avoiding wearing uniform whenever possible, a custom, which survives to the present day. The satirical *Advice to the officers of the British Army* first published in 1782, makes the following recommendations to 'young officers':

'The first article we shall consider is your dress; a taste in which is the most distinguishing mark of a military genius, and the principal characteristic of a good officer.

'Ever since the days of Ancient Pistol, we find, that a large and broad-brimmed beaver has been peculiar to heroes. A hat of this kind worn over your right eye, with two large dangling tassels, and a proportionate cockade and feather, will give you an air of courage and martial gallantry.

'The fashion of your clothes must depend on that ordered in the corps; that is to say, must be in direct opposition to it: for it would show a deplorable poverty of genius if you had not some ideas of your own in dress.

'Your cross belt should be broad, with a huge blade pendant to it – to which you may add a dirk and a bayonet, in order to give you the more tremendous appearance.

'Thus equipped you sally forth, with your colours, or chitterlin (Shirt frill) advanced and flying; . . .

'When you visit your friends either in town or country, or make an excursion to any other place where your regiment is not known; immediately mount two epaulets, and pass yourself off for a grenadier officer.

'Never wear your uniform in quarters, when you can avoid it. A green or a brown coat shows you have other clothes besides your regimentals, and likewise that you have courage to disobey a standing order. If you have not an entire suit, at least mount a pair of black breeches, a round hat, or something unregimental and unmilitary.'

General Mercer, who served during the Peninsular and Waterloo campaigns with the Royal Horse Artillery, has recorded many of the eccentricities of military dress at the beginning of the nineteenth century. The cocked hat, for instance, was subject to the various vagaries of fashion. The smartest thing to do was to wear it 'fore and aft' as in the Navy, and as soon as officers got on active service, they abandoned the feather and wore it in this fashion. It was also considered very *à la mode* to have a curved base line to the hat so that, when it was placed square on the head, the two ends with their tassels interfered with the wearer's shoulders. 'When fore and aft the foremost part hid the face, and the hinder served instead of a "hand" to scratch between the shoulders behind'.

When Mercer joined the Horse Artillery in 1804, the waist of the jacket was so high that the sash came up to the armpits. 'It was the fashion of the day for boys to imitate or try to resemble women, wearing as they did such short waists, and filling out the jacket with handkerchiefs to resemble the female figure'. The French General Marbot, who served in the Berchény Hussars during the Revolution, recalls one officer who used to wear false calves to fill out his Hungarian breeches, and the embarrassments caused when they slid round to the front during an inspection. Other 'dandyisms' consisted of wearing immensely long chains – eighteen inches at least, according to Mercer – to hold the buttoned overalls down under the instep, and trailing the sabre along the ground, a custom which applied equally to the British and French armies.

Although an order went out in 1795 abolishing hair powder in the British army, the custom was kept on by the more reactionary colonels until about 1809. One of the last regiments to obey the order was that commanded by the Duke of Kent, and even then it was only after an inspecting general had threatened to have their queues cut off on parade unless they were removed by a certain date. When the Duke was Governor of Gibraltar at the turn of the century, he issued a series of orders about hair and dress which rival those of the 'Royal Sergeant' himself. Mercer recalls that,

'The first person who boarded every ship coming into harbour was his Royal Highness's hairdresser, and no officer was allowed to land until he had submitted his head to be operated on by this functionary. On the top it was to be cut in a horseshoe form; a string put round the ear and held in the mouth decided the termination (downwards) of the whiskers. . . .'

Young officers whose hair was too short to be put into proper shape might find themselves sent on six months' leave in order to let it grow. Or alternatively, false queues of stuffed chamois leather, with a wisp of hair at the end, could be worn spliced to the wearer's own hair.

39 GREAT BRITAIN
Officer's silver shoulder
belt-plates.
Above 60th (Royal
American) Regiment, *c.* 1780
Centre 56th (West Essex)
Regiment, *c.* 1790.
52nd (Oxfordshire)
Regiment, 1800–15.
Below 73rd (Highland)
Regiment, *c.* 1780.
National Army Museum

The Egyptian campaign had a great effect on costume, both military and civilian, and design generally. Sir William Sydney Smith, the defender of Acre, was the first of a long line of Englishmen who fell in love with the desert and in particular with Arab dress. He is said to have arrived at the Admiralty with the Egyptian despatches wearing a turban and flowing robes, with a brace of pistols stuck into his sash; and most officers of either army returned home sporting a viciously curved Mameluke sabre dangling from a silken shoulder cord.

Buonaparte having defeated the fierce Mamelukes, with their shields and Saracen helmets, formed his own regiment out of them; and when he returned to France in 1799 he was accompanied by the magnificent figure of his personal attendant, Roustam. On October 13th 1801, Buonaparte, now First Consul, ordered Colonel Rapp to form a squadron of Mamelukes as part of his guard. With their prancing Arab horses and their operatic costumes, the Mamelukes became the rage of Paris and, almost overnight, turbans became the height of fashion and everyone was planning to redecorate their apartments in the Egyptian style.

General Buonaparte and his elegant wife had come a long way. The ragged *sansculottes*, victorious everywhere else, were now massed in their splendour along the coast of France facing England. Their generals – ex-smugglers, ostlers, and butcher-boys amongst them – had had the rough edges smoothed off by travel and success. The French people, tired of years of disorder and bloodshed at home, looked towards their leader to rule them; the Phrygian cap was about to give up its place of honour to the Imperial eagle, the symbol of the New Rome.

VI *Valour and Discipline*

On August 16th 1804, the battalions of the 'Army of the Coasts of the Ocean' formed up in a giant horse-shoe on the undulating downland above the town and harbour of Boulogne. They had been assembled to watch their newly-proclaimed Emperor distribute crosses of his *Légion d'Honneur* to the officers and men who had distinguished themselves in his past campaigns. As he sat on his throne, surrounded by his glittering marshals, in the centre of a vast natural amphitheatre, the August haze was dispelled by a sudden burst of gunfire from ships of the Royal Navy, tacking to and fro on their ceaseless watch over the French coast. The grandiose plan for the invasion of England required only one thing for its successful accomplishment – control of the narrow channel so that the hundreds of flat barges assembled in the area of Boulogne could transfer the Emperor and his army to British soil.

In the following December, three days after his coronation, Napoleon held an equally impressive ceremony in Paris when he presented each of his regiments with the red, white and blue standards, surmounted by their gilded eagles, which were to become the symbol of the new empire. On one side, bordered by neo-classical wreaths of palm and laurel, letters of gold recorded the number and style of the regiment, and the gift of the standard from 'The Emperor of the French', while on the other was inscribed the bleak exhortation, 'Valour and Discipline'; Arcadia had become Rome.

The destruction of the Franco-Spanish fleet at Trafalgar in October 1805 finally brought home to Napoleon the impossibility of his invasion project, and he turned his 200,000 strong army, stretched along the coast, towards Austria and Germany. As the divisions and brigades about faced and set off on their long march across Europe the right flank of the 'Army of the Coasts' became the left flank of the 'Grand Army'.

The story of the lightning campaign which ended in the defeat of the Russians and Austrians at Austerlitz on December 2nd 1805 and the subsequent career of the Emperor are sufficiently well-known. Like all Napoleon's early campaigns, that of Austerlitz and Ulm achieved more politically than any single one of the wars of the eighteenth century. In

HEADPIECE
From *Rules and Regulations for the Sword Exercise of the Cavalry,* 1796

proud imperial tones, an inscription on the arch of the Carrousel in Paris proclaims to this day that,

> 'At the voice of the Victor of Austerlitz, the Germanic Empire fell; the Confederation of the Rhine came into being; the Kingdoms of Bavaria and Würtemberg were created; Venice was reunited to the Iron Crown; and the whole of Italy ranged itself under the laws of its liberator.'

Warfare in the eighteenth century had been limited by the equality of strength and technical achievement of the opposing armies, and had invariably resulted in political bargaining rather than the destruction of one or other army. Napoleon's campaigns, short and final, altered the map of Europe time and time again.

The first and most far-reaching Napoleonic innovation was the system of *Corps d'Armée* established in 1803 in the camps around Boulogne. This was not entirely Napoleon's invention, as the glimmerings of such a system had been seen in the Duc de Broglie's army at the end of the Seven Years War and in the sub-armies of 1793; but Napoleon took the development further than anyone else. His armies now moved along separate routes, in powerful self-contained bodies, each with its appropriate portion of the cavalry and artillery, and capable of pinning down an opposing force until it could be joined by its neighbours. Moving fast over the comparatively well-developed roads of central Europe, the French bewildered and demoralised the armies of the *ancien régime*, whose inability to stand the pace is shown by the string of resounding victories won by the Grand Army. By 1809, when Napoleon's military successes had led to the establishment of a satellite empire throughout Europe, the French army was unquestionably the most efficent in Europe.

Each of Napoleon's great battles was the result of a system, developed over the years, which, in spite of his many successes has been described by some historians as nothing more than the use of the biggest bludgeon possible. Having pinned the enemy down, Napoleon next mounted a flank attack in order to force him to weaken his centre. At exactly the right moment, when the enemy was fully engaged, a hole would be blasted in the weakest point of his line by massed artillery followed by column after column of infantry accompanied by cavalry. When the enemy finally broke, a swift and relentless pursuit by light cavalry usually completed his destruction. However, the principle of divided movement meant that there was always one commander or another waiting for support, while the use of mass to break into the heart of the enemy position meant that Napoleon's battles were chiefly remarkable for their bloodiness.

Gradually Napoleon's opponents began to learn some of his techniques. In June 1808 Sir Arthur Wellesley – later the Duke of Wellington – went to Portugal, convinced that Napoleon's system of manoeuvre was unsound, and in the following years he embarked on a series of victories which proved to the world that there was nothing basically invincible about the French soldier. After 1809 the French army was continuously dissipated by severe losses, and as the quality of the new conscripts got worse so the casualties increased. After the loss of nearly half a million men in Russia in 1812, the balance swung in favour of the Allies, who were rapidly rebuilding their armies on Napoleonic lines.

In Russia in 1812 and in the long drawn out campaigns in Spain, the vast distances and the poor roads highlighted the lack of a proper supply system as one of the main causes of the undoing of the French army; and at Waterloo, Napoleon's own battle system was used against him. Short of

40 FRANCE
Embroidered dress coat, with the embroidered stars of the *Lègion d'Honneur* and the Order of Christ of Portugal, worn by Marshal Davout, *c.* 1810.
Musée de l'Empéri, Salon-de-Provence

Right
41 FRANCE
Major's shako, *Flanqueurs-Chasseurs de la Garde Impériale*, 1813–14. Worn by Baron Rouillard de Beauval.
Musée de l'Empéri, Salon-de-Provence

information, misled by his unreliable subordinates, and forced to rely on the only tactic he knew, he tried to blast his way through a strongly positoned enemy by frontal assault. For over eight hours wave after wave of Frenchmen hurled themselves to death against the rock-like British infantry. In the end it was a combination of the Foot Guards – well drilled in the 'eighteen manouevres' of 'Old Pivot' – and the light infantry – prime examples of the alertness taught by Sir John Moore – who delivered the *coup de grâce*.

As the warmth of the sun gradually soaked up the mists lingering over the field of Waterloo on the morning of the battle, the troops of the Duke of Wellington, drying out their sodden clothing and cleaning their arms, saw, spread out on the slopes of the ridge opposite them, the whole panoply of the Grand Army. Eye-witnesses describe the breath-taking spectacle as regiment after regiment moved out to take up its position, the bands playing *Veillons au Salut de l'Empire*. Later they could mark the progress of the Emperor himself, as he inspected the line, by the shouts of his men. Those watching on the other side saw all the variegated uniforms of the most colourful army ever, assembled together for the last time.

For the Napoleonic wars provided the great melting-pot into which all the different styles of the late eighteenth century – regular and irregular, practical and impractical, Classical and Romantic – were plunged, to be re-cast into the typical nineteenth century uniform. Yet in this time of change the French army was curiously conservative. On the day of Waterloo it was only in the French ranks that there appeared the fur grenadier cap, and the old *habit-veste* of the *ancien régime*. The early years of the French Revolution, with its rejection of former standards of behaviour, its Romantic conceptions of the worship of the Goddess Reason, and its new Arcadian calendar, were followed by the Empire with its emphatic demands for discipline and order. Suddenly the disciples of Liberty had themselves become tyrants, incurring the fierce hatred of 'patriots' in the conquered lands. It was these patriots, in their uneasy alliance with the surviving European monarchs, who took the development of military uniforms out of the eighteenth and into the nineteenth century.

The most superbly clad units on parade that day were without doubt the regiments of the Imperial Guard. Recruited from the most gallant and experienced of his soldiers, this was Napoleon's supreme reserve, the lynch-pin of the whole army. Formed as the Consular Guard in January 1800, it could trace its ancestry through all the various bodies, formed to protect the persons of the Government, to the Royalist *Gardes de la Prévôte de l'Hôtel*, who, on duty at Versailles during the fateful summer of 1789, rallied to the support of the Third Estate when they took refuge in the *Jeu de Paume*. In the Austerlitz campaign, the Guard was scarcely the strength of a division, having a mere 5,000 infantry and 2,000 cavalry; but at Wagram in 1809 it already totalled 25,000 of all arms. When it set out for Moscow in 1812, it consisted of 47,000 men and 200 guns, and although it returned scarcely 5,000 strong, it was rapidly built up again to enable Napoleon to prolong his resistance to the allies in 1814. At Waterloo, kept in reserve until far too late in the day, it was repulsed for the first and last time in its career.

The soldiers of the Guard were strange men; fierce, arrogant, incessant grumblers, and fanatically devoted to the person of the Emperor, they remained at heart staunch republicans, although many of them had in fact served in the Royal Army. When Napoleon formed a regiment of former noblemen – the *Gendarmes d'Elite d'Ordonnance* – in September 1806, the Guards raised such a fuss that they had to be disbanded little more than a year later. At Tilsit in 1807 a Drum-Major of the Guard, passing the King of Prussia, growled to his men 'Don't beat so loud – he's only a King'. From the outset great efforts were made to raise the standard of dress in the Guard and to make them take a pride in their appearance. Under commanders like Augerau, formerly a corporal in the Prussian Guards, and Bessières, strict orders were issued regarding dress and behaviour – the *chasseurs* were not to smoke their pipes while escorting the Council of State – and it is remarkable that the Imperial Guard, with their republican background, were still wearing queues during the Waterloo campaign. The infantry of the Old Guard made a habit of appearing on the battlefield in full dress with white gloves, their bearskin caps complete with plumes and white cap-lines, and grumbled incessantly if they were not engaged. At Waterloo they grumbled equally at being turned out in their marching order of long blue great-coats and blue trousers.

The cavalry of the Guard consisted of the *grenadiers à cheval*, originally the light cavalry of the Consular Guard, the *chasseurs à cheval* raised from Buonaparte's Guides in Italy and Egypt, the Mamelukes raised in 1801, the dragoons, two regiments of *chevaux-légers-polonnais*, and one of *chevaux-légers-lanciers*. In general their uniform changed very little during their long years of service.

The *grenadiers à cheval* in their blue *habit-vestes* with orange aiguillettes, white waistcoats, white leather breeches and boots, adopted a simple single-breasted tailed coat known as the *surtout* as an alternative to their full dress, but otherwise remained unchanged. On their heads they wore tall fur grenadier caps without front plates. The *chasseur à cheval* had two uniforms – the first was a green hussar dolman, a red pelisse, and green breeches, all copiously laced with orange braid, and the second a green *habit-veste* worn with a red waistcoat, braided in orange. The headdress was a low hussar colpack, or busby, with a scarlet bag and orange flounders, and a tall green and red plume on the left side. The green *habit-veste* was one of the favourite garments of the Emperor and appears in many of his portraits. The dragoons wore the same uniform as those of the line with the addition of aiguillettes, and white facings to the *habit-veste*.

The formation of the *chevaux-légers-polonnais* in 1807 introduced the first major innovation in French military dress since before the revolution. As early as 1797, the Polish general Dombrowski formed a legion to fight with the army of Italy against the Austrians, consisting of lancers and fusiliers wearing the by now fully developed square-topped lancer cap with leather peak, cap-lines, flounders and plume. Their dark blue jackets had crimson collars, plastrons and pointed cuffs, and were worn with a striped girdle, blue pantaloons, and hussar boots. All these features were eventually to become universal for lancer regiments. The 1st Regiment of Polish light horse were dressed in similar uniforms of the same colour; two years later they were armed with lances. The 2nd Regiment, the famous 'Red Lancers' of the Guard, raised in 1810, although dressed in Polish style with red *kurtkas* with blue facings, was in fact not Polish but recruited in France and Holland.

The uniforms of the Guard were very expensive, even the ordinary ranks having their clothing and equipment made up by the leading Paris trades-men; and between 1806 and 1810 the clothing of the Guard cost twenty million francs. Lannes, the first commander of the Guard, had to be bailed out by Augerau when he found himself unable to pay a bill of some 200,000 francs. In the period after Marengo, when the Guard was enlarged, the uniforms of the infantry battalions cost 258 francs apiece, and those of the horse grenadiers 517 francs.

The ramifications of the infantry of the Guard are a whole study in them-selves. The two original regiments of grenadiers and chasseurs each in time provided the basic cadre for a whole genealogy of regiments of tirailleur-

42 FRANCE
An officer of the *8e Régiment de Cuirassiers,* 1810–1815, *Musée de l'Empéri, Salon-de-Provence*

43 FRANCE
Officer's helmet and cuirass,
2e Régiment de Cuirassiers,
1810–15.
Musée de l'Empéri,
Salon-de-Provence

grenadiers and chasseurs voltigeurs and flanqueurs. The basic dress was the blue *habit-veste* with white lapels, white waistcoat and breeches, and white gaiters for parade, black for guard, and grey for the march. Later the grenadiers and chasseurs adopted the plain single-breasted *surtout* and later still the long blue overcoat. Both the grenadiers and chasseurs wore bearskin caps with plumes and cap-lines, the grenadiers having a brass front plate. They also had hats for undress which they carried attached to their large fur packs on the march. Also on the march they tied their plumes to the scabbards of their swords by means of their cap-lines.

In September 1803 Buonaparte raised a battalion of sailors who were to act as his escort during the crossing of the English Channel. This battalion remained in existence as the marines of the Guard, known as the 'Naval Hussars' from their hussar *dolmans* which they wore with shakos. Together with the white-clad Dutch grenadiers, raised in 1810, the grenadiers, chasseurs, and marines formed the 'Old Guard' while the remainder formed the 'Young Guard', who, to all intents and purposes, were dressed as infantry of the line except for the use of the Imperial Eagle on their cartouche boxes.

The line infantry and heavy cavalry changed very little in appearance during the Empire, but an increase in the use of light cavalry led to a corresponding abundance of new and fanciful uniform, the chief influence of which was again Polish. The hussars and *chasseurs à cheval* retained their Hungarian dress, the former in every imaginable colour, the latter in green. Both wore a variety of shako, ending up with the very tall stovepipe pattern. In 1811 eight regiments of *chevaux-légers-lanciers* were formed, the first six being French, and the remaining two Polish. The French regiments wore Polish-style kurtkas in green with a helmet with a leopardskin turban and crest similar to the traditional headdress of the dragoons, but with an Austrian style 'chenille' in place of the horse-hair mane. The heavy cavalry underwent little change after all the old cavalry regiments had been given cuirasses and helmets like the 8th Regiment. Later on, the cuirassiers, as they were now called, adopted a short-tailed jacket, and the dragoons adopted the *surtout* in marching order. The carabiniers, who had previously been dressed as horse grenadiers in blue were given white jackets, brass cuirasses, and brass helmets *à chenille*.

The French infantry of the line gradually became more weather-beaten and practical in their appearance in the course of ten years' marching to and fro across Europe. Their basic dress of blue *habit-veste*, waistcoat and breeches, lasted until well after 1812, when it was officially replaced by a short lapelled jacket of distinctly Polish appearance. As late as the 1805 campaign the hat was being worn, although a shako was prescribed for infantry in the regulations of 1804. With their republican disregard for stiffness, the French infantry usually went on campaign in grey overcoats and loose canvas trousers, with their shakos, shorn of their plumes and lines, in black waterproof covers.

By 1809, when the major part of Europe was under French domination and Napoleon had set up a whole satellite system of petty kingdoms and principalities, their armies appeared in a whole range of French inspired uniforms.

A large measure of the credit for the final undoing of Napoleon must be given to the Russian army as reorganised by Alexander I. In 1801 Paul I, whose aggressive insistence on old-fashioned Prussianism was bred partly from fear of his own unruly nobles and partly from fear of French republicanism, finally succumbed to the plottings of the former. During the latter part of his short reign all forms of radicalism in speech and dress had been ruthlessly suppressed. The word 'representative', in whatever context it was used, was like a red rag to a bull to him, and the high collars and un-powdered hair affected by the Jacobins in France were forbidden throughout Russia. On the morning of his death the pavements of St. Petersburg were packed with fashionables sporting their collars and newly-cropped hair; and a fortnight or so later the new Tsar went so far as to decree that 'everybody may dress according to his own pleasure, provided he do not violate public decorum'. Alexander I, who had been educated in the liberal principles popular amongst Europeans before the French revolution, was greatly influenced by British institutions, dress, and manners. 'He has often been heard to say' wrote an English commentator in 1815, 'that the man within whose reach Heaven has placed the greatest materials for making life happy, was, in his opinion, an English country-gentleman'. Almost immediately he succeeded to the throne he set about reforming the Russian army and removing the worst abuses of his father. By 1805 his work was completed, only to be partially undone by the Russian defeat at Austerlitz. At the battle of Eylau, however, fought in the winter of the following year, the stubborn resistance of the Russian infantry prevented Napoleon from forcing a decision. To his early reforms Alexander added others copied directly from the French. In place of the old recruiting 'Inspections', he organised the army into permanent divisions and corps. Furthermore, he established a General Staff course, in which officers of suitable education and intelligence were groomed for careers in higher command. In direct imitation of the French *Légion d'Honneur* he established the Cross of St. George for soldiers. At the same time he did not entirely relax the strict discipline of Paul's day, and his Imperial Guard, consisting, like that of Napoleon, of infantry, cavalry, and artillery, were as upright and spotlessly turned out and could goosestep and gyrate as smartly as anything that the Prussians had ever produced.

The uniforms which Alexander designed for his army were an amalgamation of all the various influences pervading Europe at the time. But perhaps he was most indebted to the quiet elegance of the English 'bucks' who surrounded the Prince of Wales. The two principles of sartorial elegance, as expressed by Beau Brummel, were firstly that a 'gentleman should blend not intrude' and that good taste in men's dress was achieved by 'certain congruities of dark cloth'. Alexander clearly approved of these sentiments, and his officers, in their tall cocked hats worn across the head, their high collars and stocks, their long-tailed dark green coats, their impeccably white leather breeches and shiny boots, would not have been out of place among the members of the *ton* strolling up and down St. James's Street.

By 1805 the infantry was equipped with its new clothing and equipment. From 1803 onwards the hat was replaced by a felt shako with a black leather peak and chin strap. On the front was a white woollen pom-pom, with a coloured centre, above a cockade made of orange and black ribbon. In February 1805 the old metal grenadier cap was abolished for all but the Pavlovski regiment. The caps worn by this regiment at the battle of Friedland were still in use in 1914, complete with bullet holes and the names of their original owners inscribed on them. The remainder of the grenadiers and fusiliers wore very tall thick horsehair plumes on the ordinary infantry shako, and a grenade badge below the cockade. *Jäger* regiments wore a felt top or 'round hat', with the same cockades as the line infantry. In 1807 they adopted the infantry shako, which in the same year was altered to have a black leather top and band and side pieces in the same shape of a 'V' directly copied from the French infantry shako. In 1809, white plaited cap-lines and flounders, and brass chin scales were added; and in 1811 the tall, fat plume was replaced by an equally tall but very thin one.

44 FRANCE
An officer of the *1er
Régiment de Chevaux-légers
lanciers*, 1811–15.
*Musée de l'Empéri,
Salon-de-Provence*

Right
45 FRANCE
Soldier's *czapka,
Chevaux-légers lanciers de la
Vistule*, 1813.
*Musée de l'Empéri,
Salon-de-Provence*

Early in 1812 the characteristic *kiwer*, or scuttle-shaped shako, probably designed by Alexander himself, was introduced. This was entirely Russian and does not seem to have been derived from any recognisable source. The leather bands, chin-scales, cap-lines and other fittings were the same as those on the upright shako. After 1808, again probably as the result of French uniforms seen at Tilsit, the Guards started wearing brass double-headed eagles on the fronts of their shakos.

The Guards and line infantry wore dark green double-breasted jackets with short tails, high open collars and so-called 'Swedish cuffs' with vertical flaps with three buttons on them, the former retaining the embroidered loops on collar and cuffs introduced by Peter III. By some obscure piece of dandyism which survived until 1914, the bottom button-hole was false, and the button itself was half set under the flap on the officers' coats. The *Jäger* at first wore a lighter green but after 1807 they adopted the dark green. In 1812 the collars of the jackets werc made lower and closed.

In 1805 the infantry wore white pantaloons – wool in winter and linen in summer – and low boots. *Jäger* wore light green until 1807 when they adopted green wool for the winter. In 1807 these were replaced by white all-in-one overall-gaiters buttoning up to just below the knee in summer, and white woollen trousers with black leather up to the knee, similar to those worn with the 'Potemkin Uniform', in winter.

Perhaps the most characteristic garment of the Russian infantryman, from now on, was to be the long browny-grey greatcoat. The Russian soldier being basically a peasant liked nothing better than loose comfortable clothing. The greatcoat rapidly became his favourite wear in the same way that the *kaftan* had been, centuries before. Now, when on active service, the dress jacket was handed in and stored, and the infantryman wore his shirt and greatcoat.

Under Alexander I, the Russian cavalry consisted of cuirassiers, dragoons, hussars, lancers and *chasseurs à cheval*. As in all the armies in Europe, the former irregular cavalry – the hussars and lancers – now became very much part of the regular army. In the Russian army the dragoons and cuirassiers wore the same headdress – a helmet partly Austrian and partly Polish in conception. It consisted of a tall leather skull with side bars, and front and back peaks bound with brass. The leather crest supported a 'chenille' of black horse-hair. The crests of the officers were white with a black and orange 'summit' and those of generals were white. On the front there was a brass plate with the Star of St. Andrew or St. George for certain special regiments, and double-headed eagles for the rest. After 1812 the white crests for officers were abolished, and cuirassiers were re-equipped with black cuirasses – both front and back pieces. The cuirassiers' jackets were white, the dragoons' dark green. In 1812, in common with the whole army, the collars were lowered and closed. In full dress both wore white breeches and jacked boots, and on service grey overalls with eighteen covered buttons and black leather strappings.

The hussars wore the classic Hungarian dress but Alexander made constant efforts, without much success, to make officers abandon gold and silver lace and braid in favour of silk. After 1803, hussars wore the infantry shako with cords and flounders. The lancer regiments which started off as two regiments of *chevaux-légers* – one Lithuanian Tartar and the other Polish – wore the classical Polish *chapska* and *kurtka* in the popular Polish blue and crimson. At first the front rank only, being the *towarisch*, or nobles, carried lances. After 1803 the two distinctions were done away with although still only the front rank had lances. The *chasseurs à cheval* wore hussar shakos and green

46 FRANCE
An officer of the *5e Régiment de Hussards,* c. 1810.
Musée de l'Empéri, Salon-de-Provence

47 FRANCE
Officer's sabretache, *8e Régiment de Hussards*, 1812. *Musée de l'Empéri, Salon-de-Provence*

Right
48 PRUSSIA
Officer's helmet, line cuirassier regiments, 1809–43. Guard cuirassier regiments had the star of the Black Eagle in place of the eagle on the front of the helmet.
Mollo Collection

Unteroffizier und Soldat des Garde Fusilier Bataillons.

49 PRUSSIA
Soldier's shako, 'Landwehr'
infantry regiments, 1813–17.
The so-called 'Landwehr
cross' was copied directly
from the cap badge of the
Russian militia.
*Musée Royale de l'Armée
Brussels*

Left
50 PRUSSIA
N.C.O. and soldier,
Garde-Füsilier-Bataillon,
1815. Coloured print by
Wolf and Jugel.
Mollo Collection

Right
51 AUSTRIA.
Soldier's shako, infantry
regiments, 1809.
*Heeresgeschichtliches
Museum, Vienna*

Page 118
Above Left
52 AUSTRIA
Soldier's grenadier cap,
1809.
*Heeresgeschichtliches
Museum, Vienna*

Below Left
53 AUSTRIA
Artilleryman's *Hut* or
round-hat, *c.* 1806.
*Heeresgeschichtliches
Museum, Vienna*

Above Right
54 AUSTRIA
Officer's helmet, German
cavalry regiments, *c.* 1815.
The inspiration for the
helmet designed by the
Prince Regent for the
British heavy cavalry in
1812.
*Heeresgeschichtliches
Museum, Vienna*

Below Right
55 GREAT BRITAIN
Infantry officer's 'Waterloo'
shako with shako plate to
the 2nd, or Coldstream,
Regiment of Foot Guards,
1812–16.
Mollo Collection

Right
56 GREAT BRITAIN
General Officer of Hussars
sabretache worn by Lord
Uxbridge, afterwards 1st
Marquis of Anglesey, at the
Battle of Waterloo, 1815.
National Army Museum

dragoon jackets with pointed instead of round cuffs.

In 1808 Alexander introduced a General Staff uniform of dark green with red collars and cuffs embroidered with leaves. This fashion which was copied from the flamboyant dress of Napoleon's marshals and generals was to become the standard staff dress for many other countries.

Alexander also instituted the *levée en masse* or militia. During the 1812 campaign the *opolchenie*, as they were called, gliding through the forests bordering Napoleon's line of retreat, played a great part in his defeat. They wore the basic Russian peasant's costume of long *kaftan* and peaked, or fur-trimmed, cap, on which was mounted their badge – a convex-ended Maltese Cross bearing the cypher of Alexander I. In the following year the Prussians would adopt the same cross for their *Landwehr*, and eventually for the decoration that was to commemorate their 'War of Liberation' – the Iron Cross.

The shattering defeat of the Prussian army at Jena in 1806 proved to be a turning point both in the development of the European army and of military costume.

As the victorious French entered Berlin, and occupied key fortresses throughout Prussia, a limit of 42,000 men was set on the demoralised Prussian army; and of these, 20,000 were impressed into the *Grande Armée* in 1812. After Napoleon's defeat in Russia, there was a resurgence of nationalism in Prussia, and in the early part of 1813 a new Prussian army, with new attitudes and new uniforms, was formed around the nucleus of the regular army. The year after the battle, a military reorganisation commission was set up under the leadership of Gerhard von Scharnhorst. This commission made no attempt to reconstruct the former Frederican army but, on the contrary, introduced many new ideas of a democratic nature aimed at abolishing the time-honoured privileges of the army. In an attempt to bring the army and the nation closer together, cadet schools were reorganised and opened to the middle classes, and in 1813 the *Landwehr* was created as a separate civilian militia. In the War of Liberation of 1813, all sections of society joined together in a great romantic crusade to oust Napoleon. 'It was in the white heat of that war, when conservative and liberal, Junker and bourgeois, forgot their differences in a new-found national unity, that the new Prussian army was forged'. The reforms affected Prussian military dress in two different ways. The regular army, under the influence of Scharnhorst and Frederick William III, was dressed, in a deliberately different fashion from that of the Frederican army, in the new style developed by Alexander I. The infantry retained their blue, but now wore shakos and jackets of Russian pattern with white or grey breeches and knee-length gaiters. The heavy cavalry adopted the Russian style leather helmet with the horsehair crest; dragoons and hussars adopted the shako; and lancers the by now well-established Polish uniform. The traditional rococo embroidered buttonholes on the coats of the officers were abolished, except for the Guard; dismounted officers were given a pack similar to those of the men but smaller and lighter. This last reform – again a direct copy of the Russians – was very unpopular amongst Prussian officers and was referred to as the 'blemish of Chivalry'. The 1809 changes were a complete reversal of the long established Prussian style, but they were the only major change in the whole history of the Prussian army. From 1809 until the introduction of field grey, Prussian and, later, German uniforms developed steadily and logically along the path set for them by Frederick William III.

The first of the nationalist revolts against Napoleon's continental system broke out in the Tirol in 1809, and from then on numerous volunteer units were raised in the various German states. The liberal students of the German

57 GREAT BRITAIN
Officer's helmet, Royal Regiment of Horse Guards (Blue), worn at the Battle of Waterloo by Sir Robert Hill.
Household Cavalry Museum

universities took a leading part in the resistance movement against the French, and as a result there was a curious and important blending of civilian and military fashion. The German student societies, no doubt influenced by the warlike nature of the times, frequently dressed themselves in pseudo-uniforms consisting of forage caps of various shapes, sometimes peaked, and long double-breasted frock coats, reaching to just above the knee. When these students joined hands with the aristocracy and formed themselves into regiments, their dress was adopted by the new units. The 'Black Corps' of 'Lützow, and the Duke of Brunswick-Oel's corps both wore black frock coats – or *litewkas*, as they were properly called – together with black shakos, gloves, hanging plumes, death's heads and other 'gothick' devices. The *Landwehr*, when it was raised in 1813, also, adopted the *litewka*, the cavalry wearing the shako and the infantry a forage cap with a peak and a floppy brim – the forerunner of the modern peaked cap. In these stirring times, Prussia, never a rich country, was forced to rely on Britain and Russia for uniforms and equipment for her new army. As late as March 1815 the Military Economy Department reported that most of the foreign uniforms had been altered or disposed of and that 'here, near Berlin, there are only some artillery units to be found which are still clothed in this manner. The Horse Battery No. 13 still wears English jackets and helmets, but with Prussian collars and shoulder-straps'.

When the war ended, the fragile alliance between the king and the liberals fell apart rapidly and the military reformers were dismissed; but not before they had managed to pass laws making every Prussian citizen of twenty years of age liable for military service – three years with the army, two with the reserve, and fifteen with the *Landwehr*. This system, which was intended to serve purely Prussian needs, was eventually to become the main twentieth century method of maintaining a standing army.

After setting the fashion for both the British and the French armies during the early years of the century, the Austrian army changed remarkably little during the Napoleonic Wars. With the exception of the artillery who wore brown, certain *Jäger* units who wore grey, certain dragoon regiments who wore green, and the lancers and hussars, the bulk of the army kept their white uniforms. In 1809 the line infantry adopted a black shako with a peak front and back, in place of the helmet, although the order for the change had been promulgated as early as 1806. Grenadiers were given a revised fur grenadier cap, also with front and back peaks. Although the German infantry retained their white breeches and black gaiters and the Hungarians their tight blue pantaloons, Austrian infantry are sometimes shown at this date wearing grey trousers or overalls. The only Austrian innovation of note in this period was the new forage cap introduced in 1813. This had ear-flaps and was the basic design which was to become the pattern for both the English side-cap and the peaked cap worn by the Austrians in 1914, and later by the Germans.

Until the expedition to Copenhagen in 1807, the British army had kept very much to itself, first preparing to repel the expected invasion of the French, and then concentrating on improving its training and efficiency for operations on the continent of Europe. Generally speaking there was very little change in dress after 1801, apart from the abolition of powder and queues around 1808. But after 1802, the disturbing influence on British military fashion, started by the *émigrés* during the Revolutionary Wars, was increased by the arrival in England of survivors of the Hanoverian army disbanded by Napoleon and later by the Duke of Brunswick's black corps. These units were taken into the British army, and the former in particular performed great service as the 'King's German Legion'. To them may be attributed the final push required to enable the Prince of Wales and several of his like-minded friends and relations – the Duke of Cumberland, Lord Paget and others – to dress certain British light dragoon regiments as hussars, and to adopt other German styles like long moustaches and even longer pipes. Through them also came the long braided 'pelisse' or greatcoat, and the small round tasselled forage cap which became all the rage by the end of the war. The former still lives on in the domestic dressing-gown, and in the braided frock coats worn by certain officers of the Household Division.

In 1808 a British army landed in Portugal and from then on, until 1815, there was constant fighting between the British and the French in Portugal, Spain, the South of France, and Belgium. As the army became more experienced in active service conditions, certain local changes of dress and equipment were made. Infantry officers adopted shakos instead of cocked hats, and overalls and trousers of all shapes and colours replaced the blue pantaloons and hessian boots worn at home. Both heavy and light cavalry adopted tall watering-caps, which were really shakos, instead of their dress hats and caps. Most of these innovations, however, were ignored by Horse Guards until 1811, when a combination of circumstances led to a series of drastic reforms in the uniforms of the British army.

In June of that year the Prince of Wales became Regent and, soon after, his brother, the Duke of York, resumed his post as Commander-in-Chief, which he had resigned when his mistress, Mrs. Clarke, was accused of trafficking in army commissions. The two brothers, aided by the Duke of Cumberland, immediately embarked on a complete change of the army's clothing. Trial patterns were made, commented on by a Board of General Officers, altered by the Regent, embodied into regulations, and finally issued to the regiments; but there were many delays and the new uniforms were not completely issued until early in 1815. Whilst the impetus for these reforms was partly dictated by practical needs, there is no doubt that it was largely the inspiration of the Regent, his love of fashion and uniforms, and his hatred of the dowdy atmosphere of his father's Court, that decided the particular styles which were adopted, and which were mainly Austrian in derivation.

The heavy cavalry were put into red *Kollette* and helmets, with white leather breeches and jack boots for dress, and grey overalls for marching order. The Household cavalry had Austrian pattern crested helmets and the dragoons and dragoon guards similar helmets but with long flowing horse-hair manes like those of the French dragoons. The light dragoons and hussars were given Austrian-style shakos, and the former what amounted to lancer uniforms, with a *kurtka* complete with plastron lapels, piped back seams, and a *Wasserfall* or piece of fringe hanging from the centre of the waist at the back. With this uniform striped girdles were worn, and officers were given dress pouches and belts exactly like those worn by Austrian light cavalry with a double G.R. in place of the double-headed eagle.

The first examples to appear in the theatre of operations caused consternation, particularly amongst the light dragoons. Wellington at once admitted that 'There is no subject of which I understand so little', and, he went on, 'abstractedly speaking, I think it indifferent how a soldier is clothed, provided it is in a uniform manner'. To him the silhouette was the all-important thing. In June 1811, a piquet of the 11th Light Dragoons was captured because they mistook the enemy for the 3rd Hussars of the King's German Legion, newly arrived in their shakos, and this rankled with the Duke. 'At a distance, or in action, colours are nothing: the profile, and shape of the man's cap, and his general appearance, are what guide us; and why should we make our people look like the French?'.

Following Pages
60 GREAT BRITAIN
Officer's jacket (epaulettes missing), 1st Regiment of Foot Guards, worn by Lieutenant-Colonel Miller at Waterloo.
National Army Museum

61 UNITED STATES OF AMERICA
Infantry officer's shako, 1814–21.
Smithsonian Institution

62 UNITED STATES OF AMERICA
Infantry shako plate (facsimile), 1812 pattern.
Smithsonian Institution

63 UNITED STATES OF AMERICA
Uniform and *'chapeau-bras'* worn by Brigadier-General Peter Gansevoort, c. 1809.
Smithsonian Institution

The infantry and artillery were less affected than the cavalry, merely replacing the old stove-pipe shako for the new so-called 'Belgic' or 'Portuguese' shako, which had a high front flap decorated with a brass plate, a plume and cockade on the left side, and cords and tassels across the front. The exact origin of this shako is unknown but it seems to be a variation of the Austrian *kaskett*, which in its turn has been described as being of Spanish origin. The belief that the Prince Regent was copying the Austrian model is strengthened by the appearance of early models with lace edgings to the fronts and neck flaps at the back.

In 1812, differences over British blockading tactics led to war between the United States of America and Great Britain. At first hostilities were confined to naval warfare, but with the abdication of Napoleon in 1814 a force of veteran British regiments was sent to North America where, apart from burning Washington, they achieved little. The opponents who got the better of them were a hastily raised force of militia backed by a tiny nucleus of regulars. The rapidity with which the militia had been raised outstripped the capabilities of the Supply Department and, instead of being dressed in their normal blue jackets, the bulk of the American infantry were dressed in grey, brown, or drab. In 1813 a high-fronted shako similar in shape to that of the British, but made of leather instead of felt, was introduced. The victories gained against the British by American units dressed in grey kersey led to a sentimental attachment to that colour, and it is to be seen to this day in the uniforms of the United States Military Academy at West Point.

VII *The Royal Milliners*

In July 1815, Europe settled down once again to enjoy the 'Eternal Peace' promised in 1814, and so rudely interrupted by the sudden return of Napoleon from Elba. After the dramatic events of the 'Hundred Days', the peacemakers returned to work in Vienna, and set about repairing the damage caused by the French crusade for liberty and brotherliness. In the years before the French Revolution some rulers had enjoyed a mild flirtation with the humanists and philosophers, but now, after twenty years of warfare, they were united in their determination to eliminate all traces of the movement that had started it all. Moreover, in the wave of reaction against 'individualism' they were supported by the bulk of thinking men; and throughout Europe the Church, both Catholic and Protestant, and the state in its eighteenth century form, were held to be the only defence against the evils of free thought. This return to the *ancien régime* was personified in the Austrian Chancellor Metternich, a firm believer in the eighteenth century virtues of balance and equilibrium. As these desirable qualities could only be brought about by order, anything which tended to create disorder had to be suppressed. The concept of a 'Holy Alliance' of European monarchs ruling in a spirit of brotherhood and charity was a mystical notion dreamed up by Alexander I, but before long Metternich had turned it into a system for policing Europe and protecting it from innovators.

With the Bourbon Louis XVIII restored to the French throne, and with liberals and absolutists joined in an uneasy alliance, the future seemed to be set fair. But the seeds of nationalism and liberty sown by the French revolutionaries were still multiplying throughout Europe. The first blow to the Holy Alliance was Britain's support of the South American insurgents in revolt against their Spanish masters. This was followed, between 1820 and 1829, by the struggle for Greek independence in which popular opinion, inflamed by the deeds and death of Lord Byron, the lure of the East, and a taste for military adventure, persuaded Russia, who had at first regarded the nationalists as mere rebels, and Britain to take action against the Turks. The naval battle at Navarino in 1827 in which a combined British, French and

HEADPIECE
Russian drill, from *The Armies of Europe* by Major-General G. B. McLellan, U.S. Army, 1861

129

64 RUSSIA
Officer's shako, line
infantry regiments, 1840–46.
*Musée Royal de l'Armée
Brussels*

131

Russian fleet destroyed the Turco-Egyptian fleet led to a further split in the alliance.

In 1830 a *bourgeois* revolution in France succeeded in placing Louis Phillipe on the throne. His protestations of peaceful intentions gained him before long the acceptance of his fellow monarchs, although hints of a revival of the Napoleonic theories of France's superiority left them uneasy. After 1830 the alliance split into two camps with the absolutist, Austria, Prussia and Russia, on one side and the liberal powers, England and France, on the other.

In 1847 and 1848 potato and grain diseases and sudden droughts brought an acute food shortage to a Europe already dangerously divided into wealthy ruling and bourgeois classes and a large and wretched proletariat. Shortage of food was followed in turn by riots, unemployment, and eventual bankruptcy; but it was not until the crisis was over that the political discontent broke out. The ensuing attempts of the 'Men of '48' to achieve political and national freedom failed because their revolutions took place at a time when the *ancien régime* was still sufficiently powerful to prevent them uniting.

In the years after 1815, the armies of Europe were mainly employed in what are nowadays known as 'internal security' operations, at home or abroad. The new Royalist French army in Spain; the Austrian army in Italy, and then in 1848 in Budapest, Prague and Vienna itself; the Russian and Prussian armies in Poland in 1831; the Russian army in Hungary in 1848; and the Prussian army in Baden in 1848, were all acting to a greater or lesser extent against the civilian population. Even the liberal minded British were not above charging unarmed rioters with cavalry. Under these conditions the first requirement of an army was that it should be politically reliable, a quality possessed by the small eighteenth century army of aristocratic officers and long-serving regulars. But there was always the fear that a conflict might get out of hand requiring forces of a size and efficiency witnessed during the Napoleonic Wars, although such large armies might be politically unreliable. Both Russia and Austria were forced to maintain large armies to preserve the status quo. The Prussian army, for economic reasons, was less menacing than either of these two, while in liberal Britain and France the army languished in unpopular isolation, hated by the working class and only barely tolerated by the wealthy and comfort-loving bourgeoisie.

These political and social struggles were clearly reflected in the dress of the participants. In the summer of 1815 all the world, starved of travel and pleasure for so long, seemed to be in Paris. Elderly English gentlemen, straight out of the novels of Fielding and Smollett, came face to face with Bashkirs and Tartars in the narrow arcades of the Palais Royal. The citizens of Paris gaped at the revelations of the Highlanders as the summer breeze lifted their kilts in the avenues of the Bois de Boulogne. The streets were thronged with sightseers – military and civilian – of all the nations of Europe. Fierce Prussians looting and attempting to blow up the *Pont d'Iéna* in return for insults received at the hands of Napoleon; Hungarian grenadiers in fur caps and tight blue pantaloons; Russians in tall brass-fronted mitre caps, wasp-waisted and elegant in long white overalls; British infantry, small and loose-limbed in stained brick-red jackets; and the returning royalist French in their new uniforms which owed much to their enforced stay in England. The Prussians looted, the Austrians introduced a system of legalised robbery, the Russians paraded, and the English either stayed in their billets, minding the baby while the parents went out to work, or went sightseeing and got drunk. On duty each army tried to outdo the others with the smartness of its turnout, and their monarchs took a childlike delight in showing them off to each other. Fashions were noted and copied. The British abandoned their new shakos and the Russians their distinctive 'kiwers' in favour of the bell-topped shako worn by the French, Prussians, and Austrians. The Prussians adopted the long all-in-one white overalls of the Russians, and gradually everyone became smarter and stiffer, and their uniforms tighter. The influences of the different countries spread to their allies and dependents. Portugal, some of the South American states and the United States of America were influenced by the British; the Italian states, particularly Tuscany, Parma and Modena, by Austria; the German states partly by Prussia and partly by Austria; while Prussia slavishly copied the Russian fashions.

With cracks appearing in the solid façade of the Holy Alliance after 1830, a great wave of romanticism engulfed the field of military costume, taking several different directions at the same time. In the early 1840s there appeared the celebrated *Pickelhaube*, or spiked helmet. This helmet was almost certainly designed by Nicholas I of Russia, and the story goes that Frederick William IV saw a prototype lying on his desk, copied the idea, and got it out faster than the procrastinating Russians. A romanticised version of an ancient Slav helmet was already appearing on coins and medals during the reign of Alexander I, but Nicholas was the first to have the brainwave of adapting existing Russian cuirassier helmets by simply removing the horse-hair crest and replacing it with a grenade finial. By 1848, it was the general headwear in both the Russian and Prussian armies, and in the British army, where it was attributed to the attentions of Prince Albert, it was being worn by the household and most heavy cavalry regiments. By 1848 uniforms had definite political implications. The slogan 'Only soldiers help against Democrats', and a whole spate of cartoons and pamphlets, gave the spiked helmet an aura of military repression which it retains to this day. The looser French uniforms and in particular the *képi* were to become symbols of liberty to patriots everywhere. In Hungary and Germany revolutionaries fought in felt hats decked with flowing plumes, and in open necked shirts. The wide-brimmed soft felt hat with a low crown, worn by Kossuth and other patriots, was taken from the hats worn by artists, musicians, poets and 'Bohemians' in general in reaction to the top hat, rapidly becoming the symbol of the bourgeoisie. Even as late as 1853 Liszt drew the attentions of the police upon himself by wearing a 'Democratic' hat in Karlsruhe. To illustrate the attention paid to such apparent trifles, it is amusing to recall that Prussian postmen were forbidden in 1846 to wear moustaches, lest they should be taken for republicans, socialists, or radicals on the run.

Of the armies of the three autocratic monarchies, that of Russia was the largest and most imposing. But beneath its glittering façade, there were serious defects in its organisation which were not to appear until 1854, in spite of continuous active service – against the Persians in 1826, the Turks in 1828, the Poles in 1831, the Hungarians in 1849 and finally the British and French, not to mention three decades of continuous warfare in the Caucasus.

After 1815 Alexander I, who had done so much to reform the Russian army, became disillusioned with mankind and with Russia in particular and, retired into a twilight of mysticism, leaving the peacetime organisation of the army to a group of ferocious disciplinarians, headed by the brutal Arakcheev. The general tightening up led to several outbreaks of unrest in the army which reached a peak during the last five years of Alexander's reign. Particularly unpopular were the 'military colonies'. Alexander's idea of putting his large and unemployed army to practical work by forming military communities, where soldiers could farm and train at the same time, was basically sound, and had been used for many years in establishing the Cossack line; but as interpreted by Arackcheev the colonies became hells on earth, where every minute of the day was punctuated by drum-beats, and

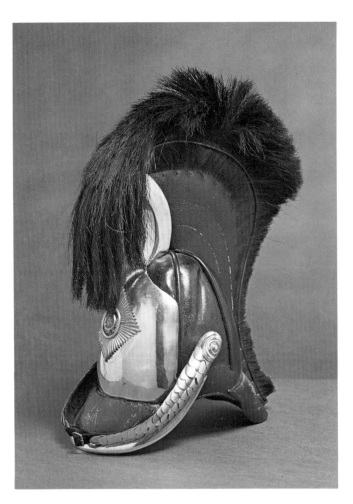

70 RUSSIA
Soldier's jacket, 1st Lancer
Regiment, 1825–55. The
blue cloth collar patches
and the white metal
epaulettes are missing.
Mollo Collection

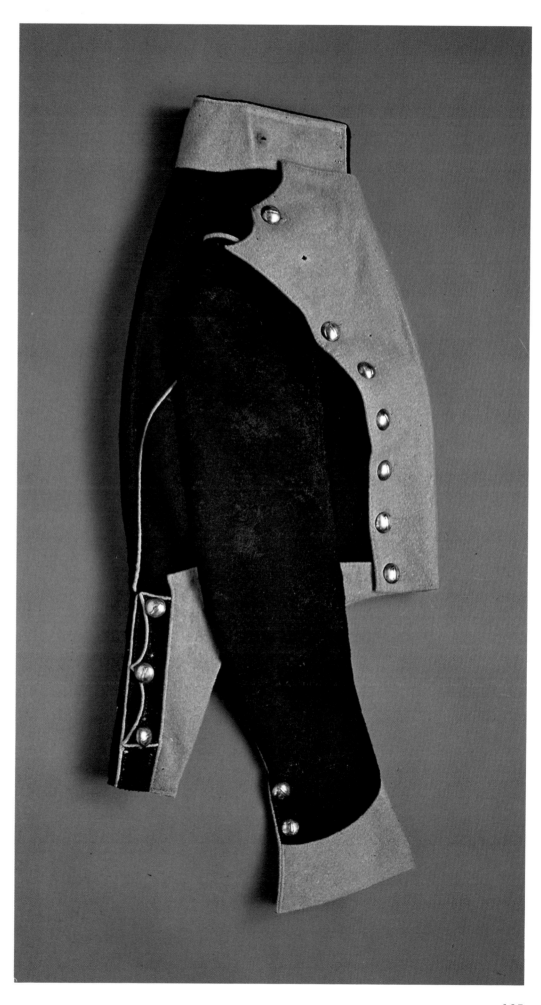

Above Left
67 RUSSIA
Officer's helmet, 13th
(Order of St. George)
Cuirassier Regiment,
1827–45.
Mollo Collection

Above Right
68 RUSSIA
Officer's cuirass, guard and
line cuirassiers, 1812–46.
Mollo Collection

Below Left
69 RUSSIA
Officer's spiked helmets,
1844–60.
Left General Officer's
helmet, *c.* 1860. This
pattern of helmet was also
worn by officers of guard
infantry regiments.
Right Officer's helmet, Life
Guard Dragoon Regiment,
1844–55.
Mollo Collection

where the miserable occupants had not only to farm but also to maintain the highest standards of parade ground discipline.

Another and more serious form of unrest was fermented among the officers, many of them of the noblest families and from the best regiments, who had been fed with liberal ideas during their time in Western Europe. Returning to Russia, animated by their new ideals, they received a rude awakening and promptly set about forming secret societies aimed at overthrowing the power of the Tsar. The assassination of Alexander, and the whole of his family, was planned for the summer of 1826, but he forestalled them by dying on November 19th 1825. There followed a period of confusion caused by the reluctance of the Grand Duke Constantine to accept the throne, but on December 14th, on the day that Nicholas I finally proclaimed himself Tsar, the 'Decembrists', as they were later called, struck. Nicholas had been warned and fortunately the coup was executed in a thoroughly half-hearted manner. The Moscow Guard Regiment and one or two other units succeeded in occupying the Senate Square in St. Petersburg, where they were finally blasted off the streets with grapeshot.

Nicholas I came to the throne to the sound of gunfire and died to the reverberations of the artillery at Sebastopol; and in the years between he was largely concerned with military affairs. Even more than Frederick William I he had a passion for formal drill and matters of uniform, and under him the Russian army became a veritable 'Spectacle of the Gods', even if conditions behind the scenes were cruel and corrupt. Only in Russia were such splendid sights to be seen as the Tsar himself, tall and straight, crammed into a crease-less uniform, piercing all and sundry with his pewter coloured eyes; or the annual appearance of the senior under-officer of the Nikolaevski Cavalry School in all his glory, known to lesser mortals as 'God on Earth'; or Sergeant Kozhemiakin of the Semenovski Guard Regiment, who could perform the foot-drill with a full glass of water balanced on the top of his head, while 'his legs in turn were raised completely parallel to the ground and the toe of his boot formed one straight line with his whole leg'. Nicholas had been severely shaken by the plot against his life, and, although only five of the 600 or so plotters were executed, he retained a hatred of the remainder throughout his life. The strict discipline and concentration on formal drill, which typify his reign, resulted from his belief that unquestioning obedience and the absence of dangerous initiative on the part of subordinates were essential to the security of the realm.

The Russian army, some 800,000 strong, was permanently organised into army corps and divisions with a separate Army of the Caucasus permanently engaged in warfare of the most exhausting and difficult kind. When not on active service, military life was devoted to reviews and inspections, which Nicholas regularly attended:

'Uniformity and organisation reached the point where a whole infantry division of four regiments of twelve battalions (not less than 9,000 men) formed in columns, performed all the movements, marching in step, not losing step in the turns and keeping the ideal alignment of rank and in depth. The manual of arms by whole regiments struck one by their "purity" . . . . In unblemished formal parades, according to the views of the times, lay the guarantee of success in war.'

But a closer inspection would have revealed several basic weaknesses. The cavalry, consisting of fifty-nine regiments of cuirassiers, dragoons, hussars and lancers was splendid but inefficient. Badly-trained by officers who knew little beyond gambling and carousing, and nothing of their jobs,

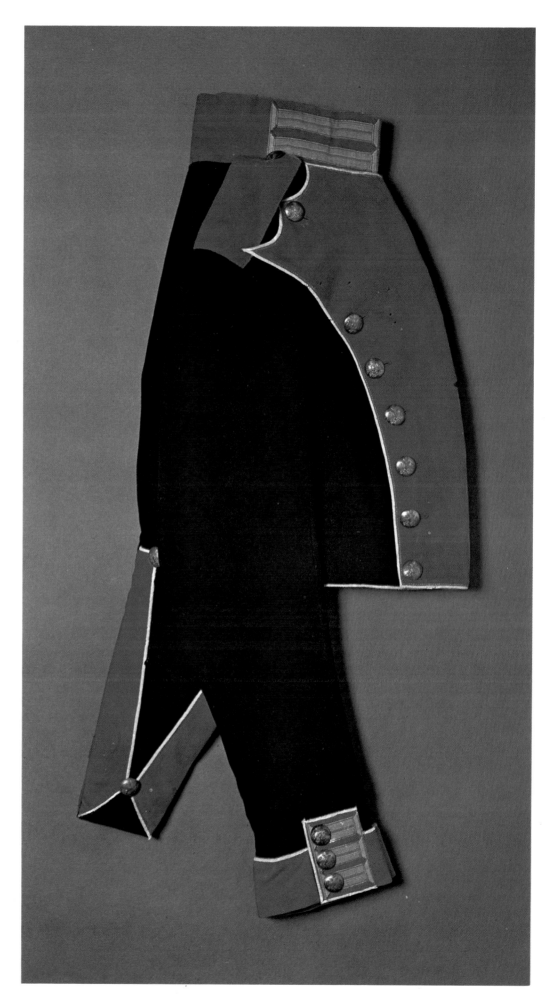

71 RUSSIA
Soldier's jacket, Life Guard
Preobrajenski Regiment,
c. 1840.
Mollo Collection

it was lacking in agility – the Russian light cavalry being comparable to the heavy cavalry of other nations, as they were to show all too obviously at Balaclava in 1854. Nicholas tried to infuse some life into them by staging vast reviews like that held at Vosnesensk, during which some 700 horses died of exhaustion. The Tsar's particular favourites were the corps of dragoons, some 10,000 strong. Nothing delighted him more than their performance which consisted of dashing forward, halting, dismounting, and transforming themselves into massed infantry battalions, and vice versa, in the twinkling of an eye.

The infantry, disciplined, devoted, and stubborn, were dreadfully weak in fire-power and flexibility. Their training was highly artificial and was entirely concerned with drill and appearance. Their performance of the parade march in regimental columns may have been perfection, but there was seldom, if ever, any ball for target practice and even if there had been, the muskets were so thinned away by polishing with brick-dust, and their screws and fittings so loosened to rattle well at drill, that they were generally useless. Only the artillery and engineers, whose duties required a sound technical training, were the equal of other armies. In the Caucasus, however, where the army was on active service for thirty years, a different system operated. In very difficult and mountainous country, interspersed with valleys, in which hostilities were confined to the most inaccessible parts, a system was gradually developed in which the low country was settled with Cossacks and posts of regulars. Roads and bridges were constructed through the mountains, and forts, which served as depots for sending out patrols of infantry, were constructed in passes and other important places. In these conditions the cavalry became adept at difficult marches and forest-fighting, and the infantry, although hampered by the quality of their weapons, at scaling cliffs and storming mountain villages. As was to be the case of the British army in India the lessons learnt in the Caucasus by the Russians were lost on the rest of their army, as there was little interchange between it and the Caucasian Corps. In military circles the Caucasus was regarded as little more than a lively sideshow and the methods used there as valueless in modern warfare.

These two schools of thought were reflected in the dress of the Russian army. The regular army, stationed mainly in north-central Russia and the Ukraine, attained a standard of spit-and-polish probably never surpassed either before or since. Nonetheless, Russian uniforms were simple in design and, as befits military clothing, of an extreme uniformity. Although the cut was extreme, with tight waists and narrow cuffs, the stuffs used, except in the Guards, were extremely coarse. The soldiers themselves made their own boots, underwear and shirts. Uniforms and greatcoats were made in the regiments – at least twenty men per company being employed on these tasks – while headdress and equipment were issued centrally, usually once every ten years. Examples of uniforms of this period reveal minute repairs and darns which testify to the husbandry of the Russian private soldier.

After 1815 the Russians abandoned the characteristic 'kiwer' and adopted the tall shako of French form, which was worn with minor modifications by the infantry, dragoons, *chevaux-légers*, hussars and artillery until the advent of the spiked helmet in 1844. In 1817 a new shako plate (which was a copy of those worn by the British Foot Guards in 1815) was adopted for all units except those of the Guard, who retained their double-headed eagle plates. The English crown was changed for that of Russia and the stars of the British regiments for that of the order of St. Andrew; but in shape and size they were identical. In 1828 this plate was changed for an Amazon shield surmounted by the double-headed eagle, in direct imitation of the plate worn by French infantry of the 1st Empire. This plate survived the change to the spiked helmet and was worn until after the Crimean War. In 1844 the Russian version of the spiked helmet, really the old cuirassier helmet, with a finial in the form of a grenade instead of a crest, first made its appearance, and was issued to regiments who formerly wore shakos, with the exception of hussars. Cuirassiers wore various modified versions of their old horsehair crested helmet until 1845, when they were issued with an intermediate spiked helmet. Those of the Guard were surmounted by a three-dimensional double-headed eagle. In 1846 an all-metal helmet was produced, again with an eagle for the Guards. Other forms of headdress were the brass-fronted grenadier cap worn by other ranks of the Pavlovski Guard Regiment (after 1825 this was worn by officers as well), the Potemkin-style helmet of the horse grenadiers, the square topped *chapska* of the lancers and the so-called 'marine shako' – which tapered towards the top – worn by marines and some other units.

The infantry, dragoons and artillery retained their traditional dark green uniforms throughout the period. One of Nicholas I's first acts was to alter the jacket from double to single-breasted, and to introduce trousers – green in winter and white in summer – for general wear, claiming to have made savings by both changes. Cuirassiers continued to wear white, lancers blue, and hussars their usual peacock varieties.

From about 1829 the Caucasus corps were beginning to adopt their own style of dress. The crack Nijergorodski Dragoon Regiment, formed in 1834, wore tall fur shakos, Cossack uniforms, consisting of blouses and baggy trousers, and *shashkas*, or Caucasian sabres, worn from a narrow belt over the shoulder; and by 1848 tunics were in common wear.

During the Crimean War, the Russian infantry were usually to be seen in their long greatcoats with the bottoms turned up, and with their trousers tucked into their boots. The spiked helmet seems generally to have been left with the baggage in favour of a peakless forage cap in company colours, or a soft white linen peaked cap, another fashion imported from the Caucasus. The cavalry, at Balaclava at any rate, were still wearing their full dress under their greatcoats, which were so thick that the blunt swords of their British opponents were unable to pierce them. The uniform of the 11th Kiev Hussars, one of the two hussar regiments present at the battle, is surprisingly accurately described by an English eye-witness:

'The dress of the Russians was a red broad-topped stiff felt shako, with brass double-headed eagle in front, and an oilskin cover overall. Underneath their great-coats they wore a dark green jacket with coarse orange worsted lace; trowsers of sky-blue, with red piping down the seams, and a narrow strapping of leather from the fork to the bottom. Their horses were in good condition; they used layers of felt, or some soft substance sewn together, under the saddle, and a blue shabracque with red edging, and their Emperor's (or some other) initials in red at the corners.'

Exactly a month before Balaclava, as the British army was making its celebrated 'flank march' round the north of Sevastopol, Sergeant Mitchell of the 13th Light Dragoons came across a stretch of road strewn with new Russian hussar jackets.

'They were sky-blue, with yellow lace, the number being on the buttons showing that they belonged to the 12th Hussars. They were of a very coarse cloth, nearly as coarse as a blanket.'

gez. von Lieder u. Krüger.   ged. von Jugel.

Berlin bei L. W. Wittich.

Above
72 PRUSSIA
Officer's *Pickelhaube,*
infantry regiments, 1842–57.
Musée Royal de l'Armée,
Brussels

Above Right
73 AUSTRIA
Officer's shako, *Banat*
Grenzregiments Nr. 10 and
11, 1854. Worn by
Feldzeugmeister Josef Graf
Jellacic.
Heeresgeschichtliches
Museum, Vienna

Left
74 PRUSSIA
Soldier, *Husarenregiment*
Nr. 5, c. 1821. Coloured
print by Lieder and
Kruger.
Mollo Collection

75 AUSTRIA
General Officer's cocked
hat, *c.* 1815. Worn by
Kaiser Joseph I.
Heeresgeschichtliches
Museum, Vienna

The army of the Kingdom of Prussia, ruled over by Frederick William III, father-in-law of Nicholas I, was similar to the Russian army in its appearance, if not in its menacing might and harsh discipline. Family ties were in fact so strong that in 1835 joint manoeuvres were held by the guards units of both countries in Prussian Poland. But the new Prussian system, aimed at providing the country with an army which would enable it to rank as a major European power, but which would not involve it in the expense of a large standing army like that of Russia, proved to have serious drawbacks. In the first place, the regular army gradually reverted to the eighteenth century attitude, whereby the officers closed their ranks to the bourgeois element, so that the gap between the regular army and the militia-like *Landwehr* gradually widened. In the second place, the annual intake of conscripts was kept low for economic reasons, so that the regular army was seldom more than 200,000 strong. During the Polish crisis of 1831 the *Landwehr* had to be embodied, to the disgust of its members and their professional comrades; and after the disturbances of 1848, when an army under Prince William of Prussia had operated in Baden, the *Landwehr* element became politically unreliable. The principle of the 'Volk in Waffen', which had been so successful in 1813, had utterly failed by 1858 when Prince William became Regent in place of his brother, Frederick William IV. Without general mobilisation the army was too small; with mobilisation it was inundated with what the French scathingly referred to as 'lawyers and oculists'. Politically it was of little importance and very much looked down upon; militarily it modelled itself very much on Russian lines, both in its appearance and in its organisation.

From 1816 to 1843 the infantry wore the bell-topped shako in a variety of forms, but generally slightly lower than the excessively tall Russian version. As in the Russian army, it was worn in an oilskin cover in marching order. In 1824 metal fronted grenadier caps, said to have been a present from Alexander I, were issued to both battalions of the 1st Foot Guard regiment, who wore them on full dress parades with white overalls, still in general use in the 1830's. In 1816 the fusilier battalions of the first 13 regiments were allowed to wear the royal cypher on their shakos, while the remainder kept the old black and white Prussian cockade. The infantry wore blue coatees, except for *Jäger* and rifles who wore dark green, and Guard regiments were distinguished by *Litzen* or lace loops on their collar and cuffs, another fashion taken from the Russians. After 1815 individual regimental facing colours were abolished and the collars and cuffs were made red throughout, while the cuff flaps and the shoulder straps which bore the regimental number were red and white alternately by corps. By 1836 grey trousers with red piping down the seams were general wear, and are sometimes shown being worn with brown gaiters for marching order.

In 1817 the *Landwehr* were assimilated into the line organisation, but were distinguished from regular infantry by having a blue edging to their collars and the *Landwehr* cross on their shakos.

The cavalry consisted of the usual cuirassiers, dragoons, hussars and lancers, together with the *Landwehr* cavalry. Cuirassiers wore Russian type helmets, white *Kollette* and brass cuirasses, based on the French pattern issued to the Prussian army from the stores at Versailles in 1814. In 1821 these were changed for steel. The *Garde du Corps* regiment wore on special occasions the black cuirasses presented to them in 1814 by Alexander I. As in the infantry Guard cavalry regiments, with the exception of hussars, were distinguished by cuff and collar Litzen'. The dragoons wore blue jackets and shakos. The hussar uniform underwent several alterations during this period, the biggest being in 1836 when the cut of the dolman was altered so that it became longer, and the looping received a different form. It is indicative of the poverty of Prussia that it was not until this year that officers received gold or silver braid on their uniforms – previously they had had camel-hair. The lancers wore blue double-breasted jackets with striped girdles and the traditional *chapska*.

The *Landwehr* cavalry were dressed and accoutred from 1815 on the lines of the regular lancer regiments except that they wore shakos. In 1822 they were given *chapskas* with *Landwehr* crosses on the fronts. The Guard *Landwehr* cavalry regiment, raised in 1817–18, remained permanently embodied. They wore Guard *Litzen* on their uniforms and *chapskas* with *Landwehr* crosses.

In the year 1843, a year earlier than the Russians, who had moved with typical lethargy, the Prussian army began to appear in its new spiked helmets. The Prussian model was different from the Russian, being custom-built, having a square peak edged with metal, and having a true spike instead of a grenade; like the Russian helmet, it had a horsehair plume for parade wear.

The Guard helmet had the old pattern eagle shako plate with the star of the Black Eagle on its breast, while the line had a new rather stiffer pattern of eagle. The *Jäger* received the helmet at first, but in 1854 they changed it for a shako with front and back peaks similar to that introduced into the British army in the following year.

With the helmet came the tunic, so that from 1843 the Prussian army acquired the characteristic appearance which it retained until 1914; and soon after the tunic, new infantry equipment was introduced which gave them an even more up-to-date appearance. This equipment, which may have been influenced by French patterns, consisted of two side braces supporting a waist belt from which hung two ammunition pouches, one on each side of the front.

The cuirassiers, dragoons and artillery also received the helmet and tunic. The cuirassier helmets were made entirely of metal, and their tunics were laced round the collar and cuffs and down the front like the old *Kollett*; furthermore they were piped on the back seams and had curious welts round the armholes. At the same time the *Garde du Corps* received *super-vestes* for court duties, and for these and ceremonial parades they wore a silver metal eagle on the helmet instead of a spike. In 1856 the *Garde du Corps* were given high jack boots and white breeches, similar to those which the British Household Cavalry had retained ever since the beginning of the century.

The uniform of the hussars continued to undergo changes, mainly of a regimental nature. Low fur busbies came in for some regiments and *mirlitons* for others. In 1855 the hussar tunic – the *attila*, worn by the Hungarian national army – was introduced, and the pelisse was discontinued. The lancers retained their jackets until soon after 1853, when the Guard lancer regiment adopted the tunic, referred to in the case of lancers, as an *ulanka*.

In 1843 tunics and helmets were adopted by the *Landwehr* infantry and cavalry. In the infantry the red piping down the front was omitted and the helmet was distinguished by the *Landwehr* cross. The *Landwehr* cavalry wore helmets similar to those of the infantry until 1852, when they were re-organised and divided into the same categories as the regular cavalry, whose uniforms they adopted with the difference of the cross on the headdress.

Writing of the Prussian cavalry in 1856, the American observer McClellan noted that 'the clothing is of excellent material, and is well made. . . .' and of the infantry that their 'march is steady, but strikes one as being stiff and awkward; for the foot is raised very high, the toe much pointed, the knee

76 PRUSSIA
Officer's *czapka,*
Ulanenregiment, Nr. 3,
1844–62.
Musée Royal de l'Armée,
Brussels

Right
77 GREAT BRITAIN
Captain Edward Wildman,
9th Lancers, 1816. Miniature
by J. Stump.
Mollo Collection

78 PRUSSIA
Officer's *Feldmütze,*
Landwehrhusarenregiments
Nr. 10, 1843–52.
Musée Royal de l'Armée
Brussels

144

much stiffened, and the foot brought down with a shock; the noise thus made by a column is something quite extraordinary. . . .'

On the subject of arms and uniform he noted that all the regiments of the Guard and at least one battalion of every line regiment were armed with the breech-loading needle-gun, which had a range of 1,000 yards and fired seven shots per minute. The material of the uniforms was very good and well made-up and generally very like the Russian uniform in style. 'Each man has a pair of cloth mittens and a pair of ear covers'.

The third army of the *Dreikaiserbund* was that of Austria. The disastrous campaign of 1805 had swept away the old army composed of long service volunteers; afterwards the military system, which had remained unchanged since the Seven Years War, was reorganised by the Archduke Charles on the principle of the 'nation in arms' first launched on an unsuspecting Europe by the French. The army was rebuilt by general conscription, and by 1813 Austria was able to put into the field well-trained armies far larger than those which had taken part in the French revolutionary war. After Waterloo, Austrian foreign policy was left in the hands of Metternich, while affairs at home were left to the Emperor Francis II and his successor Ferdinand I. The fear of the former of any form of popular movement led to severe repressive measures against anyone trying to upset the *status quo*, and gradually dis-content, bred of a combination of liberalism, nationalism and economic depression, began to spread throughout his possessions. In these conditions a large army was maintained for police activities, particularly in Austria's large Italian possessions. Being constantly employed and kept in a state of readiness, the Austrian army suffered less than any other from the effect of a long period of undisturbed peace, and was at the time considered to be the best in Europe.

In 1848 revolt broke out in Hungary under the leadership of Louis Kossuth; Prague followed suit, and in March there were riots in Vienna itself. Further risings in the Italian states kept the bulk of the army tied down there, and in 1849 the new Emperor Franz Joseph was forced to call in the aid of Nicholas I to help 'pacify' Hungary. The successful outcome of this campaign, and victory in Italy, strengthened Austria's position in Germany and for the time being halted plans to form a German state under the leadership of Prussia; but the unpopularity of vacillating Austrian policy during the Crimean war, and the result of the 1859 war against Sardinia in which she lost all her possessions in Italy except Venice, led to a decline in Austrian military prowess. Although to outside observers the Austrian army of 1859 seemed to have lost none of its effectiveness, its self-confidence had gone just as it had done in 1805.

The Austrian cavalry, which enjoyed a high reputation, consisted of cuirassiers, dragoons, hussars and lancers. Great attention was paid to the training of both man and horse, but the tactical units were apparently too large to move with speed and the men and horses too bulkily clad and accoutred. The ubiquitous McClellan was told that the men usually managed to dispose of most of it before they had been in the field for many days. Discussing the infantry, which in 1859 consisted of line infantry, grenz or frontier troops and rifles, he noted:

'Since the affairs of 1848 and 1849, the organisation of the Austrian infantry, as well as that of the other arms of the service, have been much improved. In the next war in which they are engaged the beneficial effect will no doubt be perceived. The rifles are a fine set of men, and will probably hold their own against any similar troops with whom they may be brought into contact.'

Between 1816 and 1836 there was little to differentiate the varieties of German cavalry in the Austrian army; all wore helmets and the same cut of jacket, the cuirassiers having a patch of cloth of the facing colour on each side of the collar.

In 1827 the woollen crest on the helmet was done away with, and in 1836 the hussar shako was made straighter. When the tunic was introduced in 1849, those of the cuirassiers were single-breasted with collar patches, and those of the dragoons double-breasted. In 1850, when the system of police employed in Italy was extended to the whole of the Empire, the Russian-style spiked helmet was adopted by the Gendarmerie. McClellan describes the Austrian cavalry uniforms in 1856 in considerable detail. They were well made and of excellent material. The white uniforms were popular with officers and were stated to be excellent for the field; 'it is cleaned by washing and pipe-clay; and they seem to prefer it to any other color'. The lancers alone wore epaulettes; and the 'short double-breasted frock, with a standing collar, cut away in front' was white for the heavy cavalry, dark green for the lancers and light or dark blue for the hussars. A loose 'spencer' of the colour of the coat, but with a rolling collar, was worn on certain occasions over the coat. 'The heavy cavalry wear a metallic helmet, with a high crest. The lancers the well-known Polish hat. The hussars wear a cylindrical shako, with a peaked visor.' Finally it is interesting to note that 'socks are not worn, but are replaced by linen bandages', a custom advocated by Potemkin and still current in the Soviet army.

The infantry also remained unchanged in their appearance between 1816 and 1836. German regiments wore the shako, white coatee, breeches and gaiters; Hungarian regiments the same, but with a special cuff and tight blue pantaloons; and grenz infantry the same as the Hungarians but with brown coatees instead of white. After 1830 grey trousers became the general wear for German regiments. In 1836 the peak of the shako was made straighter to help the men with their aiming, and the front plate of the fur grenadier cap was altered to a small grenade badge. At the same time, light blue trousers were introduced for officers of German regiments.

In 1849 the tunic was introduced with a system of rank badges on the collar. In the field, however, the infantry usually wore linen jackets with patches of the facing colour on the collar, and oilskin covered shakos with white curtains to protect the neck.

During the Hungarian rising of 1848–9, a national army was formed, the nucleus of which consisted of regular Hungarian regiments, forming a cadre for an entirely new national army known as the 'Honved'. The regulars wore their own uniform, substituting red, white, and green sashes and cockades for the Imperial black and yellow. The Honved troops wore shakos and tunics laced across the front in hussar fashion and, of course, Hungarian pantaloons. In this confusion the loyal Austrian regiments adopted the seventeenth century 'field-sign' in the form of a piece of white linen passing from the chin-strap attachment diagonally up to the pom-pom, and then down again. The Hungarian revolution is remarkable for the great variety of eccentric costumes worn by the insurgents, of which the most popular was a befeathered broad-brimmed hat, the 'liberal hat' in military disguise, which was to be so popular with the Confederate cavalry during the American Civil War.

In 1851 officers of Hungarian regiments adopted regulation trousers – pale blue for galas and grey for ordinary duties. On the subject of the infantry, McClellan reported that,

'The shako is of black felt, with leather top and visor; large brass eagle in

Above Left
79   GREAT BRITAIN
Officer's dress crossbelt and
pouch, 10th Hussars,
1816–20.
Mollo Collection

Above Right
80   GREAT BRITAIN
Officer's bearskin grenadier
cap, 2nd Life Guards,
c. 1830.
Household Cavalry Museum

Below Left
81   GREAT BRITAIN
Officer's helmets, 6th
Dragoon Guards, 1847–1914.
Left 1847–66.
Right 1866–1914.
Mollo Collection

Right
82   GREAT BRITAIN
Officer's helmet and cuirass,
1st Life Guards, *c.* 1830.
Household Cavalry Museum

front; wooden pom-pom, trimmed with brass; a black waterproof cover over the shako and visor; . . . The frock-coat is of excellent thick white cloth; the buttons white and plain; coat lined with thick linen; facings and cuffs different for different regiments . . . The pants are of light-blue cloth, with a white cord; always have pockets. The pants of the Hungarian and Croat infantry fit perfectly tight to the legs . . .'

'The coat and pants of the rifles are of a bluish gray, cut like those of the infantry; but instead of the shoulder-strap, there is placed at the point of the shoulder a raised crescent-shaped pad of cloth.

'Their hat is of felt, turned up on both sides, and has a large black plume of cock's feathers.'

The combination of elegance and coarseness found in Russian uniforms during the reign of Nicholas I seemed worthy of note to the eye-witnesses quoted above, because in the British army the uniforms of all ranks were made of the highest quality materials. Britain in the nineteenth century was the richest country in Europe, and the military establishment could well afford to dress the comparatively small army in luxurious fashion. But if the uniforms of the British were better in quality, they were equally if not more, impractical than those of their opponents, and army training was only slightly more sophisticated. The army which set out for the East in 1854 was technically almost the same as that which had entered Paris in triumph in 1815.

In its insistence on rigid drill, and in the harshness of its discipline, the British army was surprisingly like that of Russia for a country which prided itself on its democratic way of life. Its officers were equally ill-educated, and were primarily concerned with hunting, gambling, duelling and drinking. The men were subject to the whims and caprices of colonels like Lord Cardigan and Lord Bingham who, having paid vast sums for their regiments, treated them very much as their own private property. In spite of the industrial revolution and the growing power of the wealthy middle class, the influence of the great Duke of Wellington, who died only two years before the outbreak of the Crimean War, still counted, and his dislike of change permeated the command of the army. The expertise and grasp of administrative matters which had raised Wellington's Peninsular army to such eminence was gradually forgotten as its exponents grew old through the long years of peace-time soldiering. It was only in 1852 that Wellington's successor, Lord Hardinge, and Prince Albert started the annual training camp at Chobham. In 1853, 25,000 men of all arms were assembled there; but even so, colonels were loathe to exercise their regiments in company with others. They knew their drill – or at least their adjutants did – and if it came to a fight, their 'men had guts' and would carry the day as usual.

The cavalry were superbly mounted and equipped, but the officers knew little of their business. Their dash and fire were as bad as the slowness of the Russians; once they were let go in a charge it was virtually impossible to rally them or withdraw them in any semblance of order. From 1839 onwards the infantry were gradually re-equipped with percussion muskets, and in 1851 experiments were carried out in South Africa with the French Minié rifle, some of which were fortunately in use by the beginning of the Crimean War. In general, the British infantry retained the excellence in musketry which was to stand them in good stead at the Alma and Inkerman.

Not unlike the Russian army, part of the British army spent its time serving abroad and saw active service against a variety of savage foes. In China, Burma, India, Afghanistan, New Zealand and South Africa, British officers gained experience of actual combat, but their ideas were discounted at home, and their presence in the army sent to the Crimea was actively discouraged for the most absurd social reasons. Typical of a professional and experienced officer, whose theories were disregarded, was the celebrated Captain Nolan, who, after serving in the Austrian cavalry, the 15th Hussars in India, and making a tour of inspection of the Russian army in 1853, died at the head of the Light Brigade apparently trying to divert it away from disaster. Nolan's ideas, collected in two books published in 1851 and 1852, were generally well in advance of his time and many of them were eventually adopted. Both men and horses should be carefully selected and trained. The men should be alert, agile, quick-sighted and capable of acting on their own. The horses should be light, handy and highly manoeuvrable. The clothing, and here Nolan was relying very much on his Indian experiences, should be loose and practical. Instead of the useless and cumbersome cuirass, he suggested the adoption of steel gauntlets covering the hand and forearm. The swords in use at the time were always blunt, through being carried in steel scabbards, and Nolan advocated the use of the wooden scabbards common amongst Cossacks and other Eastern warriors. With regard to cavalry tactics he was all for 'simplicity'. He advocated always advancing 'by the centre' with a small group out in front where everybody could see them, directing the line to be taken by waving their swords. It is ironic that he met his death frantically trying to do just this.

Ignoring for the present what was going on in India, it was not until halfway through the Crimean War that there were any startling reforms in the dress of the British army. Immediately after Waterloo the general tightening up process taking place on the Continent began to creep into the British army, reaching its height of absurdity in the last years of the reign of George IV. From then on, until the reforms of 1855, clothing gradually got looser in accordance with the prevailing civilian styles. The misconception that everyone went to the Crimea tightly laced and corsetted and crammed into skin-tight overalls arises from confusing the fashions of the forties with those of the fifties. When the 'Times', in April 1854, fuming about the uniforms of the 11th Hussars, referred to the 'shortness of their jackets' and 'the tightness of their cherry-coloured pants', Lord Cardigan was quick to inform those interested that 'in the 11th the men's jackets are longer and their overalls looser than almost any other cavalry regiment in the service'. And to judge from contemporary photographs he was quite right.

The chief characteristic of the uniforms of the British army, certainly at the beginning of the period, was the lack of uniformity. Every regiment had its own special little features which distinguished it from its neighbour, and the different patterns of gold and silver lace used on officers uniforms, kept several firms very profitably occupied. The general style of the uniform was dictated almost entirely by members of the Royal Family, and this coupled with the expense and extravagance drew forth the most vehement criticisms from Whig elements of society. George IV came in for the worst of these vituperations, followed closely by the Duke of Cumberland, who, in 1837, became King of Hanover. Writing in 1837, Robert Huish had the following to say about them:

'The Prince of Wales was a soldier although the laws of the country prevented him from fulfilling the most essential part of the duty of a soldier, that of fighting; but as far as the cut of a uniform, or the adjustment of any military frippery was concerned, he was one of the most active members of the army' . . .
'The Duke of Cumberland, we beg his pardon, the King of Hanover, has punctually attended all the reviews on the continent, . . . and what did he bring back with him to his native country? New styles of dresses, new

Above Left
83 GREAT BRITAIN
Officer's shako, 65th
Regiment, 1829–44.
Mollo Collection

Below left
84 GREAT BRITAIN
Officer's jacket (epaulettes
missing), 17th Lancers,
1830–38.
Mollo Collection

Below Right
85 GREAT BRITAIN
Officer's 'Albert' shako
3rd Regiment, (The Buffs),
1844–55.
National Army Museum

Right
86 FRANCE
Officer, *1ère Compagnie des
Mousquetaires de la Garde
du Roi*, 1814–16.
*Musée de l'Empéri,
Salon-de-Provence*

harlequin uniforms, new patterns of caps and helmets, stays, padding and mustachios. He has, indeed done much for the army and too much have the people of this country paid him for it.'

William IV, although a sailor by profession, was not above trying his hand at the family hobby. There exists a set of drawings of very interesting uniforms, inspired by Russo-Prussian examples, which were obviously intended as a project for the entire British army. In the event, there were several changes during his reign which tended to simplify the officers' uniforms. The arrival of Prince Albert in 1842 coincided with the introduction of several new forms of head-dress, inspired by his rather frowsty taste. The spiked and plumed helmet of the heavy cavalry, obviously based on the Russian and Prussian models, is with us still on the heads of the Household Cavalry. In the early part of 1854, 'Punch' was quick to comment on the 'New Albert bonnet for the Guards', the forerunner of the flat forage cap, and also remarked on a curious figure 'seen in Oxford Street last Wednesday' wearing what was clearly a prototype version of the infantry tunic. 'Was it a Militiaman? and is H.R.H.F.M.P.A. experimentalising upon the gallant "fellow"?' The significance of this is that the new uniform introduced in 1855 was already in preparation before the outbreak of the Crimean War, and was clearly influenced by the Prussian model rather than that of the French uniforms encountered during the war.

The first and most noticeable change in British uniforms after Waterloo was the adoption of the bell-topped shako – already worn by some hussar regiments since 1810 and the light dragoons since 1812 – by the infantry and foot artillery. Fur caps continued to be worn by fusilier regiments and grenadier companies, and the entire 1st Foot Guards, henceforth to be known as the Grenadier Guards, in commemoration of the part they had played in the defeat of Napoleon's Old Guard at Waterloo. The basic design of infantry uniforms remained the same, but the cut became tighter and more exaggerated. By 1822 trousers were common wear – grey in winter and white in summer – and the so-called 'Prussian' closed collar was becoming general.

The cavalry reached new heights of splendour under George IV, in particular the Household Cavalry, who were issued in 1817 with cuirasses and metal helmets surmounted by an immense bearskin crest. Their coatees were double-breasted in the Continental style, with richly embroidered collars and cuffs. In 1821 their already costly wardrobe was augmented by a gigantic fur grenadier cap.

In 1830, with the accession of William IV, new dress regulations introduced further foreign features combined with certain rationalisations. All three regiments of foot guards were given the bearskin cap, which until 1835 retained the metal front plate, and thereafter acquired the appearance it has today. Gorgets were abolished together with the silver lace from the officers' uniforms of some regular regiments. Officers and sergeants of Guards and line regiments now had double-breasted coatees, with slash cuffs, while corporals and privates of line regiments retained the old single-breasted braided jacket. While the Household Cavalry and the heavy cavalry remained basically unchanged, the light dragoons and lancers, the latter first formed in 1816, were put into plain red double-breasted jackets. Hussars went into scarlet pelisses, and throughout the army in general dark blue overalls and trousers took over from the earlier grey.

The next major change was the introduction of the 'Albert' headdresses in the early 1840s. The Household Cavalry received their new helmets in 1842, and the heavy cavalry, who had received an intermediate helmet of extreme ugliness in 1843, in 1847. New dress regulations of 1846 introduced a new shako for light dragoons, and in 1847 the coatees of the heavy cavalry were shortened, and orders were issued abolishing stuffing and padding in officers' uniforms.

The British army which set sail for the East in the spring of 1854 did so wearing their uncomfortable and impractical full dress, and on their arrival in Turkey the only concession they made to the climate was the wearing of white covers over their various headdresses. Gradually, as active service conditions took a toll of their finery, epaulettes, shakos and stocks were abandoned in favour of the comfortable and practical frock coat and forage cap, although the Foot Guards were still in bearskins and scarlet as they advanced up the slopes of the Alma, and the Light Brigade made their celebrated charge in only slightly modified full dress. After the bad winter of 1854–5 there was little left of their original clothing, and the new uniforms sent out to them of the pattern devised by Prince Albert and based on Continental models, gradually came into use.

In the armies of the *Dreikaiserbund* and of Great Britain, during the period between the end of the Napoleonic Wars and the end of the Crimean War, the style of clothing was dictated rather by the stylistic whims of the monarchs concerned than by any practical considerations. Where actual combat experience was gained, if it was of an unorthodox nature it was ignored. As the tastes of the monarchs were altered with the change from classicism to gothic romanticism so the style of their uniforms altered, so that by the end of the period they were beginning to achieve the appearance which they were to retain until full dress fell into disuse after the 1914–18 war.

By 1859 the French army had become most influential in Europe, but immediately after the Restoration it went through a very bad period. The system of recruitment, favoured in France, was selection by ballot for a period of service which varied, from time to time, between six and eight years. The resulting small army of professionals satisfied both the military preference for experts over amateurs and the desire of the middle class to remain undisturbed. In this aim the latter were helped by a system of substitutes which allowed the middle and upper classes to escape military service altogether. Thus it came about that the French army despised the civilian population, who in turn thought little of the army. The aristocracy looked down on it as a breeding ground for future Buonapartes, and the middle class as a barbarous and useless survival.

After its years of Imperial glory the new royal French army was clad in a hotch-potch mixture of old uniforms with strange – to the French at any rate – foreign accretions. During the first restoration in 1814, Parisians were treated to the splendours of the new Maison du Roi – the *Mousquetaires Gris* and the *Mousquetaires Noires* in their crested helmets, red coats, black *supervestes*, breeches and high boots, and the *Gardes du Corps* in blue with red lapels, collars and cuffs, decorated with silver loops, and their trumpeters in elegant blue and white striped jackets. These uniforms were so splendidly designed and executed, and they appeared so promptly on the Restoration, that it would seem very likely that the Prince Regent had some hand in designing them while Louis XVIII was exiled in London. This theory is strengthened by the very English character of the materials and execution. In the rest of the army little was done to alter their appearance, apart from replacing the tricolour cockade with the white royalist one and changing the Napoleonic eagle for the Royal arms of France.

With the second restoration of 1815 came rather more drastic changes. The new guard infantry – six regiments in all – wore blue coats with different colour turnbacks and cuff flaps. The grenadiers wore the bearskin cap, and

87 FRANCE
Officer's 'superveste,
*1ère Compagnie des
Mousquetaires de la Garde
du Roi,* 1814–16. Worn
by Chevalier le Barsiet de la
Busquette.
*Musée de l'Empéri,
Salon-de-Provence*

88 FRANCE
Above. Officer's pouch,
*Gendarmerie de la Garde du
Roi,* 1814–16.
Below. Officer's pouch,
*1ère Compagnie des
Mousquetaires de la Garde
du Roi,* 1814–16.
*Musée de l'Empéri,
Salon-de-Provence*

Above Right
89 FRANCE
Officer's helmet, *1ère*
Compagnie des Mousquetaires
de la Garde du Roi, 1814–16.
Musée de l'Empéri,
Salon-de-Provence

Below Left
90 FRANCE
Officer's shako, *7e Régiment,*
Infanterie Suisse de la
Garde du Roi, 1814–16.
Musée de l'Empéri,
Salon-de-Provence

Below Right
91 FRANCE
Officer's shako, hussar
regiments, 1825.
Musée de l'Empéri,
Salon-de-Provence

the fusiliers the shako. In September, the plastron of the coat was abolished, and new single-breasted coats were introduced, looped across the breast with white braid in the style of the British infantry. The infantry of the line were clothed in white, except for the chasseurs, who continued to wear green, and formed into Departmental Legions of three battalions each. In 1819 the shako was made more upright; and in 1820 regiments were renumbered and given new blue single-breasted coats. In 1821 white breeches and black gaiters were replaced by white trousers in summer and blue in winter. By 1828 an iron-grey overcoat or *capote* was in general use and was carried rolled up on the pack in a blue and white ticking cover. In 1829 red trousers were introduced, although not coming into general use until after 1830.

Of the cavalry, the cuirassiers and dragoons both had helmets, the former in blue jackets and the latter in green. Hussars and *chasseurs à cheval* wore tall cylindrical shakos and the latter green jackets. As late as 1816 *Alsacien* soldiers in the 5th Hussars were still wearing pigtails and side tresses; and when they were abolished in the same year, fifty or so deserted in disgust. In 1818 *garance*, or madder-red trousers were introduced for the cavalry.

In 1830 two events occurred which were to have a great importance in the development of the French army and of military costume in general. On August 2nd, Charles X abdicated, after barricades had been erected in the streets of Paris, and was succeeded by Louis-Phillipe. A little before these political disturbances, France finally decided to settle its long-standing feud with the pirates and sea-robbers who had used Algiers as a base for nearly 300 years. On June 14th, 37,000 French troops under General De Bourmont landed at Sidi-Ferruch, and on July 5th Algiers capitulated. Almost immediately the French army began to pick up in quality and reputation.

VIII *Le Confort Français*

In 1859 there was little doubt, anywhere in the world, that France was once again supreme in the military arts. Although they little knew it at the time, the 30,000 men who landed on the North African coast in 1830, were embarking on a campaign which was to occupy the French army for the next thirty years; and one which was to change its appearance rapidly and dramatically. The special regiments raised for service in Algeria – the *Zouaves*, *Spahis*, *Chasseurs d'Afrique* and others – were to catch the imagination of the world, and were to influence not only military but civilian fashion everywhere.

The Spanish expedition had reconciled Napoleon's army to service under the white flag of the Bourbons. The African campaign restored its confidence in full, breeding a new generation of officers celebrated for their gallantry and dash. Moreover, during the civil disturbances of 1848, the realisation that the army could be useful in the protection of lives and property had gained it the grudging respect of the wealthy classes.

The Second Republic, which was established after the 1848 revolution, brought to the fore Louis Napoleon, nephew of Napoleon I, who after unsuccessful attempts at recognition, in 1836 and 1840, became its President. In 1849, in an attempt to enlist the support of the strong Catholic party, he despatched a French army to Italy to re-establish the Pope, who had been expelled by Garibaldi and Mazzini. In this, its first venture against a regular European army since 1815, the French army, sharpened by its experiences in Africa, met with considerable success.

In December 1851 Louis Napoleon dissolved the Assembly in a *coup d'état*, reminiscent of that which had brought his uncle to prominence so many years before, and in the following year he restored the hereditary empire, taking for himself the title of Napoleon III. The French army had its Emperor once again. From 1852 to 1870 Napoleon III ruled over France with varying degrees of autocracy, combining reaction and Imperial splendour at home with professed liberalism abroad. Headstrong and irresolute, he proclaimed peace but made war. In 1854 he allied himself with England and

HEADPIECE
From *The Field Exercise and Evolutions of Infantry*, 1861

159

92 UNITED STATES OF
AMERICA
Painted cap front,
Connecticut Militia, 1821.
Smithsonian Institution

Right
93 FRANCE
Soldier, *Légion Étranger*,
c. 1860.
*Musée de l'Empéri,
Salon-de-Provence*

94 FRANCE
'Casquettes d'Afrique',
c. 1840.
Left Marshal of France,
North Africa, c. 1840.
Right Soldier, *3e Chasseurs
d'Afrique*, c. 1850.
*Musée de l'Empéri,
Salon-de-Provence*

embarked on a war against Russia, in defence of the Ottoman Empire. Although it began without any sort of planning and ended only after the long drawn-out siege of Sevastopol, Napoleon emerged intoxicated with the success of his army and immediately put into operation his plan for the creation of an Italian state under Pope Pius IX. The result was the campaign of 1859, which ended in the hard-won victories of Magenta and Solferino against the Austrians. These successes were attributed by most observers to the invincibility of the French army, and between 1859 and 1870 countries as far apart as the United States of America, Turkey, and Japan hired French officers as technical advisers, or copied slavishly the convenient French dress and loose-limbed drill.

But in spite of success, there were serious defects in the French army. Although higher than ever in the public esteem, the army was kept deliberately apart from the rest of the nation. It was the main prop of the Empire, and was relied upon to carry out police duties. The officers were poor and without any of the social prestige which kept up the spirits of the equally impecunious Prussian officers. Furthermore, with little prospect of serious fighting there was little concern for military education, African experience only serving to perpetuate this attitude. The system of small mobile columns, which had been developed there, may have served to encourage dash and initiative; but the study of military manoeuvres, or of the skilful use of the three arms in battle, was ignored. Moreover, as the columns were self-supporting, there was no supply organisation. In spite of perpetuating the casual administrative habits of the First Empire, the French army continued to be victorious. In the Crimea, and in Italy, headquarters, supply and administrative services had to be created *ad hoc* and the French army acquired a reputation for efficiency in these matters only because their allies and opponents were so woefully bad at them. The French army was dominated, in the words of a contemporary, 'by an all-powerful school made up of soldiers, as fortunate as they were brave, who loudly proclaimed their contempt for the military art'. Victory justified the preservation of a system which had stood the test of time.

The general enthusiasm for French military forms current after the Crimean war is reflected in the comments of McClellan who waxed lyrical about the *zouaves*.

> 'The Zouaves are all French; they are selected from among the old campaigners for their fine physique and tried courage and have certainly proved that they are what their appearance would indicate – the most reckless, self-reliant, and complete infantry that Europe can produce. . . .'
> 'Of all the troops that I have ever seen, I should esteem it the greatest honor to assist in defeating the Zouaves. The Grenadiers of the Guard are all large men, and a fine-looking soldierly set. . . .'
> 'The appearance of the infantry of the line is by no means impressive; it requires close watching to appreciate their excellent qualities. . . .'

The infantry, armed for the most part with the smooth-bore musket, were 'allowed the utmost ease and latitude in ranks . . . much irregularity was tolerated in marching and they presented rather a slouching appearance. . . .'. McClellan has little to say about the appearance of the French cavalry except to remark that 'but little can be said in favor' of their horses; but he was evidently impressed by the *chasseurs d'Afrique*, who were such experienced veterans that 'less minute attention to details was required from the officers'.

After 1859 the fortunes of Napoleon III declined rapidly. In 1863 in an attempt to divert the attention of the Catholic party from events in Rome,

Napoleon sent French troops to occupy Mexico, where in the same year he was instrumental in having the Archduke Maximilian of Austria installed as Emperor. When the French troops were evacuated in 1867, after an ultimatum from the United States of America, the Imperial army was rapidly defeated by the republicans and the Emperor captured and shot.

In 1866 the Second Empire received an even ruder shock. The rivalry between Prussia and Austria for the supremacy of Germany erupted into open warfare and, in spite of brilliant victories in Italy, the Austrian army was soundly defeated by the army of 'lawyers and oculists' at the Battle of Sadowa. All confidence in imperialism in France burst like a bubble. Napoleon III might bluster as much as he liked at the growing power of Prussia, but, shaken by the performance of the Prussian army, he dared not use force. Certain reforms, however, were carried out. In an attempt to increase numbers to approaching the estimated Prussian strength of 1,200,000, the old *garde nationale* was reformed as the *garde mobile*; and certain improvements were made in armaments, notably the introduction of the Chassepot breech-loading rifle, which had a range up to 1,600 yards compared with the 600 yards of the Prussian needle gun. But in the vital fields of staff work and administration, in the planning of mobilisation and in the use of railways, in all of which the Prussians excelled, the French made little headway. When war finally came in 1870 the French army was as ready as it had been 'for the Crimean War, for the Italian War, for the Mexican adventure, for all the military enterprises of that era'; what it was not ready for was that the era itself had changed.

The army despatched to Algiers in May 1830 consisted of three infantry divisions, a composite regiment of cavalry, and the usual supporting arms and services. They embarked in their normal uniforms but with white linen covers over their shakos. The cavalry consisting of one squadron of the 13th *chasseurs à cheval* and two of the 17th – one armed with lances – was given the title of the *Chasseurs à cheval d'Afrique*. They wore white covered shakos, braided dolman jackets, and red overalls. The infantry wore shakos and covers, blue single-breasted jackets, red trousers and white gaiters. With them they took their grey greatcoats, packed into cylindrical blue and white ticking covers, strapped on top of their packs. It was not long before active service and the ferocious heat made some changes necessary. The infantry left their shakos and jackets in store and wore their greatcoats with various forms of peaked forage cap, some like a tapering shako and some like the Russian and Prussian peaked cap. These caps became so common that in July 1833 it was ordered that 'Troops serving in Africa will no longer use their shakos or *bonnets de police*; in place of these items they will receive a cloth cap, together with a waterproof linen cover'. This *casquette*, as it was called, was a tall and narrow cloth shako which in due course was to develop into the famous *képi*. At the same time the infantry crossbelts, with pouch, sabre and bayonet, were discarded in favour of a black waistbelt, with a pouch in front and a bayonet frog at the side.

By 1840 French tactics had resolved themselves into the light column system, by which all heavy baggage, including sabres, cross-belts and pouches, was left in store, while the column marched as close to the enemy as possible and formed an encampment. Here further items were stored under guard while the main body set off in light marching order consisting of the *casquette*, worn with a white neck flap, rations for two days, and reserve ammunition rolled up in the tent and worn over one shoulder.

With the expansion of operations in North Africa came new units which were to gain world-wide renown – *chasseurs d'Afrique*, *zouaves* and *spahis*. The first were formed in 1832 after the 13th and 17th *chasseurs à cheval*

Left
95 FRANCE
Officer's helmet and cuirass,
line cuirassier regiments,
1845–54.
Musée de l'Empéri,
Salon-de-Provence

Above
96 GREAT BRITAIN
Officer's shako, 34th
(Cumberland) Regiment,
1855–61.
National Army Museum

Below
97 UNITED STATES OF
       AMERICA
Officer's shako, 3rd U.S.
Artillery, 1821–31.
Smithsonian Institution

98 FRANCE
Officer's sabretache and
pouch, *Artillerie à Cheval*
de la Garde Impériale,
1852–70.
Musée de l'Empéri,
Salon-de-Provence

were returned to France. In 1834 the native element in the three regiments became so large that it was formed into separate regiments of *spahis*. The dress of the *chasseurs* was romantic and practical at the same time. A pale blue *habit-capote à la Polonaise* – a long frock coat – with scale epaulettes, voluminous red and blue sashes, and baggy red trousers. Their full dress headdress was a lancer *czapka*, with a red top, black skull, and horizontally placed peak, while on service they wore a red *casquette d'Afrique*. The *spahis* at first wore native costume of various colours, the only uniform item being the green burnous they wore on service. In 1841 they were given a uniform consisting of blue arab trousers and waistcoat, and a red jacket, worn with the green burnous. The *zouaves* were originally formed in 1830 from tribesmen of the Zouaoua tribe who came forward to help the French. By 1832 they consisted of one battalion of ten companies, eight of which were French nationals. At first their dress was very varied and their French officers frequently affected arab dress consisting of:

'. . . tricolour turban with an aigrette, blue Turkish jacket, embroidered in gold, red mameluke trousers, with gold trimmed pockets, silk sash full of pistols, and a curved sabre, but they found these disguises so grotesque, they hurriedly abandoned them. They were still allowed to choose their own guise, but their first attempts had sufficed and one saw only European costume amongst the French officers. . . .'

By the time of the Crimean war the uniform of the *zouaves* had become world-famous and had resolved itself into a headdress consisting of a red fez with a long tassel, which was wound round with a turban for full dress, a blue waistcoat fastening at the back, a blue jacket, which left the neck unencumbered, and baggy scarlet trousers tucked into yellow leather gaiters. McClellan was told that 'this dress is the most convenient possible' and that the men prefer it to any other'.

The military left in France disapproved of all these fripperies. The grumpy Marshal de Castellane makes many irate references to the permissiveness of the African army in his memoirs, but willy-nilly the ideas tried out in Africa were gradually passed on to the whole army. The year 1845 saw new dress regulations which completely altered the appearance of the French army. Needless to say, Castellane was not too pleased:

'A circular of March 2nd 1845 from the Minister of War announces that the trials made in various regiments have proved the necessity of reducing the size of the cartouche box, replacing the crossbelt with a waist belt and substituting a tunic for the coat. It is a real revolution in clothing, for officers will have a tunic like the men. They have done away with the old *redingote* and cloak and replaced it with a *caban*. Infantry officers will now have their sabres trailing like the cavalry; they do their best to suppress anything that is dignified.'

In 1839 a battalion of *chasseurs à pied* was formed at Vincennes and dressed in a uniform based on African models; a double-breasted blue tunic, baggy grey-blue breeches piped in yellow, *zouave* type gaiters, a hooded cloak made of waterproof material, and a shako sloping forward from the back. In 1840 ten battalions of *chasseurs* were assembled in camp at St. Omer under the Duc d'Orleans and their dress was modified to a single-breasted tunic. Apart from differences in dress, the *chasseurs* were armed with better weapons than the line, were trained to precision in fire, bayonet fighting, and marching at the *pas gymnastique*.

The new regulations introduced in 1845 settled the basic pattern of French uniforms until 1870. The main changes for the staff were the introduction of blue *képis* and the reduction in the size of the cocked hat, which now acquired that particularly low French look which it still has today. It was now always to be worn fore and aft (*en colonne*), as opposed to athwartships (*en bataille*), although certain reactionaries like Castellane continued to wear their hats in the old way for many years.

The line infantry and the light infantry, differentiated by the former having blue collars, red cuffs with a blue flap, and yellow buttons, and the latter yellow collars, blue pointed cuffs piped in yellow, and white buttons, wore the new shako, tunic, waistbelt equipment, and red trousers. Their greatcoats were altered so that the skirts could be buttoned back on the march. The officers' *caban*, mentioned by Castellane, was a loose ample overcoat of blue cloth lined in red. It fastened down the front with a series of olives and loops of black cord and had gold or silver braid rank markings on the cuffs, in the form of Austrian knots. The officers were differentiated from the men, when wearing the tunic, by their gold or silver epaulettes and their gorgets. As the old sword frog, worn under the coat, was impracticable with the tunic, a waistbelt with two sword slings was adopted by the infantry.

The appearance of the cavalry was not altered much by the 1845 regulations, which served rather to codify various changes which had already taken place. The two regiments of carabiniers, the cuirassiers and the dragoons wore helmets and coats, the first pale blue, the second dark blue and the third dark green. All wore red trousers so heavily strapped with black leather that only a tiny portion of the red could be seen at the side. The lancers, who since 1837 had been wearing blue *kurtkas*, were given a *képi* embroidered in front with crossed lances. The *chasseurs à cheval*, dressed in green, underwent various experimental uniforms including, in 1839, a *palto*, or braided dolman which descended to below the hips. In 1843 they were given fur busbies with plumes on the left-hand side, which were replaced in 1848 by red shakos. Hussars wore shakos, short braided dolmans and strapped trousers, the colouring of which differed for each regiment.

The reforms of 1845 consisted essentially of the adoption of tunics in place of coats, waistbelts instead of crossbelts, and in the rationalisation of the headdress. But in 1854, with the formation of the *Garde Imperiale*, in direct imitation of that of the First Empire there was a return to the past. The luxury of the Second Empire – the *style Rothschild* – is fully reflected in the costly and Ruritanian uniforms of Napoleon III's Guards. The infantry, consisting at first of grenadiers and *voltigeurs*, wore tunics with white plastrons in imitation of the jackets of the First Empire, but in 1860' these were changed to single-breasted tunics with braid loops down the front as in 1815. The *chasseurs* of the Guard wore tunics piped in yellow, grey-blue breeches, and *zouave* gaiters. In 1854 the cuirassiers of the guard in dark blue and light blue tunics, the lancers in white *kurtkas* with pale blue facings, the dragoons in green and white, the chasseurs in green, red facings and white lace, the guides in green, red facings and orange lace, and the artillery in busbies and blue dolmans braided with red, created a kaleidoscopic effect as they paraded in the streets of Paris.

In 1861 a new smaller shako was introduced, and in 1862 a shorter double-breasted tunic. In 1868 dragoons and lancers were issued with tunics, while at the same time, a trial was made of a long hussar dolman, which did not finally come into use until 1872. The *gardes mobiles* were given the normal infantry uniform with grey-blue trousers. In 1868 various volunteer units known as *francs-tireurs* were formed and attached to the *garde mobile*.

167

99 UNITED STATES OF
     AMERICA
Staff Officer's dress coat,
1832–51.
Smithsonian Institution

These wore a variety of strange costumes usually consisting of a wide-brimmed felt hat decorated with feathers, grey, brown or blue blouses, baggy trousers and *zouave* gaiters. During the war of 1870, the Germans refused to recognise these units as authorised combatants, and many were shot when captured. Later on they were dressed, as far as possible, like the *garde mobile*.

The revolution in uniform did much to alter civilian dress in ways which are with us still. In 1815 the British were the leaders of male fashion, largely on account of their expertise in handling the hard cloths favoured by the country gentleman. Their bluff no-nonsense mode of dressing was smartened up by Beau Brummel, with the result that standards of tailoring were far higher than they had been in the eighteenth century. With the return to absolutism, tightly cut coats of dark colours became the general wear for men. With them, however, came certain items culled from the wardrobes of the military: baggy Cossack trousers, peaked caps, frock coats, long braided 'great-coats', and overall trousers, worn over ankle boots, and strapped under the instep. Women's clothes, on the other hand, had suffered from the years of isolation from Continental fashions, and British visitors to Paris were renowned for their extreme dowdiness. After 1815 Paris once again took the lead in female fashion, and held it undisputed until our own times.

A combination of radicals and democrats on the one hand and romantics on the other brought about a reaction against the top hats and frock coats of the wealthy classes, while the new fashions imported to Paris by the veterans of North Africa, led to a proliferation of loose clothing. The officers' *caban* was the first link in a series of loose box-like coats, which in turn developed into the lounge suit of the late 1850s. The costume of the *zouaves*, which together with Garibaldi's famous red shirt created a furore in the 1860s, led to the adoption by women of the blouse and bolero jacket, and by men, of knickerbockers for shooting and other sports . . . and to the invention in England by 1869 of the 'Norfolk suit', consisting of a loosely cut short jacket, pleated back and front with two large box pleats, and knickerbockers. By 1870 men's clothes had reached a point of development from which they were to alter only slightly. Lounge suits, peg-top trousers, cloth caps, wide-awake hats and bowlers had taken over from blue swallow-tail coats, white trousers and top hats, for the bulk of mankind.

The most wholesale copying of French military styles took place in the United States of America. After the 1812 war the regular US army was very small in size and relied, in times of crisis, on the assistance of the various state militias and volunteer regiments. There was no regular cavalry at all until 1832 when, as a result of increasing clashes with mounted Indians, a battalion of mounted rangers was formed. This was expanded in 1833 to form the 1st Dragoons, and in 1836 a second dragoon regiment was raised. In 1846, after several years of friction over the independent Republic of Texas, the United States declared war on Mexico. After sixteen months of fierce fighting, the Americans defeated the Mexicans, stripping them of two-fifths of their territory. Texas had already gone; now California and New Mexico became part of the United States. During the war a third regiment of dragoons was raised. Hard service on the frontier and in Mexico turned the dragoons into a fierce and business-like body of men. Distinguished by their moustaches and long hair, they hardly ever wore their full dress, which consisted of a tall cylindrical shako, blue double-breasted jacket faced with yellow, and blue-grey overalls, and was reminiscent of that of the British light dragoons. Instead they were usually to be seen in blue peaked caps and short blue shell jackets trimmed round the collar and cuffs and on the back seams with yellow braid. Their officers wore single-breasted blue frock

100 UNITED STATES OF
    AMERICA
Shako, 1st Pennsylvania
Artillery, 1840.
Smithsonian Institution

Far Left
101 UNITED STATES OF
    AMERICA
Dragoon Sergeant in winter
dress, 1833–50.
Smithsonian Institution

Left
102 UNITED STATES OF
    AMERICA
Union infantryman in
marching order, 1865.
Smithsonian Institution

Right
103 UNITED STATES OF
    AMERICA
Soldier's dress shako,
Union Light Artillery, 1865.
Smithsonian Institution

coats with gold buttons, and the specifically American invention of rank badges worn on embroidered straps on the shoulder, originally the loops through which the epaulette passed, all finished off with red sashes. In 1846 a regiment of mounted riflemen was formed wearing similar uniforms but with green as their distinctive colour. Early in 1850, five years after the revolutionary French changes, a general order announced the introduction of a new basic uniform for the whole army – the tunic and French *casquette*. According to the announcement, 'a large number of officers of the Army, probably more than half, have applied since the war with Mexico to have a uniform less expensive, less difficult to procure and better adapted to campaigns and other service'. The 1851 Dress Regulations, which followed this decision, gave mounted units the cap and tunic, dragoons having orange distinctions, mounted riflemen green, and artillery red. The cap was decorated with a coloured pom-pom and an eagle badge, mounted regiments having lines with thick braided flounders. In 1854 the short jacket was restored to mounted units, and in 1855 the famous 'Hardee' or 'Jim Davis' felt hat first appeared on the heads of the newly formed 1st and 2nd Cavalry. These regiments wore the cavalry uniform with yellow trimming but were also issued with a curious garment, described as a 'Gutta-Percha Talma', with large loose sleeves, which extended to the knees. The hats were looped up on one side and adorned with black ostrich feathers, and were named after Secretary of War Davis and Major Hardee of the 2nd Cavalry, who is supposed to have invented them; they were also known as 'Fra Diavolo's', after Auber's celebrated opera.

During the Mexican War period, the infantry wore their fatigue dress of a blue peaked forage cap, sky-blue shell jacket trimmed with white braid, and trousers. White crossbelts, a black painted pack, and a red rolled blanket completed their equipment. The officers wore the blue frock coat, with silver buttons and rank badges, and the red sash.

In 1851 the infantry were given the shako-cap and tunic, with black leather equipment consisting of a waistbelt and plate, from which hung the bayonet, and a crossbelt and cartouche box; their arm colour was now 'Saxony blue'. At the same time they were given a short, four-button 'blouse' which, worn with the *képi* forage cap, became the general and celebrated dress of the Civil War period. The officers were given the French *caban*, complete with sleeve rank markings, virtually the same drawing that appears in the French dress regulations being used to illustrate the US regulations. In his report to the US War Department, after the Crimean War, McClellan has the following to say on the subject of the dress of the US cavalry. Devotees of American 'cavalry versus Indian' films will instantly recognise how many of his suggestions were in fact adopted.

'I would recommend that the scale epaulette be entirely dispensed with for regimental officers; it is useless, expensive, and inconvenient: the strap on the undress uniform is a sufficient distinction of rank.

'For the men, I would replace the scales by straps of cloth, of the same shape as that on the old fatigue uniform, but sewed fast to the jacket.

'They should also have a police cap, without visor, and of such a nature that it can be folded up and carried in the pouch, or whereever may be most convenient; the Scotch bonnet, Turkish fez, a Greek cap of knit or woven wool, a flexible cap of the shape of the old forage-cap – any of these would answer.

'For service on the prairies, the men should have a loose flannel coat, leaving their uniform coat in garrison; the ordinary dark-blue sailor's shirt, cut open in front, and provided with a lining and pockets, is as good as any thing that can be devised.

'The French fashion of giving the men a merino scarf in the field, instead of a stock, is worthy of consideration.'

When, on the morning of April 12th 1861, the guns echoed out across Charleston Harbour, the northern states of America found themselves in grave peril. The small regular army was scattered in hundreds of tiny posts, while the growing forces of the south were threatening the capital. It was the state volunteer militia units that came to the aid of Lincoln. Throughout the years of peace these local units had dressed themselves up in whatever they liked. There were highlanders in feather bonnets and kilts, 'Highland Fusiliers' in tartan trews, exact copies of the British Foot Guards complete with bearskin caps, 'German Artillery' in spiked helmets, lancers in *czapkas*, 'The New York Garibaldi Guards' in *zouave* pantaloons, red shirts, and *bersaglieri* hats adorned with cock's feathers; but above all there were *zouaves*.

In the years after the Crimean war, a penniless clerk by the name of Elmer E. Ellsworth became friendly with a French fencing instructor who had served in the Crimea with the *zouaves*. With his aid, Ellsworth raised a company of *zouaves* in Chicago in 1859. Within five weeks they had mastered the rapid drill, and, in 1860, they made a very successful tour of the east, taking part in drill competitions and spreading the *zouave* craze. The company was disbanded but, capitalising on his success, Ellsworth issued an elaborate printed plan for clothing companies, regiments, or for that matter the entire US army in 'the greatest degree of comfort and convenience to the soldier', by which he meant a sort of *zouave* costume of grey cloth. He chose grey 'because it is less expensive and wears longer than any other colour except white or scarlet, besides being very neat and properly our national color'. Finally, in 1861 he returned to New York to command the 'New York Fire Zouaves', by which time the craze had so developed that both sides during the Civil War had several *zouave* units who, in the early years at any rate, went into action in full Arab costume.

In August 1861 the Quartermaster-General placed an experimental order in France for 10,000 complete equipments 'to be uniformed as the Chasseurs à Pied', and the whole of the US army was very nearly clothed in this fashion. One regiment certainly was: the 83rd Pennsylvania Infantry so distinguished themselves in 1861 and 1862 that they were issued with these new uniforms as a reward. The entire regiment appeared in the uniform of the *chasseurs de Vincennes*, consisting of '. . . a shako, two jaunty, tasteful suites, dress and fatigue, with cloak, two pairs of shoes, two pairs of white gloves, two night caps, gaiters, sac le petit, containing five brushes for various purposes, needle case with combs, thread, spool, cloak pin, and various other conveniences'.

One of the many tragedies of the tragic American civil war was the lack of distinguishing marks between the two sides. Contrary to popular belief, the northern troops were not clothed exclusively in blue, nor the southerners in grey. The Dress regulations for the army of Georgia, the first state to secede, dated February 15th 1861, specify a 'blue flannel sack for fatigue dress and a single-breasted frock-coat of 'Georgia Cadet gray' for full dress. The hat was to be of black felt, although officers were permitted to wear caps 'according to Pattern "No. 9" "French officers" '. The enlisted men of North Carolina were to wear a 'sack coat' and trousers of North Carolina grey cloth, and felt hats. Officers when off duty could wear 'French forage caps'. The southern cavalry, traditionally better horsemen than the industrialised northerners, affected a very dashing Kossuth-Garibaldi appearance with felt

Following Pages
Above Left
104 CONFEDERATE STATES OF AMERICA
Jacket worn by General John S. Mosby, 1865.
Smithsonian Institution

Below Left
105 AUSTRIA
Soldier's *Hut, k.k. Jägerbataillon, Nr. 5*, 1861.
Heeresgeschichtliches Museum, Vienna

Above Right
106 UNITED STATES OF AMERICA
U.S. Cavalry officer's buckskin jacket, as worn during the Indian wars, c. 1870.
Smithsonian Institution

Below Right
107 GREAT BRITAIN
Officer's tunic, 34th (Cumberland) Regiment, 1856–68.
National Army Museum

108 GREAT BRITAIN
Pattern of Rifle uniform for wear by the Volunteers. Plate No. 3 from R. Ackermann's *Costume of The Volunteer Corps*. Drawn by Orlando Norie and published on February 6th, 1860.
Mollo Collection

hats and feathers, short grey jackets with the yellow lining button backed, and French rank braiding on their cuffs; but by the end of the war, poverty and shortages had reduced all their finery to a collection of civilian rags.

After the Civil War the regular army continued to wear their pre-war uniforms until new regulations were issued in 1872.

In the thirties, forties and fifties, the Italian states, who mostly had rather small and ineffectual armies, dressed them in accordance with the sphere of influence – Bourbon or Hapsburg – to which they belonged. One army, however, stood out in particular; that of Sardinia. The long military traditions of the ruling house of Savoy had been so well preserved that by the end of the Crimean war McClellan was able to report on the Sardinian detachment which took part in terms only second to those in which he describes the *zouaves*. The part played by Garibaldi's 'Thousand' in their red *képis* and shirts, and the Sardinian army in the war of 1859 and the subsequent struggle for the unification of Italy, was admired throughout the civilised world and led to the spate of 'Garibaldi' fashions.

When Italy was finally united, Victor Emmanuel, King of Sardinia, became its first king, and his army became the model for the subsequent royal Italian army. The uniforms and tactics of the Sardinian army were closely modelled on French patterns. The uniform was generally shakos or blue *képis*, blue tunics and pale blue-grey trousers. The exceptions were the famous *Bersaglieri* formed as early as 1833 by General Lamarmora. This officer had carried out a complete survey of all the light infantry of Europe and his regiments were intended to embody all their best features. The *Bersaglieri* were dressed like the French chasseurs, with blue tunics and baggy trousers, but with their very distinctive round hat which they wear today; after the Crimean war they adopted the *zouave* fez as an undress cap. All their movements were carried out at the double, and their barracks were built without staircases, entrance and exit being effected by means of ropes. Their rifle, the prototype of which was made by General Lamarmora with his own hands, had a built-in spike in the butt to assist in climbing hills. According to McClellan the *Bersaglieri* in the Crimea wore dark blue great-coats and trousers, and the hat was 'of felt, with a flat rim three inches broad; the rim is stiff and covered with oiled linen, the crown is round; there is a plume of black-cock feathers'. Of the rest of the infantry he says that their appearance was strikingly like that of the US infantry. In the Crimea the infantry wore their greatcoats, the tunics being left at home, and they wore an Italian fisherman's cap 'something between the Greek cap and the Turkish fez'. He sums up in the following complimentary terms: 'The organisation, discipline, instruction, and personal appearance of the Sardinian infantry are excellent'.

All the cavalry wore dark blue tunics, grey-blue trousers and greatcoats; and they usually wore a low French-type shako in a yellow waterproof cover, the hind flap of which fastened over the top. '. . . they may be re-garded' says McClellan, 'as among the best troops in Europe. The appearance of the Sardinian Cavalry, as indeed of their whole army in the Crimea, was excellent; indeed, the general appearance of their army was superior to that of either of the allies.'

Their opponents, the Austrians, had changed little in appearance since the introduction of the low shako and tunic in 1849. In 1861 a new tunic was introduced with shorter rounded skirts and a turned down collar. During the campaign of 1866 the infantry usually wore their greatcoats over their shirts, the skirts of the coat being fastened back, not outside, in the French manner, but inside.

As regards the regular cavalry, the cuirass was abolished in 1860; and the cuirassier regiments were absorbed into dragoon regiments in 1868. Perhaps the most significant development in the Austrian army at this time was the formation of a number of volunteer Hungarian regiments raised for service in the Italian war. These regiments, both horse and foot, which were later taken into the regular army, carried on the romantic traditions of the national army of 1848–9. They appeared in a variety of curious costumes based on Hungarian folk dress with added dashes of 'Garibaldism'. But from all this mass of fur, feathers, pelisses, blouses, knickerbockers and big boots emerged, as early as 1866, the prototype of the modern service dress jacket with flapped pockets on the breast and hips.

After the Crimean war the British army showed a curiously schizophrenic attitude towards France. On the one hand there was a considerable distrust of France's military power, which was largely traditional, and was typified by Lord Raglan's habit in the Crimea of occasionally referring to the enemy as the 'French'; and by his petulant remark on the evening of the Alma as the French trumpets shrilled out over the darkening battlefield, 'Ah, there they go with their infernal *too-too-tooing*; that's the only thing they ever do'. On the other hand in the reforms which took place immediately after the war, much attention was paid to the French military forms, particularly in the matter of dress.

The new uniforms of 1855 which gradually permeated out to the front lines introduced the tunic to all regiments of the army except the Royal Horse Artillery. The uniform of the Life Guards, Blues and Foot Guards, now reached a point in its development which, with but minor alterations, it still retains today.

The heavy cavalry continued to wear the spiked helmet except for the Scots Greys, who retained their fur grenadier caps; and all wore scarlet tunics with the exception of the Royal Horse Guards, and the 6th Dragoon Guards (the Carabiniers), who wore blue Light Dragoon *attilas*. The shape of the helmet was altered in 1873, and the decoration simplified, when it achieved the appearance it has today. Expensive regimental patterns of gold and silver lace virtually disappeared, except on pouch and sword belts, and rank badges were worn on the collar, which at first was cut very low and rounded in front, while the cut of the whole tunic was rather loose and the trousers very baggy.

The light dragoons and hussars were given braided *attilas*, the former with French shakos. In 1861 the remaining light dragoon regiments, four of which were former regiments of the Honourable East India Company, were turned into hussars. The hussar regiments were distinguished by the colour of their plumes and busby bags; and the lancers were given double-breasted tunics with coloured revers. Up to about 1868 leather-booted overalls were still in general use for mounted troops.

In 1855 the infantry, with the exception of the Guards, were given a shako which was a cross between the French and Austrian patterns having, unlike the French shako, a peak at the back. These shakos, decorated in front with a pom-pom, were found as inconvenient as the Albert shakos, and they were soon abandoned in the Crimea in favour of the round forage cap. In 1860, flank companies were abolished and in 1861 a new cork shako was introduced, covered in blue cloth – green for rifles and light infantry – which was only four inches high in front. In 1869 yet another shako appeared, this time with a chain chin strap.

The original double-breasted tunic was altered to single-breasted in 1856. Epaulettes and wings were discontinued, together with shoulder sword belts and regimental plates. Rank badges were now worn on the collar and the sash over the left shoulder. Highland regiments were given a curious piece

109 RUSSIA
Officer's *képi*, 13th Hussar
Regiment, 1862–81.
Mollo Collection

Right
110 RUSSIA
Uniforms and equipment of
the four infantry regiments
forming the 15th Infantry
Division, 1862–81. From the
official lithographed
schemae published from
time to time by the
Prototype Institute of the
Office of the Chief Intendant.
Mollo Collection

111 RUSSIA
Officer's shoulder-boards,
1855–1914.
From left to right Junker,
Constantine Artillery School
for Officers; Colonel, Suite
of Nicholas II; Captain, 16th
Grouzinsky Grenadier
Regiment; General-Adjutant,
Horse Guard Regiment
(Suite of Alexander II);
General-Adjutant, Life
Guard Ataman Cossack
Regiment (Suite of
Alexander II); Lieutenant-
Colonel, 55th Artillery
Brigade.
Mollo Collection

15я ПЕХОТНАЯ ДИВИЗIЯ

57й Пѣх. Модлинскiй п.

58й Пѣх. Прагскiй п.

59й Пѣх. Люблинскiй полкъ.

60й Пѣх. Замосцкiй Ген Ад. Гр. Коцебу и.

179

of Victorian romanticism called a 'doublet' which consisted of a tunic with four pointed flaps decorated with false buttonholes and buttons instead of skirts, the original double-breasted version having square or lozenge-shaped buttons.

By 1864 an undress blouse with four buttons down the front and a single breast pocket with flap was being worn in some regiments. Officers wore very low flat *képis* and frock coats in undress, sergeants wore caps similar to those of the officers, while the men retained the Crimean period round forage cap.

The traditional liberal pacifism of the middle classes in England was changed dramatically by the Crimean war and the Indian mutiny into the militant patriotism or jingoism which was to be such a noticeable British characteristic for the rest of the century. The sudden realisation of the size of the French and Austrian armies engaged in Italy, and a fear of Britain being 'prostrate before hordes of Chasseurs de Vincennes and black-muzzled African legions' resulted in a public demand for some form of volunteer army. As a result, between May 1859 and June 1860, some 130,000 Volunteers were raised and formed into a small corps, the nucleus of which was formed by various rifle clubs which had existed before the Crimean war. In spite of initial opposition from Prince Albert and the Duke of Cambridge on the age-old grounds that an amateur army would get in the way of the professionals, or that they would be an 'armed and dangerous rabble', the Volunteer movement turned out to be of considerable value to the regular army and the country as a whole. Its high-minded moral tone, its junketings, picnics, balls, and outrageous dress may have been ridiculous, but it brought to the army the skills of a class which had previously had little to do with military service. In the first place the Volunteers were very efficient; and when in 1860 the myriad small units were consolidated into battalions, Britain was in possession of a very respectable reserve army. Furthermore, they were well trained in science and industry, and many technical inventions and improvements stemmed from volunteer sources. The Crimean war had underlined the importance of supply and administration and the amateurs of the volunteer movement brought the precision of the counting-house, mill or factory, to their military activities. Eight years before the dramatic German mobilisation in 1870, a volunteer-inspired pamphlet contained a plan for rushing troops by railway to any point of the British coast which might be threatened by an invasion. In the social field, the granting of Volunteer commissions broke yet another barrier in the social equality of the moneyed and landed classes.

The recommended dress for Volunteer units should be, according to War Office instructions, 'as simple as possible'. The rifle uniform was grey with red piping and black braiding, inspired by that of the dreaded *Chasseurs de Vincennes*; a low *képi*, a single-breasted grey tunic, baggy grey knicker-bocker trousers, and yellow *zouave* gaiters. The greatcoat was voluminous and hooded. Artillery units had a similar uniform but blue with red piping and black braiding, and black gaiters. In the event, however, admiration for Garibaldi and all his works got the better of some unit commanders, and when 3,000 Volunteer officers were presented to the Queen, in March 1860, they appeared in 'every shade of grey and green, drab-blue and tartan knickerbockers and blouses, wide-awake headdresses, helmets, shakos and caps with any quantity of horsehair and feather plumes, and belts of black, white and buff leather'. The North Cornwall Corps was particularly outstanding in 'scarlet shirts, blue serge trousers tucked into boots, and a wideawake hat with a small plume'. Some corps, however, were a bit less exotic and wore uniforms based on sporting clothes or the smock of the rustic labourer.

The end of the Crimean war saw the collapse of the system of Nicholas I and the beginning of the end for Tsarism in Russia. The death of the Tsar on February 18th 1855 from pneumonia, brought on in a typical fashion by refusing to wear a greatcoat at a review, ushered in a period of 'thaw' which was in the end to prove disastrous. Alexander II, who succeeded to the throne, while a typical mid-nineteenth century monarch, was a kindlier and less diehard character than his father and was soon prevailed upon to ease the growing discontent in Russia by inaugurating a series of liberal reforms. Commissions were set up to examine the status of private and state owned serfs, conscripted factory workers, and the army, and the results of their deliberations were embodied in a series of reforms which started in 1863 with the liberation of the serfs. The consequent breakdown of the old feudal structure and the appearance of a new *déclassé* intelligentsia for whom no reforms went far enough, sowed the seeds of the Russian revolution. Coupled with these reforms there was rapid development in the building of factories and railways in an attempt to catch up with the rest of Europe.

In foreign affairs, the period after the Crimean war marked the beginning of the *Entente Cordiale* between France and Russia which was to last until 1914. Even before peace was made in 1856 a Russian ambassador had been fêted in Paris. Soon after Alexander II visited Napoleon III, who was looking towards Russia as a new ally in the coming struggle against Prussia. But apart from the second Polish uprising of 1863 which was easily suppressed, Russia was left to carry out her expansionist policies in the Caucasus and central Asia uninterrupted. In 1864 the redoubtable Shamyl was captured and the Caucasus was finally conquered; and in 1870 the Russians were pushing eastwards to Khiva, Bokhara, and Turkestan.

Reform in the army took the form of a new recruiting system based largely on French principles. Under Nicholas I, landowners or others possessing serfs were ordered to provide a certain number of recruits – a system which was capable of endless graft and which resulted in the army being saddled with the dregs of society. The new ballot system, in which the proportion of lucky or unlucky tickets was varied depending on how many recruits were required, resulted in a better class of recruit. The terms of service were reduced to five years with the regular army followed by service in the first and second reserves; and there were exemptions for only supporting-sons, bread-winners of families and families who already had one son serving.

The reform of military education and staff work was started by the formation of more officers' schools and by the establishment of military historical and scientific associations. The technical improvements in arms – the needle gun and breech-loading artillery – were copied from the other armies of Europe; and in place of the tight stiffness of the period of Nicholas I, the new loose style of clothing was introduced.

In 1855 the short-tailed jacket or coat was abolished and the tunic or *demi-kaftan*, already worn in the Caucasian corps under Nicholas I, was extended to all arms. The spiked helmet, which like the British shako, had been rapidly discarded in the Crimea, was abolished except for the Preobrajenski Guard Regiment – who retained it with modifications until 1881 – and was replaced with the tapering 'Marine shako'. The double-headed eagle with outstretched wings, set on an amazon shield, was changed to an eagle with upright wings after the Austrian manner. In 1862, a French shako was introduced for all arms except lancers, together with a *képi* for undress. The Caucasus Corps, always ahead of its time, never received the shako but continued to wear either the white peaked cap or the fur *papacha*.

181

The cuffs, collar, epaulettes, and other details of the tunic remained the same as they had been under Nicholas I but the cut was made looser. During the siege of Sevastopol, Russian officers were unable to obtain the capes or surtouts they normally wore in winter and had to adopt soldiers' greatcoats. They adopted an ad-hoc system of rank markings which consisted of sewing onto the soldiers' regimentally coloured cloth shoulder strap, strips of gold braid – three for field officers, and two for captains and subalterns – and adding the rank stars from their epaulettes. This is the origin of shoulder boards still worn in the Russian Army. These straps were so obviously more practical than epaulettes that they gradually replaced them on the tunic for everything except full dress.

Thus, by 1870, the armies of the civilised world had, almost without exception, modified their previous impracticable full dress into their conception of a practical working dress, as inspired by the example of the victorious French armies. In 1870 the situation was to be reversed with the crushing defeat of those same armies by the heirs of the Great Frederick grown powerful once again.

IX *Kaisermanöver*

On July 19th 1870, France declared war on Prussia, and within a matter of weeks she had suffered a crushing and humiliating defeat. After a lightning mobilisation, the Prussians defeated the French at the battles of Froeschwiller and Forbach, and bottled up the Army of the Rhine in Metz. On August 30th, MacMahon's relieving force was surrounded, and three days later Napoleon and his entire army were taken prisoner at Sedan. Meanwhile, the three other major powers, on one pretext or another, remained neutral spectators at the birth of a unified Germany.

The Franco-Prussian War '. . . in which the territory of the French was completely overrun, their capital and central city besieged and captured, and the nation made to pay a ransom such as modern statesmen had not dreamt of' ushered in a period of rearmament and militarism which was to culminate in the destruction of the old Europe in the holocaust of 1914–18. The declaration of a new German Empire at Versailles in January 1871 led to the emergence in the centre of Europe of a state of over forty million people and to the upsetting of the balance of power. In the resulting arms race, the influence of the winning side was paramount, so that in 1891 an American observer, discussing the development of armies throughout the world, could say that '. . . everywhere the tried and approved precepts of Prussia have served as an example', thus giving the armies of the great powers of Europe many features in common.

In the infantry, the old distinctions between grenadiers and fusiliers, *Jäger, Schützen*, rifles and zouaves, were purely titular; as far as their recruitment, equipment and training were concerned they were the same as any other infantry. Guards units as well, which in the Russian and Prussian armies amounted to a corps of all arms, enjoyed the same organisation and employment as the rest of their respective armies. The only truly specialist infantry were the twelve battalions of *chasseurs* raised and trained in France for mountain warfare, and the Austrian army's twelve battalions of Tyrolean *Jäger* who fulfilled a similar function. With regard to infantry weapons, France's original lead in the introduction of small-calibre rifles and smokeless powder was soon over-hauled, and by 1890 all the major powers, with the exception of Russia, had rifles with magazine loading and ranges of the order of 3,800 metres. Although the French had *mitrailleuses* or machine-guns in the Franco-Prussian war, they had made very little use of them; and the Russian army in the Russo–Turkish war of 1876–8 could only boast 'several *mitrailleuses* and Gatlings'. The weapon was little regarded, except in colonial wars where it had proved itself useful in stopping hordes of tribesmen dead in their tracks. As far as relative strengths were concerned, commentators of the time credited the French and the Russians, then recently allied, with a superiority of 150 battalions over the members of the triple alliance – Germany, Austro–Hungary, and Italy.

The retention of different categories of cavalry – cuirassiers, horse, dragoons, *chevaux-légers*, uhlans and hussars in Germany; dragoons, *chasseurs à cheval*, cuirassiers and hussars in France; uhlans, hussars and dragoons in Austria; and dragoon guards, dragoons, lancers and hussars in Great Britain – was little more than a historical curiosity. The ideal of uniformity, much admired at the time, existed only in Russia where, apart from the ten regiments of the Guard cavalry, the rest were either dragoons or Cossacks. The training of all these different types of cavalry, with the possible exception of the Cossacks, was uniform throughout Europe. There was some minor difference in their weapons, however; in Germany the cavalry were armed throughout with lances made of steel tubing; in France only the front ranks of dragoon regiments had lances; in Russia only the Guard and some Cossack regiments; and in Austria nobody at all, including uhlans. Some military thinkers were beginning to see in the increased range and efficiency of fire-arms, the end of the cavalryman in war, and in the British army in particular, more attention was being paid to training him to shoot, and to fight dismounted. In the Russian army, also, the cavalry were equipped with rifles and bayonets, and were required to carry large amounts of ammunition for this purpose. The lead in numerical strength of cavalry in 1890 was taken by Russia with her almost inexhaustible supply of Cossack formations; the German and French cavalry were about equal, so that in cavalry as well as infantry the French and Russians had the edge over their likely opponents.

The transformation of the Prussian army from insignificance in 1859 to invincibility in 1870 was the work of three people – the first Emperor William I, Bismarck, and von Moltke. William I, the first professional soldier to ascend the Prussian throne since the death of Frederick the Great, immediately he became Regent in 1858 set about providing Prussia with a cheap but effective army. The proposals put forward by his adviser, von Roon, caused such political uproar that in 1862 the Assembly refused to make any further grants for the army. At this juncture, the King summoned Bismarck as Minister-President, the Assembly was dissolved, and within six months the Prussian army was in action against Denmark. The subsequent quarrel with Austria swung liberal opinion firmly behind Bismarck, and the political crisis was forgotten in the afterglow of the victory of Sadowa.

By 1867, not only did Prussia possess a remodelled and victorious army, but also she was being reinforced by the armies of the new North German Confederation. Under the new constitution, the King of Prussia was commander-in-chief of the federal army, which was divided into twelve areas embracing Prussia, Schleswig-Holstein, Hanover, Hesse, Nassau, Frankfurt and Saxony. Gradually the Southern German states joined the confederation, so that in 1870 Prussia had at her disposal some 1,180,000 men.

The startling superiority of the Prussian mobilisation in 1864, 1866 and 1870 was the result of years of hard work by General von Moltke, who had been appointed chief of the General Staff in 1857. This meticulous officer quickly realised that the old-fashioned direct personal command of an army was no longer feasible in the days of railways and long range firearms. Both made the wide dispersal of units desirable, and he promptly set about developing a system by which all the various parts of the large, lumbering armies might be controlled. With infinite care and patience he trained a whole generation of staff officers who, by 1870, had carried his own ideas to every corps, division and brigade in the army. Analysing past mistakes, appreciating future problems, and making detailed mobilisation plans, after Sadowa Moltke and his officers held all the reins firmly in their grasp.

With the formation of the Imperial army in 1871, the whole of the land forces of the German Federation came under the direct control of the Emperor. It was an awe-inspiring array and was closely studied by its possible allies and opponents. Two of its main concepts were immediately copied by everybody with the exception of Great Britain. The first was the Prussian theory of compulsory and personal service, whereby every able-bodied person was bound to serve in the army and defend his country while in his full physical strength and health; this was copied by all except Great Britain, who preferred to rely on the volunteer regulars. The second concept, that of a General Staff system whereby widely scattered commands and units worked together in a prearranged and unified way, was also copied, and henceforward far more attention was paid to such matters as planning, administration, supply, military and scientific education. Finally, throughout the world, those armies which had been trained or influenced by French ideas turned to Germany as a new and better source of inspiration.

In 1888 William I died and was succeeded by his son, the Crown Prince Frederick – son-in-law of Queen Victoria. This liberal-minded prince died of cancer fourteen weeks later and was succeeded by his son. William II – the last of the German Emperors – rejected the liberal tendencies of his parents and harked back to the Prussian military virtues of simplicity, frugality, and honesty displayed by his grandfather. Throughout his life, he was unable to shake off the effects of his strictly English upbringing, and retained, like Alexander I, a deep admiration for the way of life of the English gentleman, while at the same time behaving like an eighteenth century Prussian land-owner. Nervous, tense, and lacking in self-confidence, he committed or allowed to be committed a whole series of blunders, from the dismissal of Bismarck in 1890 onwards, which resulted in his losing the dynastic friend-ship of Britain and Russia, and of driving both into the French camp.

During his reign, Germany – a rapidly expanding modern state – was ruled according to the forms and ideals of the *ancien régime*; and instead of trying to right the situation, the bourgeoisie and trade unionists tried to ape the forms of the court. 'The dream of being ennobled, or at least becoming an officer in the reserve, helped to mould the political views of the average citizen. Militarism was endowed with an air of dedication. . . . The Prussian lieutenant stalked through the land like a young God, the bourgeois lieute-nant of Reserve like a demi-god.'

The German officer-class, traditionally of high social status, tried to compete with the material display of the wealthy bourgeoisie in a manner entirely alien to the old traditional Prussian austerity, with the result that by the end of the century there was a return to rightness of dress and concentra-tion on externals which recalled the days of Nicholas I. No sooner had he ascended the throne than William II, in a circular, felt the need to reprove those officers who wore uniforms of ultra-fashionable cut, pointing out that if the regulations on uniforms needed amendment, he was the one who would do it. In an attempt to foster comradeship between officers, the monarchy tried to keep them from bad company, luxurious excesses, gambling, duelling

Above Left
112 PRUSSIA
General Officer's
Pickelhaube, with parade
plume, 1894–1914.
Mollo Collection

Above Right
113 PRUSSIA
Soldier's grenadier cap, *1er
garde-régiment Kaiser
Alexander, Füsilier bataillon,*
1824–1914.
Mollo Collection

114 PRUSSIA
Standard bearer's gorget,
guard infantry regiments,
1898–1914.
Mollo Collection

115 RUSSIA
Officer's 'superveste', Life
Guard Chevalier Guard
Regiment, 1846–1914.
Mollo Collection

116 AUSTRIA
Officer's *czapka*, 1st
Uhlan Regiment, 1868–1914
*Musée Royal de l'Armée,
Brussels*

and horse-racing by isolating them in their regimental messes or 'kasinos', but this policy only resulted in a system whereby impecunious officers spent their all without ever leaving the mess.

Thus were nurtured those incredible figures who people the cartoons of Thöny, sneering at civilians, artists and foreigners, endlessly bored. Brutish ox-like generals with monocles and scars, Guards adjutants with skull-like faces glaring from underneath their *Pickelhaube*; bored hussar subalterns, hands thrust into greatcoats pockets, trying to find something to do in Berlin on a Sunday; uhlans, cuirassiers; be-mitred grenadiers, they are all there with their carefully trimmed moustaches, their cigars, and their incredibly high stiff collars. German officers had so many different orders of dress that when two British officers, Count Gleichen, a subaltern in the Grenadier Guards, and Colonel Montagu of the Blues, were sent to attend the new Kaiser's first manoeuvres in 1888, they found it

'. . . rather difficult to know what uniform to wear whilst we were distributing our pasteboards. According to my ideas, undress uniform was quite sufficient, but Oliver Montagu thought differently. He did not think that his own full dress, with cuirass, white breeches and long boots, was necessary; on the other hand, of his undress, he had only brought a blue patrol-jacket, and left his blue frock-coat at home. So he compromised on the strength of the German custom for such social duties – 'Kleine Uniform mit Helm'; and not only did he wear a plumeless helmet with a patrol-jacket, which looked quite a decent kit, but he ordered me to conform to the German idea too and wear my bearskin with my blue frock-coat!'

Another Englishman, who served in the Prussian hussars, found that German uniforms were much cheaper than their British counterparts. The sky-blue, gold-braided full dress *attila* cost me rather less than a British infantry officer's tunic, and it was just as well tailored. . . .'

The new German Imperial army of 1871 contained units from all over Germany. These retained their own uniforms and badges, but were re-numbered consecutively with the Prussians. On their headdresses the different states wore two cockades, one red, white and black for the German Empire and the other of the state colour.

Lieutenant-Colonel Exner, writing in *Armies of To-day* in 1889 remarked that 'The uniform of the German army is handsome and practical' although 'a few changes, however, are just now being contemplated'. Throughout the period 1870–1914 the German infantry wore the spiked helmet and blue tunic, with grey-black trousers for normal duties and white duck for parades, when horsehair plumes were worn in the helmets in place of the spike. The helmet itself was altered on numerous occasions, ending up in 1900 lower and rounder with curved front and back peaks. In 1887 the brass border round the front peak, and the brass chin scales, were abolished, the latter being replaced with a black leather chin strap. In 1891, however, the border was restored and certain regiments were permitted to wear brass chin scales again. By 1898 troops on manoeuvre were to be seen wearing grey cloth covers over their helmets, but otherwise in full dress. *Jäger* and *Schützen* continued to wear the *kappi* or shako with front and back peaks, and in 1894 the *Kaiser Alexander Garde-Grenadière Regiment* appeared for the first time in the historic Russian mitre caps, which were handed over to them when the 1st Foot Guards were given a new model based on the Prussian mitre of Frederick the Great's days. In undress, officers wore a peaked cap which during the latter part of the eighties became very tall and stiff; the men wore a similar cap without a peak.

The tunics, dark blue for infantry and pioneers, and dark green for *Jäger* and *Schützen*, altered in shape over the years, becoming gradually shorter in the skirts. During the 1866 campaign, shoulder straps of twisted black and silver cord, with the rank stars from the epaulettes, were introduced, and epaulettes abolished completely, but William II restored them for wear 'at grand parades, court festivals and for full toilet'. The campaigns of 1864, 1866 and 1870 established for all time the custom of wearing trousers inside the boots on active service; and by 1889 black cloth riding breeches and black boots were being worn by mounted infantry officers, as well as generals, staff, and officers of the mounted branches.

In the last years of William I's reign, certain rationalisations in equipment took place in an attempt to lighten the load of the German infantryman. The cloak was no longer worn across the body *en banderolle*, and, except for the guard and line grenadier regiments, black leather equipment replaced the white. The 'Standard' of September 1888 gave the following note on the new German infantry equipment:

'. . . In fighting the Knapsack proper can be laid aside. The belt holds up the whole equipment. The bayonet, which is shorter than before, hangs on the left; two cartridge boxes are fastened in front and one behind. Those in front contain 30 cartridges each (15 for Non-commissioned Officers) and are fastened, not to the lower edge of the belt, but to its outer surface. The cartridge box worn behind contains 40 cartridges, and serves as a support for the knapsack. . . .

'The breadbag is now of brown sackcloth, and hangs from the belt on the right, the flask being fastened to it by a hook. The cooking utensils are now strapped horizontally to the knapsack. The cloak is rolled round the knapsack.'

In 1894 further attempts were made to lighten the equipment. The rear pouch was abolished and the front pouches made to hold forty-five rounds each. The skirts of the tunic were shortened and the leather belts made narrower; at the same time, aluminium helmet mounts were suggested, together with an undress blouse with a turn-down collar.

The smartness of the *Erstes Garde-Regiment zu Fuss*, to which Count Gleichen was attached during his visit to the German manoeuvres, was wonderful, but he was surprised

'. . . at the comparative slackness in barracks – the men seemed to let themselves go, and in their dirty brown canvas fatigue-suits compared unfavourably, I thought, with ours at home. As to kit, each man had no less than five tunics; but they were passed on from man to man as his time was up; and as there is no smoke and very little dirt in the Potsdam air, the dark-blue tunics lasted much longer than our scarlet ones in London.'

Changes in cavalry uniforms were of an even more minute nature than those in the infantry; the biggest changes being in the footwear. After 1870 the bulk of the mounted arm were wearing breeches and boots which came up to the knee with a slight scooping-out at the back. Cuirassiers, however, wore high soft boots, known as 'Brandenburg boots', which were cut off square at the top at mid-thigh. These were replaced between 1886 and 1888, by ordinary boots, except for officers of guard cuirassier regiments, who wore high jacked boots and white breeches for full dress. Cuirassiers retained their original helmets and white *Koller*, the several regiments differing by the

117 AUSTRIA
General officer's cocked
hat, c. 1900.
*Musée Royal de l'Armée
Brussels*

118 AUSTRIA
Officer's helmet, Dragoon
regiments, 1868–1914.
*Musée Royal de l'Armée,
Brussels*

Above Right
119 PRUSSIA
Officer's helmet, *Garde du
corps*, 1889–1914.
Mollo Collection

Below Right
120 PRUSSIA
Officer's fur cap,
Leibhusarenregiment, Nr. 1,
1861–1914.
*Musée Royal de l'Armée,
Brussels*

Far Right
121 PRUSSIA
Officer's sabretache,
Leibhusarenregiment,
Nr. 2, 1853–61.
*Musée Royal de l'Armée
Brussels*

colour of the braiding and sleeve piping; but cuirasses were by 1889 only worn at parades, and no longer in the field, as they were found to oppress and hinder the men. In the field and in undress, officers of all regiments, all rank and file of the two guards regiments, and n.c.o's of line regiments, wore dark blue tunics piped and braided in the same way as the white *Koller*.

Dragoons retained their spiked helmets and cornflower blue tunics; and the lancers their *czapkas* and dark blue *ulankas*. In 1888 all German cavalry were given lances with pennons in their state or national colours, those of the n.c.o's having the full state arms instead. In 1867 an eagle plate was added to the front of the *czapska*, which by then was made entirely of leather, with a coloured cloth cover for the top part which could be worn for parades. The *ulanka* had a plastron which was dark blue on one side and the regimental facing colour on the other; in full dress it was worn with the coloured side showing.

Hussars' uniform, according to Colonel Granville Baker, writing in the 1880s, 'had retained much of its pristine cut and colour'. The various regiments were distinguished by the different colours of their *attilas* – black, dark-blue, light-blue, brown, scarlet, and crimson, with white or yellow braiding. Pelisses were the same colour as the *attila*, except for the guard and 3rd Hussars who wore blue with their red *attilas*. Officers and men wore a low fur cap with a coloured bag, plume, cap-lines, and various devices – cyphers, death's heads, honour scrolls, and the like. Both the traditional hussar barrel sash and the *sabretache* were retained by German hussars.

All troops of the guard corps were distinguished by gold or silver, or yellow or white, loops on collar and cuffs. The colour, style, equipment and uniforms of the non-Prussian army corps differed in several regards from the Prussian army. In Saxony, for instance, the cavalry kept their light-blue tunics and the artillery dark green, while in Bavaria the predominant colour of the infantry was light-blue and that of the cavalry green.

Austria's vacillating policy during the Crimean war had resulted in the loss of the support of the other great powers, and, at the Peace of Paris, she was forced to evacuate the Danubian provinces which she had been allowed to occupy. After the Italian war of 1859 she retained only Venice, and even this she had to give up under the terms of the Peace of Prague, which ended the war with Prussia in 1866. As if being pushed out of Italy were not enough, in the following year she was edged out of the German confedera-tion, and as a result the Emperor Franz-Joseph I was forced to come to terms with his dissident Hungarian subjects. In June 1867, he was crowned King of Hungary, and the 'dual monarchy' of the Austro-Hungarian Empire came into existence.

Under the new system the empire consisted in effect of two states with separate governments, in Vienna and Budapest, of which only the ministries of war, finance, and foreign affairs were common to both. The Emperor him-self, impressive-looking and hard-working, much admired and imitated throughout his empire, was the only person with enough power to resolve the various nationalist interests, which were in the end to cause the downfall of the Hapsburg dynasty, but he was too detached from them to interfere. Austria was kept out of the Russo-Turkish war in return for being given the administration of Bosnia and Hertzegovina, but her alliance with Germany led to the intervention of the latter when the two provinces became a crisis spot in 1908 and 1909. The central powers' diplomatic victory on this occasion was a hollow one which served not only to humiliate Russia, and warn Great Britain and France, but also to pave the way to World War I.

The Imperial and Royal – known as the *K und K* (Kaiserlich und König-lich) army was the instrument of the dynasty and the exclusive concern of the Emperor; but although its organisation looked simple on paper, it was in fact very clumsy and complicated. Of the 340,000 men serving in 1882, a large part were not under the direct control of the army itself. In 1867 a new Hungarian army or *Honved* was formed, consisting of cavalry and infantry, which, although under the operational control of the emperor, was responsible to the Hungarian parliament. To balance this, there was the equivalent purely German *Landwehr* run by the government in Vienna. To add to these complications all regiments were recruited provincially, which meant that the men of any one regiment might speak German, Czech, Polish, Ruthenian, Hungarian, Italian, or Serbo-Croat, or a mixture of all. German was the official command language, while the regimental instruction language was that of the men.

At the head of the *K und K* army was a *Kaisertreu* officer corps. But although Vienna could boast the possession of what was reputed to be the best General Staff Academy in the world, the average Austrian officer was ill-educated and very bored. Scattered over the wide plains of the empire, the little garrisons achieved a depressing sameness according to a contemporary account:

> '. . . Two buttons on a uniform could not more closely resemble each other than does one Austrian provincial garrison town another . . . barracks, a riding-school, a parade-ground, an officers' mess, and in addition three hotels, two cafés, a patisserie, a wine-bar, a dingy music hall with faded soubrettes who, as a sideline, most obligingly divide their attentions between the regular officers and the volunteers. Everywhere soldiering entails the same busily empty monotony; hour after hour is mapped out in accordance with antediluvian regulations, and even one's leisure does not seem to offer much in the way of variety.'

Fortress garrison duty was not much better, and the better elements among the young officers were often forced to seek refuge by getting attached to a school or course, or even the *Honved*.

The rationalisation in the dress of the Austrian army, which took place after the Franco-Prussian war, was to last with little change as a full dress until 1914. The infantry abandoned their time-honoured white uniforms, which were henceforth only worn by general officers, for a simple dark-blue tunic with collar and cuffs of the regimental facing colour and a black shako. Austrian regiments wore blue-grey trousers, while Hungarian regiments kept their special cuffs and tight pantaloons. Officers had gold lace round their shakos, gold waist sashes, and piping down the front of their tunics.

By 1882 an undress uniform, based on the folk costumes of the *Landwehr* volunteers, was coming into general use. For officers it consisted of a black *képi*, and a dark-blue *Bluse* with four outside pockets, and a collar with patches, or *paroli*, of the regimental colour, on which the rank stars were placed. The men had a similar *Bluse* with pockets and *paroli*, and a pad, or *Achselrolle*, on the right shoulder to prevent the rifle slipping off. At the same time the men were given a light-blue cloth *Feldkappe* with a black leather peak, a metal cockade and two ear flaps which buttoned up in front. This cap was the forerunner of the famous model worn by the Afrika Korps in the last war, and by most armies since. Greatcoats were blue-grey with coloured *paroli*; and a kind of glove, with only three divisions for the fingers, was issued for winter campaigns.

The *Jäger*, consisting of the twelve battalions of the Tyrolean *Kaiser Jäger*,

122 RUSSIA
Officer's cuirass and helmet,
Life Guard Horse Guard
Regiment, *c.* 1860. A
similar pattern was in use
from 1846–1914.
Mollo Collection

Above Left
123 RUSSIA
Officer's sabretache, Life
Guard Hussar Regiment,
His Majesty's, 1855–81.
Mollo Collection

Above Right
124 RUSSIA
Non commissioned officer's
'*mundir*', 3rd Sumski
Dragoon Regiment,
1881–94.
Mollo Collection

125 RUSSIA
Officer's helmet, Life Guard
Horse Grenadier Regiment,
c. 1900. A later version of
the 'Potemkin' helmet,
re-introduced in 1854.
Mollo Collection

and thirty independent rifle battalions, wore, by 1891, a field uniform similar to that worn by the infantry but of a different colour. The *Bluse*, cloak, cap, and trousers were all of *hechtgrau*, or light grey. The paroli and piping down the trousers were grass-green and the buttons were yellow. In full dress the uniforms were grey with green facings worn with the round hat which in 1871 replaced the old *Corsehut*.

The Austrian *Landwehr* infantry wore a light-grey *Bluse* like that of the infantry in style, with grass-green paroli and shoulder-straps with the number of the battalion sewn on in white cloth, blue-grey trousers with a green stripe, white metal buttons and a blue-grey *Kappe*, like that of the permanent infantry. The *Honved* infantry wore a dark-blue frock with red braid on the collar and cuffs; light-blue Hungarian breeches piped in red, and the usual field-cap.

Dragoons wore a black leather helmet, with front and back peaks, a very high curved crest, gilt or brass ornaments, and a plate with the Imperial arms and the double-headed eagle. The field-cap was the same pattern as that of the infantry except that the body and peak were made of madder-red, or *krapproth* cloth. The single-breasted light-blue tunic had collar and cuffs of the regimental colour, plain metal buttons, and a black and yellow cord on the left shoulder for the revolver strap. The *Pelzrock*, made large enough to be worn over the tunic, was light-blue, lined with fur, and with a black astrakhan collar. Plain madder-red breeches and black boots cut straight at the top completed their uniform.

Hussars wore a shako of distinctive regimental colour, with a straight black horsehair plume, and a field-cap the same as the dragoons. The *attila* was light or dark blue cloth trimmed with black and yellow cord, and the pelisse was similar but trimmed with black astrakhan. The breeches were tight, made of madder-red cloth and edged with black and yellow braid, worn with Hessian boots.

Lancers wore the *czapka*, the upper part of which was of the regimental colour, with a drooping black horsehair plume; light-blue *ulanka*, with three outside pockets and madder-red collar and cuffs; light-blue pelisse, madder-red breeches and boots like the dragoons. Dragoons, hussars, and lancers were all armed alike with the cavalry sabre and carbine, officers and n.c.o's having a revolver instead of the carbine.

The Austrian *Landwehr* cavalry consisted basically of dragoons and lancers. The former were dressed like the permanent dragoons, except that all regiments had madder-red facings and white metal buttons. The latter were the same as the regular lancers except that they wore, instead of the *czapka*, a Polish *tartarka* of fur with a madder-red crown. The *Honved* cavalry were dressed like hussars with a shako of regimental colour, madder-red field-cap, dark-blue frock with red facings, dark-blue pelisse trimmed with white fur and red braiding, madder-red breeches with red braiding and Hessian boots. By 1890 the full dress headdress was only worn on service by the cavalry and horse artillery, other units wearing the field-cap.

The war of 1870–71 conditioned French attitudes up to 1914. Bitter and humiliated by the terms of the Treaty of Frankfurt, in which Alsace-Lorraine was annexed by Germany, the French desire for 'la pevanche' was sometimes buried but never dead, and the peace was regarded in some circles as little more than a truce. Gradually the French established myths about their defeat. Their soldiers had been brave, their commanders mediocre, the high command inadequate, and the French soldier's best quality, his aggressive spirit, had not been properly employed. The French General Staff were determined never to be defeated in such an ignominious way again, and concentrated on planning an all-out attack for the next round when it should occur.

Such thinking kept France proud in her misfortune and eager to become a powerful nation once more. The rebellion in Algeria in 1871 and subsequent colonial ventures in the eighties provided practical renovation, and by 1890 the confidence of the army had been in a great measure restored. These same colonial activities had, however, estranged relations with Great Britain and, threatened as she thought by the Triple Alliance, France found herself isolated in Europe. In order to redress the balance, a secret military pact was formed with Russia. The *Entente Cordiale* with Britain, which started in 1904, subsequent German diplomatic blunders and interference in the Balkans crisis, all strengthened the alliance between France, Britain and Russia against Germany and her allies. At the turn of the century, the general majority felt that war was inevitable, and there was in consequence an increased interest in military affairs. In 1891 a French general could write in an article for international circulation that 'after the woes of Sedan', France 'will have, if it please God, the joy of another Jena. The duel is not yet ended, but at the next *reprise* the engagement will no longer be unequal'. The general military interest led in turn to spy fever, xenophobia, anti-Semitism, and finally to the celebrated *affaire Dreyfus* of 1894–1906 which set off an anti-militarist reaction.

Under the Third Republic set up in 1871, the Imperial Guard was naturally enough abolished – the 'garde Républicaine' who took their place was in fact the metropolitan gendarmerie, and in no way corresponded to them. The chief changes in the army were made in 1872 and included the disbanding of the national guard. In matters of dress, apart from the abolition of the Imperial cypher and other emblems, the most obvious alteration was in the angle of the peaks of shakos and *képis* from horizontal to a moderately drooping one inclined at an angle of thirty degrees.

In the infantry of the line the 1872 uniform for the rank and file remained the same as that of 1867, except that the yellow pipings were abolished, the collar only remaining yellow as before. The officers wore a tunic similar to those of the men until 1884, when it was replaced by the *dolman*, similar to the British officers' 'patrol' jacket, with seven loops of black braid across the chest. In the following year the officers' shako, previously similar to the mens', was also discontinued and the officers in full dress differed entirely from their men, the latter having plain double-breasted tunics, and a blue shako, and the officers single-breasted *dolmans* and a red *képi*.

From 1886, however, a stiffened red *képi* replaced the shako for the men. In 1893 a short loose tunic was ordered for officers, single-breasted and plain, with seven buttons down the front. This had a red collar and a red flap on each blue cuff. Finally, in 1899, the tunic was adopted for officers and men and once again they were dressed to correspond with each other. Also epaulettes for officers, which had been discontinued during the *dolman* period, were restored for review order.

Chasseurs à pied went through the same modifications, retaining their distinctive colouring and white metal buttons.

In the cavalry, the dragoons underwent similar changes but in their case the men also were given the braided *dolman* for a time. In the cuirassiers, officers were permitted to wear the *dolman*, but not the men. In 1882 the heavy cavalry was still wearing a tunic with long skirts and with three buttons to each pleat at the back. The bottom of each skirt was turned up for mounted duties, showing the red lining. This tunic was replaced a year or so later by a shorter version, the skirt of which was not worn turned up. All cavalry and mounted services had the same type of leather booting coming up to the knee and with a small V in the front. Heavy cavalry wore the

127 RUSSIA
Officer's *czapka*, Life
Guard Lancer Regiment,
His Majesty's, 1881–1914.
Mollo Collection

Left
126 RUSSIA
Officer's 'Attila', Life Guard
Hussar Regiment, His
Majesty's, 1881–94.
Mollo Collection

128 RUSSIA
Left General Staff. General
Officer's shako, or '*kiwer*',
1908–14.
Right Officer's '*kiwer*',
Artillery of the Guard,
1908–14.
Mollo Collection

199

black waist-belt over, and light cavalry under, the tunic. The light cavalry wore a light-blue *dolman* with nine cord brandenbourgs across the chest, red collars and black shoulder cords. The light blue shakos had a bugle on the front for *chasseurs à cheval* and an Austrian knot for hussars, a fashion copied from the Hungarian volunteers.

The trousers of the entire French army were *garance* or madder-red. The infantry had yellow buttons and the cavalry white. By 1880 cloaks and overcoats for the whole army were full grey-blue.

In 1881 a trial helmet for light cavalry was introduced, shaped like the British 1878 infantry helmet but without the spike. Covered in pale blue cloth, they had black leather front and back peaks, a chain link strap passing diagonally across the front, which was decorated with a small tricolour cockade, a bugle horn for *chasseurs* and an Austrian knot for hussars. These helmets were in fact issued to one regiment, the *11th Chasseurs à Cheval*.

In the 1890s, riding, or 'knicker', breeches became fashionable for officers, and by 1897 cyclists and *Chasseurs Alpins* were wearing leg-bandages, or *puttees*, copied from the British. The latter also wore large blue berets, blue tunics with turn-down collars, and grey-blue knickerbockers.

In Russia the era of great reforms did not last long. By 1870 Alexander II's liberal inclinations had started swinging back to reaction as the revolutionary movement grew. Abroad, Russia continued her expansion in eastern Asia, all the while keeping an eye on the ailing Turkish Empire. As the grip of the Ottomans relaxed on the conquered Slav territories in the Balkans, so a spirit of liberty and independence began to flourish there. The methods used by the Turks to repress a revolution in Bulgaria roused Russia to intervene by forming a volunteer army to fight for Bulgarian independence; and in 1877, fired with an idealistic desire to help brother Slavs and co-religionists, war was declared and a Russian army crossed the Danube. The war, which was fought on two fronts, one in the Caucasus, and the other in the Balkans, brought the Russian armies to the gates of Constantinople, where they were abruptly halted by the threats of the British navy. The Congress of Berlin was summoned to resolve the situation, but in the end the Russians came away with feeling themselves cheated out of the fruits of their victory, largely by Bismarck. Under the peace terms, the state of Bulgaria was created, and Serbia and Roumania were liberated from Turkish rule, while Austria was rewarded for supporting Germany by being given the administration of Bosnia and Hertzegovina. As a result, in spite of the strong family ties which existed, relations between Germany and Russia grew steadily worse.

In 1881 Alexander II was assassinated and was succeeded by Alexander III, a staunch reactionary, who, while rejecting any suggestion of reform, embarked on a policy of 'russification', which interfered with the lives of his subjects to such an extent that half the Russian empire was turned into potential enemies. Under these conditions the seeds of revolution continued to flourish. In the year of his accession the Triple Alliance was renewed and Russia began to look towards France to redress the balance, with the result that a very close alliance was formed, a great deal of French money was invested in Russia, and there was a direct interchange of ideas between the two armies.

Compared with the Crimean army, the Russian army in the Russo-Turkish war was a modern fighting force, although its effectiveness was tempered with barbaric splendour and inefficiency. Archibald Forbes, a British war correspondent with the Russian army in the Balkans, classified the various schools of Russian officer as follows:

   '. . . the old ignorant school, the young ignorant school, the old refined

129 RUSSIA
Officer's tunic, or *'mundir'*,
Artillery of the Guard,
1908–14.
Mollo Collection

200

school, the young cultured and scientific school, and the young dashing reckless refined school, fluent in languages, knowing not much of the art military, but fine gallant soldiers. . . .'

Elsewhere he noted their want of means, their shortage of education, the corruption, favouritism, and general absence of responsibility. The men were still severely drilled, but even so did not present the smart appearance of most European armies. Their pay was small, and their rations consisted mainly of black bread, a small quantity of meat, and a 'good deal of Kasha', or buckwheat groats. He obviously liked them though, and sums up the typical Russian soldier as 'small-eyed, pug-nosed, stalwart, hardy, well-built, hard as nails, brown as a berry, of vast energy and gaiety but strong of odour'; and finally, 'a love of intoxication is among his greatest faults'.

There were no changes in the basic uniform of the Russian army during the remainder of Alexander II's reign, apart from the introduction of a new sash for officers, silver woven with black and orange lines, and fastening in front with a *pass* like a lancer girdle. The prolonged wars in central Asia, however, were responsible for the practical campaigning dress, consisting of the traditional Russian shirt, with an upright collar buttoning on one side, worn outside the trousers, with a belt over it. It was further embellished and given a military air by the addition of cloth shoulder straps from the tunic, the whole garment being known by the new name of *gymnasterka*. The *képis* were worn with white covers and neck flaps, and, in Turkestan in particular, rawhide trousers, dyed bright red, known as *chambary*, were worn as a protection against scorpion bites. Forbes describes the Russian troops in the Balkans in 1877 as wearing blue trousers, tucked into heavy boots, a white blouse, a tunic, a thick overcoat, and a cap 'which fitted over his ears'. The boots were very high and soft, so that when the tops were pushed down to just below the knees they fell into large concertina-like folds.

Alexander III abolished the tight buttoned tunic in November 1881, and introduced a new uniform which was intended to be standard for the whole army. The official reason for the change was economy of time and money, but the real reasons lay more in Alexander's chronic meanness, and a romantic wish to restore the 'good old days' of pre-Peter the Great Muscovy. All the line cavalry regiments were converted to dragoons and were given the *dragoonka*, or small round fur cap, with a top of the regimental facing colour, a green double-breasted *kaftan*, which fastened down the front with hooks, baggy trousers and soft boots. The *kaftan* was made very loose, with gathers at the waist and pockets at each side for carrying extra cartridges. In undress uniform the officers and senior n.c.o's wore peaked caps, while the rank and file wore peakless round caps. The dragoons were armed with rifles and bayonets, together with the *shashka*, or sabre, which was introduced in various forms for the whole of the army, and was worn from a narrow shoulder belt hanging back to front in the Caucasian manner.

The infantry had a similar uniform, with the difference that their full dress cap was a small fur pill-box. The guard infantry and dragoons were given the new-style uniform with their old embroidered collars and cuffs, the Pavlovski regiment retaining its mitre caps. The remainder of the guard, cavalry, artillery, engineers, and other units retained their old uniforms.

This was the uniform which was still in use during the Russo-Japanese war, ten years after Nicholas II came to the throne in 1894. The humiliating defeat suffered by Russia spread despair throughout the Russian army, and, in 1908, certain changes were made in an effort to restore morale. The *kaftans* of first the infantry and then the cavalry were given their buttons back, and the unpopular fur caps were abolished and replaced by the undress caps, embellished for a short time with the eagles and honour scrolls from the former. The dragoon regiments were given back their former titles and uniforms, except for the cuirassiers who kept the title of dragoons although they were restored their old uniform. In 1909, in a final burst of romantic militarism, the guards regiments were given back their distinctive *plastrons* and a modernised version of the old 1812 *kiwer*, smaller and made of cloth with a leather top.

To Great Britain, involved in her ever-growing empire, the crushing military efficiency displayed by the Germans in 1870 came as a nasty shock. Suddenly the possibility of Britain becoming engaged in a European war of similar proportions, woke up the authorities to the fact that the British army was anything but up to such a struggle. Although certain reforms had been effected after the Crimean war, they were not sufficient. The construction of the permanent camp, and then the barracks at Aldershot, had done a lot towards improving the living conditions and health of the soldier. The responsibility for clothing him had been removed from regimental contractors and centralised under the War Office; he was now given a free issue on recruitment and many abuses were done away with; and in 1867 the length of service was reduced to twelve years. In 1859, after the Franco-Austrian campaign, rifled artillery superseded smooth-bore, and after the Austro-Prussian war of 1866 the Enfield rifle was converted into the breech-loading Snider. But this was not enough, and in 1871 two major reforms were introduced by Lord Cardwell. The first was the abolition of the time-honoured custom of purchasing commissions, and the second was the formation of double-battalion regiments. By this, all corps which had only one battalion were amalgamated into two battalion regiments, of which in normal times one served abroad and the other at home. In 1881 a further rationalisation of the infantry took place, much to the fury of the traditionalists, who regretted the passing of numbers as much as the passing of the titles which replaced them are regretted today, when the regiments were given territorial titles. The various reserve units – volunteers and militia – were added to their local 'County' regiment as third and fourth battalions.

Nevertheless the last quarter of the nineteenth century was not a good one for the British army. At the root of the trouble was the Commander-in-Chief, the old Duke of Cambridge, during whose lengthy term of office conservatism of the worst sort flourished. Such new-fangled ideas as a permanently formed expeditionary force, mobilisation plans and staff work fell upon stony ground. Even lectures for officers on the cavalry of Europe were frowned upon, on the grounds that Britain's was just as good. As a result, the life of officers and men stationed at home stretched before them in an endless vista of boredom and routine.

But unlike the other armies the British army had constant practical experience of warfare, albeit on a small scale, in its constant fights with 'savages' of one sort and another, and gradually there emerged a group of educated officers who looked towards the coming struggle in Europe. They studied military history – even wrote books on it – and attended Continental manoeuvres whenever they could, and gradually began to work out theories of their own about the place of the British army in a European war. In Whitehall, Lord Wolseley and Sir Evelyn Wood, and in India, Lord Roberts, together with their various disciples, were hard at work thinking constructively about how the army should develop in the modern age. Yet even these visionaries could describe the British officer in 1889 in the following terms:

'It is the varied experience, and frequent practice in war, provided for our

130 RUSSIA
Officer's forage cap, Life
Guard Hussar Regiment,
His Majesty's, 1881–94.
Mollo Collection

131 RUSSIA
Officer's caps, Life Guard
Pavlovski Regiment,
1825–1914.
Left 1878–1914.
Right 1825–78.
Mollo Collection

132 GREAT BRITAIN
Officer's helmet, The
Gloucestershire Regiment,
1881–1901.
National Army Museum

133 RUSSIA
Officer's full dress
epaulettes, 1880–90.
Left Field Marshal's, worn
by the Emperor Wilhelm I
of Germany, *c.* 1880.
Centre Colonel, 4th Finnish
Rifle Regiment, *c.* 1900.
Right. Field Marshal's, worn
by Wilhelm I as
Colonel-in-Chief of the 5th
Kalujski Infantry Regiment,
c. 1880.
Mollo Collection

officers by the nature of our wide-extending empire, which makes them
. . . the best in the world. A far larger proportion of them know the
sensation of being under fire than those of any other army. Other things
besides . . . make the English officer what he is. As an English gentleman,
he is by birth what we believe to be the representative of all that is
noblest, most manly, brave and honorable in human nature . . . You will
find him climbing Alpine mountains, crossing Swiss glaciers, tiger shooting
in Bengal, hunting lions in equatorial Africa, or other big game amid the
snows of Thibet. To ride well to hounds is one of his cherished ambitions,
and, as a matter of course, he loves cricket, polo, and all manly out-of
door games. All these experiences train him to a self-reliance unknown to
the men of other nations . . .'

This complacency reached its height in 1898 with the culmination of Lord
Kitchener's successful expedition to Khartoum, which displayed both the
oldest and the newest elements of warfare. The stately advance of the
British infantry against the Dervish *zarebas* at Atbara with bands playing and
colours flying, or the wild charge of the 21st Lancers at Omdurman, recalled
all the glories of Waterloo and Balaclava. But in fact the campaign was won
by new weapons, Maxim guns, Lee-Metford rifles, and by precise logistics
and mobility, the use of steamers and railways. Then less than a year later
came the Boer war, the early disasters of which shattered the glorious image
of the British army. The self-reliant, manly British were revealed to the whole
world pinned down on the baking veldt while untrained Boer farmers potted
at them from behind rocks.

The army emerged from the war with even greater practical experience
than it had had before. From then on until 1914 the emphasis was on musketry for both cavalry and infantry, to such an extent that in 1914 the
Germans often mistook British rapid rifle fire – sixteen rounds per minute
sometimes working up to thirty – for an abundance of machine guns.

In 1906 the reforms discussed for so long were put into hand by the new
Liberal secretary of State for War, Lord Haldane. An expeditionary force was
formed at home and the 'Territorial Army', incorporating the Yeomanry
Volunteers and Militia, complete with all supporting arms was established
as a reserve force. Improvements were made, even if staff procedures and the
publishing of the 'Field Service Regulations' was a belated attempt to
provide a basic system of organisation to which 'every officer would
automatically conform and would be known to conform'. Between 1909 and
1914, at home as well as in India, attempts were made to conduct manoeuvres
and 'Staff Rides' which were aimed at a close study of the French and German
armies in preparation for the war which, from 1911 onwards, appeared
inevitable.

The British Expeditionary Force, when it finally went to war, was the
best-trained and prepared army the country had ever possessed at the
beginning of a war. Highly disciplined, able to shoot faster and more
accurately than any of its allies or opponents, supported by cavalry infinitely
superior to the enemy in dismounted work and marksmanship, and backed
up by brilliant artillery and a well organised administrative service, it gave
a good account of itself in the early mobile part of the war. It was only
when it came up against the defensive preparedness of the German army that
the trouble set in. The Germans were found to have a damaging superiority
in artillery and machine-guns, together with a whole range of lesser items,
hand-grenades, flares, and camouflage suits for wire-cutting at night, which
had been noted as early as the 1908 manoeuvres, but which the British
government was too mean to provide.

Soon after the Cardwell reforms of 1871 the new 'valise equipment' was issued to the infantry. For the first, and last, time the pack was carried well below the line of the shoulders, the separate cartouche box on a shoulder belt was abolished and replaced by two pouches for twenty rounds each, worn on either side of the waistbelt clasp, with a 'ball bag' for a further thirty rounds slung below the right-hand pouch.

Various small modifications were made in the design of the tunic, but the biggest change came in 1878, when the German-inspired spiked helmet, or 'blue gooseberry' as it was affectionately called, came into use for all infantry except the guards, fusiliers, and highlanders. These helmets, which had gilt or brass fittings for regular regiments, and silver or white metal for Volunteers, were blue except for the rifles and light infantry who had green, and the Volunteers who had grey.

In 1880 the rank badges of officers were removed from the collar and placed on twisted cord shoulder-straps; and in 1881, when regiments were 'territorialised', there was an attempt to simplify the system of regimental facing colours. Royal regiments were given blue facings, English and Welsh regiments white, Scottish yellow, and Irish green, and at the same time the pointed cuffs on the rank and file uniforms were altered to round cuffs. These changes were apparently an economy measure connected with the addition to regiments of militia and Volunteer battalions and reservists, it being decided that it would have been too complicated and expensive to keep the myriad different patterns in stock for issue on mobilisation. But, predictably, these changes were very unpopular, and gradually the old traditional colours crept back in.

The scarlet uniform was still the fighting dress of the British infantry and when on manoeuvres at home, or in marching order, black leather gaiters and full equipment were worn with the full dress tunic. On these occasions staff officers usually wore a blue 'patrol jacket' profusely decorated with black mohair braid. Other officers gradually adopted a 'frock' or 'red serge' jacket, based on the sporting Norfolk jacket, in place of the tunic; and by 1898 this had become the service dress of the whole army. The colour and regimental distinctions of the serge jacket repeated that of the full dress tunic but was provided, rather like the Austrian *Bluse* with breast and hip pockets.

In spite of these attempts to achieve some sort of practicality, the visionaries were far from pleased. Lord Wolseley, writing in 1889, summed up the situation as he saw it in the following uncomplimentary terms:

'. . . We have lately done something to improve our style of soldier's dress, but no man tied up as ours are in tight fitting tunics can do a satisfactory day's work during war. We dress our sailors for the work they have to do, but we still cling to a theatrical style of garments for the soldier. There are, however, some difficulties attached to this question of dress in an army raised, as ours is, on a system of voluntary enlistment. We must make the soldier's clothing acceptable to the men who have to wear it, and, strange to say, they like very tightly fitting coats and trousers, to swagger about in with their sweethearts. They like those ridiculous forage-caps stuck on the sides of their heads, and which are no protection from either sun or rain. . . .

'Is there anyone outside a lunatic asylum who would go on a walking tour, or shoot in the backwoods or the prairies, trussed and dressed as the British soldier is? This applies to all ranks, for I confess to a feeling that the dressed-up monkey on a barrel-organ bears a strong resemblance to the British General in his meaningless cocked hat and feathers of the last

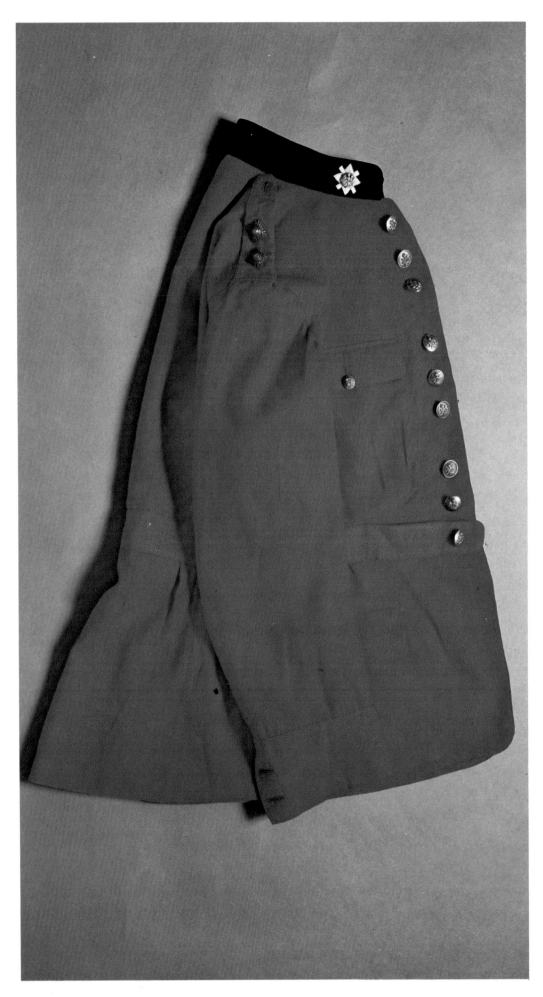

134 GREAT BRITAIN
Scarlet 'frock', Scots Guards,
1882. Worn by Major
Drummond-Moray in
Egypt.
The Guards Museum

century, and his very expensive coat, besmeared both before and behind with gold lace.'

The general officers who are still to be seen attending the Queen's Birthday Parade dressed in identical uniforms to those worn by Lord Wolseley and his contemporaries would hardly thank you to be compared with organ grinders' monkeys; nevertheless they serve to illustrate the drastic changes in military fashion which were to arrive with the new century. Between 1870 and 1900 there was a constant tug-of-war between the advocates of ease and comfort and the admirers of smartness and tightness, and it became increasingly obvious that the soldier had to have two uniforms, one for working and fighting and the other for parades. Thus for the first time 'service dress' became distinct from 'full dress'. Further impetus was given to this development by British experiences in colonial fighting, and by the Boer war. Finally, in 1900, the Boxer uprising in China brought to Peking a motley combined force of British, Indian, American, French, German, Russian, Italian and Japanese troops; a great deal of comparing notes was done, and for the first time everybody could examine the advantages and disadvantages of that purely British invention, *khaki*.

x *Drabber and Drabber*

The great increase in the efficiency and range of military weapons during the second half of the nineteenth century raised in the minds of a few military thinkers the question of camouflage, or concealment. The dark green which had been popular for forest-fighting in the late eighteenth century, began to be replaced by grey by such units as the British volunteer Rifle Corps, in imitation of the Austrian *Jäger*. But there was still no proper appreciation of the differing effects of climatic and geographical conditions. Thus, scarlet, the normal colour of the British infantry, particularly when it was beginning to get war-stained, stood out less in a hot parched landscape than dark-green, blue, or white. This was noted by eye-witnesses on various occasions, notably in the Peninsular war, during the battle of the Alma, and during the Egyptian campaign of 1882 when scarlet was worn in action for the last time. Even as late as 1899, the *Navy And Army Illustrated* could ask, after the Volunteer Review held on Horse Guards Parade in June:

> 'Why do people say that the traditional red coat of the British soldier is so very conspicuous? As the Volunteers poured out from beneath the shadow of the trees on Carlton House Terrace and flowed into the sun-light the red was not, on the whole, more visible than the green or grey. In the shade it was more distinct than the green, but in the sunlight the green stood out much more sharply. The grey, again, made a very clear mark in the shade, and was quite visible enough in the sun. . . .'

With the exceptions mentioned above, the regular armies of Europe dressed in dark obvious clothing, and, on the occasions when they had to fight in a hot climate, they went to the opposite extreme and wore white. Gradually, however, the notion of a uniform in the middle colour range was adopted largely through the influence of sportsmen. If concealment was necessary, then the sort of clothes worn for shooting should, by rights, be ideal for soldiering. Thus the wheel had come round full circle. The native and civilian clothes adapted by Garibaldi, and others, became the models for the

HEADPIECE
From *Infantry Training*, 1914

210

Norfolk suit, which in turn became the model for the military service dress.

But even before the long lines of foot guards, in bearskins and scarlct, moved off on their slow and stately ascent of the Alma heights, the word *khaki*, and its variants *khakee*, *Kharkee*, and *kharki*, were already well-known in the frontier provinces of India. It all started in the late 1840s when a certain Harry Lumsden raised the Queen's Own Corps of Guides, for military and political duties in the Punjab. At that time the dress of the Bengal irregular cavalry was left very much to the wishes of the commanding officer, and Lumsden, having 'conceived the highly unorthodox notion that a tight scarlet tunic with a high stock was not the most suitable garment in which to wage war in the plains of the Punjab in the hot weather', decided to 'do them all brown'. In 1846 he issued his men with a smock and wide pyjamas, made of coarse homespun cotton, turbans, sheepskin jackets, and wadded cotton over-jackets, all dyed with *mazari*, a local plant which gave a drabbish grey colour, and which was used by the locals as a form of camouflage. The leather items, which would not take mazari, were dyed with mulberry juice which produced a yellowish drab shade. The resulting colour was described as *khaki*, from the Persian *khak*, meaning earth, or dust.

In 1848 Lumsden tried to obtain drab coloured cloth from England to clothe both his cavalry and infantry in what he described as 'mud colour', but the experiment was not a success and subsequently the cloth was dyed regimentally. In December 1849 the 'Mudlarks', as the Guides were now being called, went into action in their khaki clothing which was thus seen on the battlefield for the first time. The comment of the commander-in-chief, Sir Charles Napier, was brief and to the point: 'Yes, it's not a bad colour for work'.

In 1835 it was noted that the 43rd, 71st and 85th Light Infantry regiments, ordered to Canada, 'are to be clothed in grey – a cloth very much the colour of the bark of a tree. This is a popular change, as there will be much bush-fighting, and our 'red-coats' will not be so good an object for the American or Canadian riflemen'. The first reference, however, to khaki being worn by a regular British regiment, occurs during the 8th Kaffir war of 1851–2, when the 74th Regiment wore a battledress consisting of a forage cap, trousers, and a holland bush shirt. This seems, however, to have been an isolated instance and during the Crimean war, anyone with Indian experience having been turned down, the British army fought in full dress.

With the outbreak of the Indian mutiny in 1857 there was a dramatic change. New regiments raised in the Punjab were dressed in khaki, and before long the regular Queen's regiments started to follow suit, dyeing the white clothing, issued as a matter of course to troops serving in India, with mud, coffee, tea, tobacco, black and red office ink, and anything else that came to hand. At the same time many irregular and experimental articles came into use, particularly the sun-helmet, usually the crested type, which allowed air to circulate through the front of the crest, wound round with a puggaree, or turban of muslin, and curtains or a veil down the back to protect the neck. The infantry wore either these pith helmets, the now infantry shako in a white or khaki cover, or forage-caps with turbans and quilted curtains, the rest of their uniform consisting of either shirts, blouses, tunics, or 'jumpers', in red, blue, khaki, or white. The 93rd Highlanders wore the kilt, and feather bonnets, with a quilted puggaree wound round the lower half, the 'very ugly brown coats of stout cotton material with red collars and cuffs, intended for boat work in China', rolled greatcoats, haversacks, and waterbottles. Other units, like the European artillery and the cavalry, wore forage-caps with white muslin turbans, and either white or full dress uniforms.

135 UNITED STATES OF
AMERICA
General officer's khaki
tunic worn by General
L. Wood, 1898.
Smithsonian Institution

136 GREAT BRITAIN
The original 'Sam Browne'
belt worn by Lieutenant-
General Sir Samuel Browne,
V.C., c. 1860.
National Army Museum

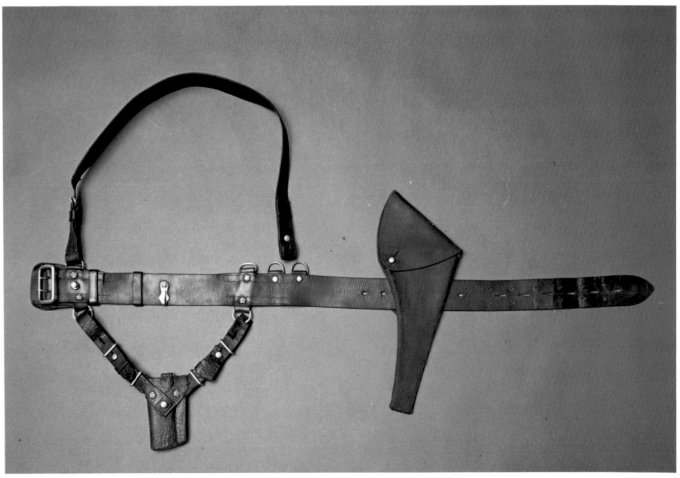

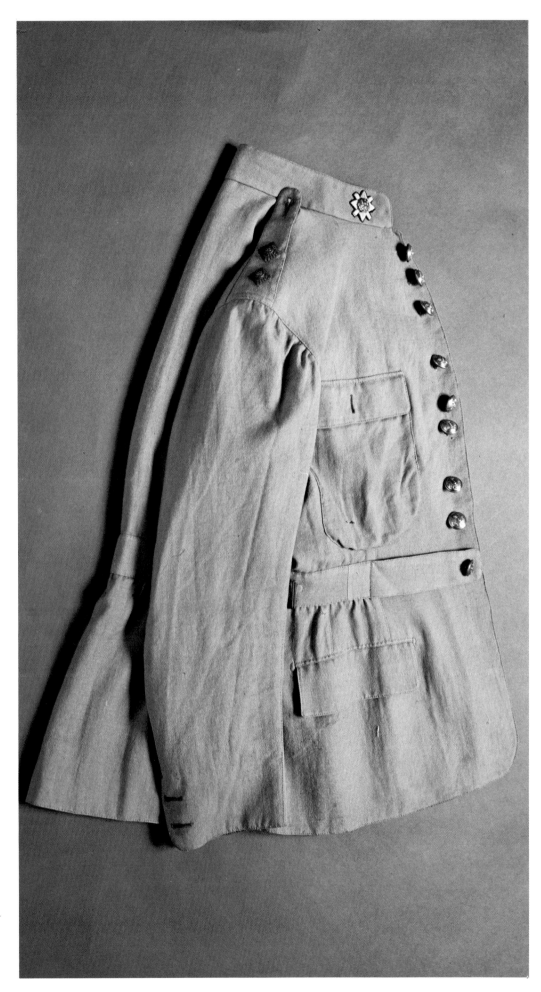

137 GREAT BRITAIN
Khaki frock worn by Major
Drummond-Moray, Scots
Guards, in Egypt, 1884.
The Guards Museum

After the mutiny khaki went rather out of fashion, but it was reintroduced as a working dress in 1861, only to be abolished three years later. At this time the normal dress for British infantry in India was a white tunic and trousers, and a white crested sun-helmet. Officers wore white trousers and an Indian undress jacket of red cotton, known as a 'five button jumper'. In the regulations of 1865 battalions in China, Ceylon, and Mauritius were to be issued with 'Wicker helmet and puggaree', and they were to have a serge frock every other year instead of a tunic. During the 1867-8 campaign in Abyssinia most regiments wore their full dress with white crested sun-helmets.

In 1873 another milestone in the development of khaki was reached. Sir Garnet Wolseley as he was then, was put in command of an expedition 'organised for the purpose of putting a stop to the intolerable cruelties and depradations of the Ashantee monarch on the West Coasts of Africa'. A memorandum, listing his ideal kit for an officer taking part in the expedition, includes, amongst other items:

> '. . . A haversack of stout canvas; A cork helmet with puggaree all of a khaki brown; Telescope or racing glasses; Good watch; A pocket filter; A clasp knife with tweezers; A respirator for use at night; A Norfolk jacket, pantaloons, and gaiters of strong brown canvas and shooting boots for use during the day in the bush. . . .'

This typical sportsman's outfit was probably worn by the officers only and purchased at their own expense, for scarlet continued to be worn in action both in the Zulu war, and in the Boer uprising which led to the British defeat at Majuba in February 1881. In both these campaigns the infantry wore the red serge frock and a white version of the full dress helmet, with the spike and badge removed, which in some cases was dyed khaki.

In India, however, the well-known British foreign service dress which was to influence the armies of the world was beginning to take shape. In the Afghan war of 1878-80, the entire infantry wore white drill dyed khaki, including the helmet, while the cavalry wore khaki helmets and blouses, full dress breeches and boots, pouch-belts, revolver cords, and brown leather waist-belts. Swords were being carried in the 'Sam Browne' frog, although not all officers were wearing the cross-brace.

The Sam Browne belt, which is now an accepted piece of military equipment throughout the world, was the brain-child of General Sir Samuel J. Browne, V.C., who, as a lieutenant, formed the 2nd Punjab Cavalry in 1849. The belt itself was born during the mutiny, when Sam Browne lost his arm, and, it is said, finding great difficulty in carrying his sword when dismounted, perfected an idea which he had had in his mind for some years, namely, a belt which would not only support the sword in comfort when mounted, but which would also carry the pistol safely. The original belt and cross-brace – sometimes two were worn – pistol holster and sword frog, all of brown leather, differed very little from the pattern still worn. In fact, the basic elements had been seen before; Cossacks had for years worn their *shashkas* from a narrow shoulder belt, and their pistols in leather holsters attached to a waist-belt and secured to the wearer by means of a cord. Sam Browne combined the two in a typical piece of Victorian pseudo-functionalism.

A second curious feature which started in India was the wearing of chain-mail shoulder-straps by officers of mounted units, a custom which is continued today in some cavalry undress uniforms. One of Sam Browne's officers started wearing pieces of chain on his shoulders, during the mutiny as a defence against sword cuts, and advising his Colonel to do the same, gave him two pieces of chain. When he was killed a short time after, they were found to have come from two of his bridles.

A third feature was the adoption of *puttees*, which were described in a contemporary dictionary as 'A piece or strip of cloth, bandage; . . . used in lieu of a gaiter, originally introduced from the Himalaya, and now commonly used by sportsmen and soldiers'. Puttees were a variant of the foot-bandages used by the Russians, with the difference that, instead of being wound round the foot in place of socks, they were wrapped round the socks and top of the boots in place of gaiters. Smartness required that they should be arranged tightly and neatly, with the result that they became uncomfortable and their true usefulness destroyed.

Thus by 1880 the basic elements of modern service dress were already well developed in India; but in other theatres of war the adoption of khaki still lagged behind. The authorities in England still hankered after grey, and during the Egyptian campaign of 1880–2 uniforms of this colour were to be seen alongside scarlet, the blue or white of the Egyptians, and the khaki of the units sent direct from India. Count Gleichen, who served with the Heavy (Cavalry) Camel Regiment, formed from detachments from the various guards regiments, has left a graphic description of their appearance during the campaign:

'. . . Clad in their light-grey tunics, cartridge bandoliers over their shoulders, Bedford cord breeches, blue putties, brown lace boots, spurs, white helmet (subsequently stained brown with tea), carrying no kit but a haversack and a water-bottle, and, finally, adorned with a puggaree and blue goggles, our men certainly presented a somewhat different appearance from their comrades on Queen's Guard – especially later on when nearly everyone grew a beard. Red tunics we took with us in our kit-bags, but practically never wore; and more useful were the blue jerseys and fishermen's caps with which we were served out for the voyage and took up-country with us'.

In 1884 an official khaki field service dress of helmet, tunic, trousers, and puttees was authorised for troops in India; and although a fast dyed khaki was invented in Manchester and patented the same year, the new service dress continued to be dyed regimentally for some years. Meanwhile in England laborious attempts were being made to invent what amounted to a rival service dress to that developed in India. In January 1884 the 1st Dorsetshire regiment were issued with an experimental service dress, which was illustrated and described in *The Graphic* on February 2nd of the same year. The uniform consisted of a version of the full dress spiked helmet, tunic and trousers of 'a kind of warm drab-grey, selected as coming as near invisibility as possible'. The loosely-cut tunic, which was embellished with red piping on collar, cuffs and shoulder-straps, had pleats in front, like the Norfolk jacket, which could 'be undone on service, so that the garment became a loose one', pockets, and 'two removable slips of cloth, fastened by loops to buttons on the breast, each made to hold six cartridges' – an idea taken from the Cossacks. Another idea 'borrowed from the Italians', or more correctly the Austrians, was the hard pad on each shoulder intended to prevent the rifle slipping off on the march. The loose trousers were worn with boots and anklets, which, together with the belts and accoutrements, were made to 'assimilate, inasmuch as pipeclay and blacking are to be banished and grease substituted'. The uniform was intended to be worn in place of the red serge frock on service, during manoeuvres, and in undress, and was to be universal, the only distinguishing mark being the regimental title embroidered on the shoulder-strap. The whole concoction was somewhat of a failure; the shoulder-pads had to be removed, as they interfered with the wearing of greatcoats, and the cartridge loops were found to be useless because the cartridges fell out when the men lay down to fire. It is not certain how many regiments received this outfit, which one writer has described as a ' "dunduckety mud-coloured" coat, with buttons in all sorts of places'.

The failure of this new uniform delayed the introduction of service dress for several more years, and in 1889, Sir Garnet, now Lord Wolseley, was still fulminating on the subject:

> '. . . The change hoped for generally is that we should have two costumes – one for active service and field manoeuvres, of the colour we use in India – it is a light tawny, resembling that of the hare – and fitting very easily everywhere, especially about the throat; the other scarlet and very smart, and ornamented with braids and buttons as at present, to satisfy the young soldier and his 'Mary Anne'. . . . In all our recent little wars we have used a special dress made for the occasion, and what we now want is to make that special dress the undress uniform of the army. . . .'

Lord Wolseley finally became Commander-in-Chief of the British army, in succession to the Duke of Cambridge, in 1895, and in the following year a pattern of khaki frock was established. In the Soudan campaign of 1897–8 khaki was worn by all the troops taking part and thereafter it became the universal dress for foreign service. In 1899 the pattern was altered, to conform to the Indian frock, by the addition of three pleats on the sleeves above the cuffs, and by changing the stand-up collar for a stand-and-fall collar fastened with hooks and eyes. The white pith helmet had a khaki cover and spine-pad, and in order to identify regiments, it was ordered that the shoulder straps from the old serge frocks were to be sewn on the sides. A newspaper correspondent at the Cape found there was little to distinguish in the all-prevailing khaki, but took some consolation from the fact that 'if you pass to starboard, you catch sight of a three inch square of scarlet cloth sewn on the khaki coloured helmet cover, with some such legend (in white letters) as "Yorks", "Essex" or "L.N. Lancs", and you recognise the line man'. Some regiments invented their own devices, the Highlanders usually sewing a small patch of tartan on the sides of their helmets.

The khaki service dress prescribed for South Africa entailed an entire change of dress – helmet, clothing and boots – but fortunately a reserve of 40,000 suits, sufficient to equip the entire force, had been gradually built up since April 1899. Although representations from South Africa to the effect that serge would be more appropriate to the climate than cotton drill were approved by the Commander-in-Chief in August of the same year, the first three divisions embarked with the latter. Fortunately the time of year was suitable, and serge clothing was eventually sent out to them. Up to May 1900, troops embarking for South Africa took one suit of drill and one of serge with them, and thereafter two suits of serge.

While the fighting was going on in South Africa, troops on manoeuvres at home began to adopt some of the ideas which had been found practical there. Thus both cavalry and infantry could be seen in red or blue serge frocks, draped around with webbing cartridge belts, and with khaki slouch-hats on their heads. Finally, in 1902, an Army Order introduced a universal service dress, intended to be worn on all but full dress occasions. At first it was confined to regimental level, general and staff officers retaining their blue frocks. The new service dress for officers consisted of a khaki peaked cap, tunic and trousers, worn with a Sam Browne belt. Mounted officers wore breeches and boots and dismounted officers puttees. The different arms of the service were distinguished by coloured braid trimmings on the shoulder straps, while ranks were indicated by a curious system of drab braid loops and knots on the cuffs. A wide-brimmed 'slouch' hat, with one side turned up, was provided for foreign service. This style of hat, which was very popular with colonial forces, first appeared in Britain during the jubilee celebrations of 1897. On that occasion an American observer described the uniforms of the Australian contingent as being:

> 'As a rule light brown or drab in colour, simply made, with little or no ornamentation. High boots, or leggings, were worn, and broad-brimmed soft hats of the same color as the uniform, turned up on the side. In some cases feathers were fastened to the side of the hat, which was turned up. There was a dash of the Texan ranger or frontiersman about the uniform, which harmonised perfectly with the stalwart form and martial bearing of the men themselves.'

The dress of the men consisted of a khaki peaked cap, tunic, 'pantaloons', and puttees. At first the shoulder straps were made of pieces of drab cord, regiments being indentified by curved strips of coloured cloth, embroidered with the regimental title; but, after 1907, the shoulder straps were made of khaki cloth and bore metal regimental titles. For a short period the men were inflicted with the ugly peakless 'Broderick' cap, but by 1905 it had been replaced, once and for all, by the khaki peaked cap with a small regimental badge.

Staff officers continued to wear blue for manoeuvres until 1911, when the khaki uniform became optional wear. In 1913, when the modern style tunic with open lapels was introduced, it became compulsory for all officers. The method of distinguishing the rank of officers, up to the rank of Colonel, was changed in 1904, for a system combining the traditional stars and crowns with braid rings on the cuffs, which, although not officially abolished until 1920, was given up in 1915, in favour of bronze metal badges worn on the shoulders, as the cuff badges provided too good a mark for snipers.

After khaki, the next most important development in military clothing and equipment was the gradual replacement of leather equipment by canvas or 'webbing'. The development of webbing had its origins in the Indian fighting in the American west. The introduction of rapid-firing and repeating weapons meant that the soldier had to carry far more ammunition on his person than had previously been the case; moreover it was found that, in the close fighting with the redskins, which at times resembled stalking as much as anything else, getting ammunition out of pouches was virtually impossible without revealing one's position. Gradually the custom grew up of adding leather loops to the waist-belt to hold individual cartridges. However, further experience revealed that when the leather loops got wet, they corroded and spoilt the metal cartridge cases, and experiments were made with canvas. In 1867 a Captain Anson Mills, of the United States Army, patented an improved cartridge belt made of canvas on webbing; but the problem still remained how to make such a belt, and it was not until 1880 that a loom was designed which could weave the belt and loops all in one piece, which was vital if they were not to become unstitched through wear and tear. The first 'Mills woven cartridge belt' was adopted by the U.S. Army in 1880, to be followed, in quick succession, by such improvements as double and triple cartridge belts, cartridge wristlets, and, when magazine rifles became more common, belts with small pockets, to contain cartridge clips, each with its own covering flap, all integrally woven. During the South African war, thousands of webbing bandoliers, cartridge belts, rifle slings, and waterbottle straps were supplied to the British army, but owing to an unfortunate misunderstanding webbing came out of the war with a very bad name. This was entirely due to the introduction of flimsy pre-loaded, expendable bandoliers, intended to cater for the extra ammunition required in South Africa, which the troops in the field tried to treat like the normal webbing cartridge belts. After incessant use, however, they fell to pieces and many thousands of rounds of ammunition were lost on the veldt. The result was that, in 1903, the old buff leather Slade-Wallace equipment was replaced by a new equipment consisting of a leather bandolier, and a waistbelt with two leather pouches. The Mills Woven Cartridge Belt Company, who were still the sole manufacturers of webbing equipment, refused to despair, however, and eventually sold the idea to the Royal Navy, which was very pleased with the results. Finally, after nearly four years of hard selling, their faith was rewarded and the 'Pattern 1908 Web Infantry Equipment' was approved by the Army Council. On January 30th 1908 it was demonstrated to Edward VII at Buckingham Palace, and thereafter came into general use. The basic equipment consisted of a waistbelt with two cartridge carriers of five pockets each, totalling 150 rounds, from which was hung the bayonet frog and entrenching tool carrier; two 2-inch braces crossed at the wearer's back and passed through diagonally set buckles on the back of the belt; from the bottom ends of these braces were hung the haversack and water-bottle. The large pack was carried fastened to the back of the braces, resting in a cradle formed by two cross-supporting straps, so that the load was balanced whether the belt was fastened or not; moreover, the whole equipment could be put on and taken off in one piece. With various modifications this equipment was worn right up until the introduction of battledress in 1938, when, together with the old service dress, it was relegated to the use of cadet forces.

In India and other hot weather stations, khaki drill continued to be worn with the sun-helmet; and by 1908 khaki drill 'shorts', worn with stockings, or 'hose tops', and puttees were coming into wear.

Apart from its contribution to the development of webbing equipment, the United States Army added little to the store of new ideas in military costume during the last part of the nineteenth century.

After its rapid expansion and modernisation during the Civil War, the army returned to carrying out its former task of guarding the last frontiers of the United States, and occasional police duties. The regular army, recruited mainly from Irish and German emigrants, was much reduced, and in 1890 was only some 25,000 strong, backed up as before by State volunteer units. Frontier service consisted mainly in fighting Indians; and as the cavalry were useful for this purpose, they were increased to ten regiments. In the late 1890s, the situation changed drastically with the worsening of relations with Spain over the question of conditions in Cuba, and in 1898 war was declared and a mixed expeditionary force of regulars, volunteers and militia was sent to the island. In the 'splendid little war' which followed, the United States annexed Cuba, Puerto Rico, and the Philippines, thus suddenly joining the ranks of the colonial powers. In 1900 an American force was despatched to China to assist in the relief of the Legations at Peking, beleaguered in the Boxer rising, and from then on, United States influence spread throughout the world, particularly in Latin America and the Far East.

As in Europe, the general trend in American uniforms was the gradual development of separate dress for service and full dress. In 1872 a new uniform was introduced which copied the Prussian fashions then paramount in Europe, but in a very short time it had been relegated to use on parade, while a more comfortable and practical dress was adopted in the field.

The Prussian influence was most obvious in the black felt spiked helmet, which was introduced in 1872 for wear by mounted troops. The helmet, which had a front and back peak edged with black leather, was surmounted with a gilt or brass spike and horsehair plume, a metal eagle front plate, and cap-lines ending in flounders and tassels. The plumes, and the cap lines of the rank and file, were in the colour of the arm of service: yellow for cavalry, red for light artillery, and orange for signal troops. With the helmet came a dark blue single-breasted tunic and blue-grey trousers. Collar and cuff patches, tunic pipings, and trouser stripes were of the branch colour. Officers had gold cap-lines and double-breasted tunics, furnished with extremely ugly epaulettes consisting of twisted cord straps and large pad-like crescents, reminiscent of Russian and Prussian lancer epaulettes. The undress of the men consisted of a dark-blue képi, and, after 1874, the dark-blue 'five-button blouse', the collar and pointed cuffs of which were edged with braid of the branch colour.

The cavalry field-dress, immortalised by the 7th Cavalry, who were massacred together with their Colonel, George Armstrong Custer, at the battle of the Little Big Horn, consisted of a black slouch hat, the five button blouse or a plain blue shirt, black leather boots worn over the canvas reinforced blue-grey trousers, and gauntlet gloves. The officers wore double-breasted shirts, which were sometimes trimmed with white or yellow braid. The typical Indian-fighting cavalryman was armed with the 1861 pattern sabre, worn from a black leather waist-belt with slings and a cross-brace, not unlike the Sam Browne, a carbine and a revolver, and preferred his home-made cartridge belt to the regulation pouch.

The slouch, or campaign, hat presented somewhat of a problem. The 'Hardee' hat of the earlier period had proved very oppressive in hot weather, while the képi gave no protection at all from sun and rain. In their search for something more suitable, the authorities resurrected the 'Andrews' hat, which had been issued to part of the 2nd Dragoons when they were serving in the south-west in 1851. This hat, made of pearl or stone-coloured felt, had a very wide brim which could be turned up on two sides, in the manner of the eighteenth century soldier's hat, to form a cocked hat. The 'campaign hat' of 1872 copied this design, but being made of black 'velvet-finished' fur felt it was soon found wanting under active service conditions. The general complaint seems to have been that it lasted 'in the field about three weeks; it then becomes the most useless uncouth rag ever put upon a man's head'. After several attempts to improve it, it was finally replaced with the more solid 'bush hat'.

The infantry wore a shako, based on the French model, until 1881 when they were given a modified version of the felt helmet. This and other changes, made at the same time, were the results of the deliberations of a Board assembled, in 1879, to discuss and examine the whole question of army equipment, in spite of opposition from the celebrated veteran, General Sherman, who had the following to say on the subject:

'Changes in uniform should be very rare. . . . The uniforms worn during the Civil War became familiar to every man, woman, and child, in the country, and should *never* have been changed; and if any change is now to be attempted, it should be back towards that then worn and made historic.'

The infantry tunics were similar to those of the cavalry, but with bright blue

138 RUSSIA
Left Officer's khaki service dress jacket and 'Sam Browne' belt. Guard and line infantry regiments, 1908–17.
Mollo Collection

139 RUSSIA
Officer's khaki service dress cap, 1908–17.
Mollo Collection

140 FRANCE
Left Soldier's képi, 15e Régiment d'Infanterie, 1914.
Right Soldier's képi, line infantry regiments with active service cover, 1914.
Musée de l'Empéri, Salon-de-Provence

trimmings. When the helmet was introduced, it was given a white plume, and in 1884 the blue distinctions on the jackets were changed to white. The equipment of the infantry, introduced in 1872, consisted of a valise, worn on the small of the back and supported by means of two leather 'suspenders', and a waist-belt with two pouches in front. In action, however, the American soldier gradually reverted to the old custom of carrying his belongings in a blanket roll slung across the body, and, as in the cavalry, cartridge belts began to take the place of pouches.

Between 1880 and 1898 there were various small modifications in U.S. uniforms. In 1881 cork or 'paper' summer helmets covered in white drill were introduced, and in 1892 officers, who had been wearing their own version of the five button blouse with the old Civil War rank badges on the shoulders, were given an elaborate frogged patrol jacket, similar to that worn in the British army. In 1895 this was replaced by the dark-blue 'sack coat', which was buttonless and edged all round with blue mohair braid. At the same time they were given a new képi, which had a stiff crown and a straight up-and-down peak like the British.

When the Cuban war broke out, a khaki tropical service dress had already been adopted, but few troops were issued with it, and most of the expeditionary force wore one variant or another of the field uniform and campaign hat in use in the 1880s. This consisted generally of the drab campaign hat, blue shirt, blue-grey woollen trousers, and brown canvas leggings. Infantry equipment consisted of a blanket and belongings wrapped up in a shelter half, slung over the shoulder, and a web cartridge belt from which hung the haversack and bayonet. The hurriedly raised volunteer units wore an assortment of clothing; the famous 1st U.S. Volunteers Cavalry, Theodore Roosevelt's famous 'Roughriders', at first were issued with campaign hats, brown leggings, and the brown canvas cavalry stable dress blouses and trousers.

With the stationing of considerable garrisons in the Far East, the khaki, introduced in 1898, gradually came into general use, although it was not universally popular:

'. . . The khaki uniforms furnished, are objectionable in every respect. The material is poor and the clothing ill-fitting, badly made, and the original diversities of colour are multiplied with every washing. The material . . . is fit neither for campaigning nor garrison purposes.'

Finally, in 1902, the universal 'olive-drab' service dress was introduced. This consisted of the drab campaign hat, a tunic with a high closed collar, bearing the branch insignia in bronzed metal, khaki breeches, brown leather boots for the officers, and canvas leggings for the men. In 1903 a new pattern web cartridge belt, containing nine separate covered pouches, was introduced. From the belt, which was pierced by a series of holes, hung the haversack, bayonet and entrenching tool, the remainder of the soldier's kit being carried across the body in the blanket roll, as before. In 1910, however, a completely new system of equipment made its appearance, in which the blanket roll, haversack, bayonet, and entrenching tool were all attached to a 'pack carrier', which was carried on the back in 'papoose' fashion. This basic design of equipment, although modified in various ways, survived in its essentials until 1956.

When the United States entered the World War in 1917, the A.E.F. was issued with the 'overseas cap' of a design that is still worn today. The rapid expansion of the American army caught the supply departments on the wrong leg and, as a result, many items of British origin had to be issued to the troops in France. Amongst these were puttees, steel-helmets, gas masks, Sam Browne belts, and even British tunics complete with brass General Service buttons bearing the royal arms.

The next major power to adopt khaki was Russia. In 1908, at the same time that certain changes were made in full dress in an attempt to restore the army's morale after the Russo-Japanese war, a khaki service dress was established, which was to be worn 'in all regions affected by war activity'. This consisted of a khaki peaked cap bearing the oval Russian cockade, and a *Kittel*, or jacket, of khaki cloth, with pockets for the officers and without for the men. Two years later, the *Kittel* of the rank and file was abolished in favour of a khaki shirt, or *gymnasterka*, of traditional Russian cut, which was the same for all regiments except those of the 1st Division of the Guards, who had a white braid strip along the edge of the flap which closed the collar, and a white braid band round the cuffs. Infantry wore khaki trousers or breeches, and the cavalry and horse artillery full dress blue-grey breeches.

Officers, at first, wore their normal gold or silver laced shoulder-boards on the *Kittel*, but after some time these were replaced by special shoulder-boards made of khaki braid. The men wore reversible shoulder straps, khaki on one side, and of the same colour and design as in full dress on the other.

The officers' equipment, up till 1912, consisted of a brown leather waist belt, with two narrow cross-belts which supported the revolver holster on the right hip, and the *shashka* on the left. A brown leather binocular case was worn from a third narrow leather cross belt. In 1912 this arrangement was changed for a British-style Sam Browne with two braces.

The men had a waistbelt with one ammunition pouch on the right side, a large haversack and a waterbottle over the left shoulder, and a large blanket roll over the right shoulder, the ends of which were tucked into the mess-tin.

The year 1913 saw the last pitiful attempts of the *ancien régime* to turn the clock back in the realm of military fashion when, as part of the tercentenary celebrations of the House of Romanoff, the khaki uniform was adapted to make it more of a full dress. To the *Kittel* of the officers and the gymnasterka of the men was added a false plastron, with buttons and collar attached, and false cuffs. The absurdity of this *tenue*, and its shoddy functionalism, is one with the evening dress 'dicky' of silent comedy fame; and it was, of course, found to be most impracticable. Some officers went to the trouble and expense of having special full dress *Kittel* made up, but because, on the regulation uniform, the bottom corners of the breast pockets showed beyond the edges of the dicky, their made-up uniforms had to be provided with two false breast pockets. With this 1913 uniform, tall tapering fur caps, of a pattern made popular by the Young Turks movement, were worn. There were other examples of such attempts to decorate service dress, but they were all doomed to failure from the start, for full dress and practical combat dress were drawing rapidly apart for all time.

In spite of the strong alliance with France, and the French finance which had been employed in the smartening up of Russian uniforms after the Russo-Japanese war, there was very little of French influence or style to be seen in the results. If anything, the influence was German, the Russian war ministry at one point seeking the advice of the celebrated uniform historian and artist Richard Knötel. At the same time, however, 'Englishness' was considered extremely smart when on service, with the result that when the First World War broke out, Russian officers started appearing in the long, loose, service dress jacket with huge pockets, known, perhaps as a compliment to the British Commander-in-Chief, Sir John French, as the 'French'.

The Russians fought until 1917 in the 1912 service dress, which remained unchanged except that certain 'Shock Battalions', formed after 1915, were

141 AUSTRIA
Above left 'Hechtgraue
Kappe' or field service cap,
infantry and artillery,
1908–15.
*Heeresgeschichtliches
Museum, Vienna*

Above Left
142 PRUSSIA
Soldier's field-grey
Pickelhaube, infantry
regiments, 1910–17.
*Musée Royal de l'Armée,
Brussels*

143 FRANCE
Left Officer's helmet, line
cuirassier regiments, 1914.
Right Soldier's helmet, line
cuirassier regiments with
active service cover, 1914.
*Musée de l'Empéri,
Salon-de-Provence*

Right
144 GERMANY
Above Field Grey Ulanka,
Garde-Ulanen, 1910. The
yellow piping denotes
Regiment No. 3. Shoulder
straps missing.
Below Soldier's field grey
tunic, Infantry regiments,
modified 1910 pattern,
c. 1915
Imperial War Museum, London

issued with French pattern steel-helmets which bore on the front the Russian double-headed eagle.

After 1917 the opposing 'red' and 'white' armies were still clad in vestiges of Tsarist uniform, although the Bolsheviks abolished all the officers' badges. In 1919, however, certain élite units of the red army appeared in a curious uniform, which harked back to the days of the streltsy. The head-dress was a pointed khaki cap, with a cloth peak and folding ear flaps, while the uniform itself consisted of a khaki gymnasterka with four bars of orange braid across the upper part of the breast, and a long khaki greatcoat with three similar braid fastenings. The whole affair, which was very reminiscent of the old Russian boyar costume, abolished by Peter the Great, was not introduced by the revolutionary government as a reaction to Tsarism; on the contrary, it turned out to have been yet another project for a new uniform for the Romanoff celebrations of 1913. That the last essays in military romanticism of the Russian Imperial family should have become the symbol of the new régime, is one of the most ironic of all the vagaries of fashion.

The 'boyar' uniform lasted, with various modifications, until 1924, when the Soviet army gradually returned to the basic uniform of 1914. In 1943, during a period of great nationalistic and patriotic fervour, the old Tsarist shoulder boards were introduced, together with the old-style gymnasterka with a stiff collar. But although the general principles are the same, the cut and shape of the present Russian uniform has a character all of its own.

The last of the main protagonists on the allied side during the First World War had, in spite of numerous trials and experiments, been singularly unsuccessful in developing a satisfactory service dress. In the French colonies, which by the turn of the century consisted of Indo-China, West Africa (Senegal, mid-Niger, and Chad) and East Africa (Madagascar), apart from her North African possessions, and outposts in the Caribbean, the Pacific, and China, white sun helmets with khaki covers, white or khaki clothing, and black or khaki puttees were worn by European troops; but in metropolitan France the red képi and trousers of the French infantry survived every time that some other style of clothing was suggested.

In 1903 the first of several experimental uniforms was launched on an unsuspecting French public. It was grey-blue, consisting of a slouch hat, turned up on the right side, a tunic without pockets, and trousers. Full dress epaulettes were worn on parade, and there was a simplified system of rank markings on the cuffs. The dress sword belt was a curious version of the Russian officers' sash with a *pass* at the front instead of a buckle. The men had the slouch hat, a loose *vareuse*, with a wide turned-down collar and pockets in the shirt, trousers, and leather anklets. Perhaps, not surprisingly, when a company clad in the new uniforms marched past the President at a Longchamps review 'the opinion of the army and the public was strongly against the change, and the projected change was abandoned'.

Next, a French medical officer of high rank proposed to replace the képi with a 'light helmet or casque of aluminium', but this was not much more of a success. The *Graphic* in an article accompanying a sketch of a metal helmet with leather chin strap, chain link strap across the front, front plate of grenade and flags, lion crest in front, and a separate floral crest at the rear, judged it to be:

'. . . neither beautiful nor imposing in appearance . . . the recumbent lion in the front has anything but a military appearance, and only serves to detract from whatever little smartness the headdress might have presented. . . . Still as its inventor claims, the new headdress would be durable and impervious to wet; . . . There is, however, nothing particularly French about its appearance, and, whatever its advantages, it is doubtful whether they would be sufficient to counterbalance the French soldier's affection for his time-honoured red képi.'

The *Graphic* was, of course, quite right.

In 1911, another experimental uniform was introduced, this time influenced by British and German models. It was khaki, with a low, cloth-covered helmet piped in red; a blue scarf; a khaki vareuse with a turned-down collar; khaki trousers and puttees; and the normal French leather equipment.

In 1913 the celebrated battle-painter Edward Detaille was asked to design a new helmet. The result, which was reminiscent of a seventeenth century pikeman's combe-helmet, was tried out by a company of the 28th Infantry Regiment in Paris and was very quickly withdrawn, although it was subsequently used by the 3rd Battery of Horse Artillery attached to the 1st Cavalry Division.

In 1914, on the eve of the outbreak of war, the British *Handbook of the French Army* describes the full dress uniform of the French army in great detail, but adds a rider, which incidentally gives rise to doubts as to the gullibility of the British Military attaché, to the effect that:

'. . . It is probable that a new pattern of uniform will be shortly introduced, which will be made from a material manufactured from wools of blue, white and red colours, interwoven in such a way as to render the cloth as invisible as possible. . . .'

When the war did, in fact, commence, the French army left to take up its positions on the frontier in the uniforms of 1914, but the bright colours, amongst which the *garance* of the képis and trousers were most noticeable, were gradually abandoned. The cuirassiers, dragoons, and chasseurs wore khaki covers over their glittering helmets, and the infantry blue covers over their képis. At the start of the campaign the troops were given metal *calottes* to put inside their képis, which, being of doubtful usefulness and notorious discomfort, were usually used as receptacles for water, although they did, in fact, save some lives. Gradually the uniform of the French army was changed and, in the spring of 1915, metropolitan troops were issued with the famous *bleu horizon* uniform consisting of the képi in a cover, *capote, vareuse,* trousers and puttees. At the same time, the *casque Adrian,* or steel helmet, sometimes referred to as a *borguignotte,* was introduced. This was the final distillation of the *casquemanie* that had afflicted France since 1900. Its skull, front and back peaks, and crest were all of steel painted light blue, and on the front there was a small badge of the arm of service. At the same time, the colonial troops were given a khaki uniform.

In 1919, France was left with an army completely different in appearance from that which had started out on the war, but in 1928 it was decided to stop the manufacture of horizon bleu material and to replace it with khaki. The blue was still in occasional use, however, as late as 1935.

From Britain, France, Russia, and the United States of America, we now turn to their opponents, the so-called 'Central Powers', which consisted of the German and Austro-Hungarian empires and their allies. The Austrian army, which could with justification take the credit for the invention of service dress when it introduced the *Bluse* and field-cap in the early 1880s, was slow to follow this development to its logical conclusion. It was not until 1909 that a light-grey service uniform started to be introduced into the infantry and the Austrian *Landwehr*. The jacket of this new uniform was cut like the *Bluse,* which it replaced, and the trousers and greatcoat were made of the same material as the jacket. The field cap remained the same for the men, and officers were provided with similar ones in place of the blue képis they had previously worn.

It was in this uniform that the Austrian infantry entered the First World War. The colour of the caps, jackets, and trousers was a very bluish grey, known as 'pike grey', but it was later changed for the greyer colour worn by *Jäger* regiments. The *Bluse*, which was fly-fronted, with pointed pocket flaps, had *paroli* on the collar of the old facing colour. Those of the men had the right shoulder-strap constructed in such a way that it could be rolled up to form a pad, a feature which was retained right up until the nazified Austrian army was issued with German pattern tunics after 1938. Officers wore breeches and brown leather leggings, and the men, trousers and puttees; Hungarian regiments, however, retained their traditional tight breeches and laced boots. Officers also wore the traditional gold and black tasselled sash, but they were soon discarded, together with their swords, under active service conditions.

While the infantry were dressed in this comparatively practical manner, it was, apparently, inconceivable to allow the cavalry to do likewise, and they went to war in all the glory of their traditional full dress. Before long, however, they were issued with grey covers for their shining helmets, their red trousers were changed for grey, and, later still, they were given grey *Blusen*, cut like those of the infantry, and pelisses.

Since the 1880s, Germany had been busily engaged in acquiring herself an empire, which she had done with such effect that, by the turn of the century, she had possessions in East and West Africa, the Cameroons, Togoland, New Guinea, Samoa, and a foothold in China. The *Schutztruppen*, and police, responsible for the maintenance of law and order in these overseas territories, wore a variety of clothing inspired by British colonial models. The 'protective force' in South-West Africa, for instance, which was raised from European volunteers on a seven-year engagement, wore, according to a British source:

> '. . . Norfolk-jackets of grey cord and of khakee drill, with facings of cornflower blue; trousers of the same material with stripes of cornflower blue, and brown laced ankle boots; grey cord riding breeches with brown field boots and jack spurs; grey forage caps with cornflower blue piping and band. For parade purposes a grey felt "Billy-coke" hat, turned up on the right side is worn. . . .'

It is obvious that this grey uniform, with its coloured pipings, and its riding breeches and boots, contained many of the features which were to become representative of German field uniforms during the two world wars; but although khaki drill, which the Germans christened *Braundrell*, and grey cloth were equally acceptable in the colonies, the military authorities at home were still in two minds about its suitability for wear in Europe. That they approached this problem with typically Teutonic thoroughness is evident from the following report published in the *Navy and Army Illustrated* on September 2nd 1899:

> 'The question as to which colour affords the best or worst mark for firing at on the battle-field does not seem to have been finally decided upon even yet . . . Germany recently indulged in a series of experiments, the results of which would seem to prove that previous ideas were somewhat fallacious. The first test was to discover which colour disappeared from sight first. Ten men were dressed, two in dark grey, two in scarlet, two in blue, two in light grey, and two in green. The first to vanish . . . were the pair

145 PRUSSIA
Soldier's field service
czapka, Garde-Ulanen-
Regiment, 1910–17.
*Musée Royal de l'Armée
Brussels*

146 PRUSSIA
Officer's field service attila,
hussar regiments, 1910–17.
*Musée Royal de l'Armée
Brussels*

attired in light grey, and, contrary to all expectations, those dressed in red were the next. . . . Dark grey, blue, and lastly, green, were successively lost to sight. Another, and probably more important test was that made at the rifle range to discover which colour was the more readily hit by the marksman, and this, stranger still, proved that red was a long way the most difficult colour to hit.'

In the following year German troops took part in the defence and relief of the legations at Peking; and during the campaign a variety of field clothing was worn alongside the blue home service uniforms, amongst which blue cotton jackets, or *litewka,* and bandolier equipment made their appearance. A British correspondent described German troops, arriving in Peking after its capture as:

'. . . magnificently drilled men, quite machine-like, but apparently too heavy in build for colonial warfare. They were beautifully armed, but their clothing and hats seemed more adapted for suburban summer gardening in Germany than for war purposes. Allowing khaki clothes to be of real use, the incongruity of khaki clothes with an enormous white straw hat, which must have been very difficult to keep on one's head on a windy day, was palpable.'

Meanwhile, back in Potsdam, the Kaiser and his advisers were hard at work, and in the spring of 1901 they despatched the incredibly smart Sergeant Homberger to London to 'show German Army equipment to the King and to the War Office authorities'. A photograph of the sergeant shows him in the experimental grey felt spiked helmet, fly-fronted grey *Bluse,* grey trousers and brown boots and equipment. This uniform appears to have been issued to certain units serving in the Far East, probably on a trial basis. A more important step forward was taken during the same year with the introduction of special machine gun detachments, which were dressed in grey-green uniforms and shakos.

The British *Handbook of the German Army* (*Home and Colonial*), published in February 1907, mentions that a 'loose blouse (*litewka*) is provided for fatigues and drills within the unit', and also that 'a new grey uniform has recently been experimented with, with the idea of its universal adoption throughout the army. It is understood that a change to some such uniform is now taking effect but nothing definite is known in this connection.' Patterns of this new field-uniform, made out of *feldgrau* cloth, were apparently issued in 1907, but it was not until February 1910 that it was introduced for wear throughout the army for service in the field, and for all field exercises 'except against a marked enemy'.

Full dress was still being worn on manoeuvres as late as 1913 but when the war broke out the whole of the front-line units of the German army took the field in the *feldgrau* uniform which, while practical and reasonably in-conspicuous, was firmly based on traditional designs. The reserve formations, however, went into action in their blue uniforms.

The infantry service dress, made of light-grey cloth, consisted of the full dress helmet in a grey cover, a tunic, or *Waffenrock,* cut on the same lines as the full dress tunic but with a stand-and-fall collar and two buttoned pockets on the skirts, grey trousers and leather boots. The *Waffenrock* was piped in scarlet and had dull white metal buttons stamped with the state coat-of-arms; and the shoulder straps, which were of the corps colour, bore the regimental number of the cypher of the Colonel. Guards regiments retained their *Litzen* in grey braid. *Jäger* and *Schützen* wore shakos and similar uniforms in green-grey material. Officers wore brown leather belts, and their sword scabbards were blackened.

The tunics of the cavalry stuck closely to the patterns of their full dress. Thus cuirassiers and dragoons wore field-grey *Kollers*, hussars braided *attilas* and lancers piped ulankas, together with their respective full dress head-dress in grey covers. The new pattern of leather equipment, introduced in 1911, was worn by cavalry as well as infantry.

As with the other participants, various modifications were made as the war proceeded. The first things to go were the officers' swords and the red cloth numbers on the helmet covers, together with their sashes, which were replaced by brown leather belts; and the light *Feldgrau* was gradually changed for the *grüngrau* of the *Jäger*. In 1915 a new 'War and Peace' grey uniform was announced, in which coloured collars and cuffs, and, in the case of lancers, coloured plastrons were added to the *Waffenrock*, to convert it to full dress, while its place was taken on service by the fly-fronted blouse. This project for converting service dress into full dress seems to have been an elaboration of the scheme tried out in Russia in 1913, and it is interesting to note that the German uniform historian and artist, Richard Knötel, who was an adviser to German War Ministry, was also employed by the Russian government. In fact, the full dress *Waffenrock* does not appear to have been issued, and for the remainder of the war the German soldier wore the *Bluse*. The final change was the introduction of the very characteristic steel helmet in 1916.

When the war ended, in 1918, the German and Russian empires were in ruins, with the Kaiser deposed and the Tsar and his immediate family assassinated. In both countries revolutions were in full swing and, as always in a revolutionary situation, the symbols of tyranny were being ruthlessly destroyed and the armies democratised. France being in a seriously weakened condition, Britain and the United States of America emerged from the conflict as the apparent victors, whose fashions were henceforth to influence military uniform. In the harsh economic conditions that prevailed immediately after the war, the victory of service dress over full dress was complete, and traditional coloured uniform although retained by the guards units of certain countries, was relegated to little more than an extension of court ceremonial. Gradually, as the political situation clarified and a new breed of right-wing dictators appeared, a new form of political uniform emerged in which the wardrobes of the *ancien régime* were rummaged through to provide new variations to an old theme.

The concept of clothing political ideology in a particular style of uniform, while not new, was brought to a fine art in Adolf Hitler's Third Reich. The now notorious uniforms of the Nazi Party were, however, by no means a purely German invention but the final crystallisation of three separate lines of development, two of which owed much to Great Britain. One stems directly from the Boy Scout movement, founded in 1908 'for the purpose of training boys in the essentials of good citizenship' and for developing a spirit of service to the community. Founded by the hero of Mafeking, Colonel Baden-Powell, the Scouts were dressed in a mock South African service dress, which consisted of a slouch hat, khaki shirt and shorts. Badges of rank and proficiency were manufactured separately and sewn on to the shirt by those entitled to them.

The second line of development stems from Russia where, during the civil war, the Tsarist, or 'white' armies, formed elite officers' battalions, whose black uniforms, cut on the lines of the British service dress, large amounts of which had been sent to Russia after the demobilisation of the British army, were decorated with the death's head badge. The third stems from Hitler's birthplace, Austria. The N.S.D.A.P. was originally formed in Munich, the capital of Bavaria, which shares a common frontier with Austria, and where, as in Austria the *Kappi*, or 'ski-cap' was commonly worn. This, together with the Austrian system of collar rank badges, was adopted first by the S.A. and then the S.S., to be followed by many of the other para-military formations of the Third Reich.

It is not surprising that both the German National Socialists, and the Italian Fascists, should have modelled their uniforms on those of Russia, when they had already imposed on their respective countries a totalitarian system of a kind that had flourished in Russia for centuries. Moreover, in the case of Germany, one of Hitler's earliest disciples, and one who exerted considerable influence on his thinking during the formulative years of Nazism, was the 'white' Russian émigré philosopher Alfred Rosenberg.

There can be little doubt that these developments, which were romantic in inspiration, helped to delay the invention of a truly functional combat dress. Uniform became the weapon of the propagandist. The dress of the Boy Scouts, which was deliberately intended to suggest healthy adventure, with undertones of moral education, was soon added to and adapted to promote a more sinister ideology.

During the Third Reich the morale of the army was deliberately fostered by a return to traditional uniform features, and gradually the somewhat seedy uniforms of the Weimar Republic were replaced by something akin to the glories of Germany's military past. Thus the struggle between romantic traditionalism and true functionalism was carried on until the Second World War, and after, when it was finally resolved, largely through the development of airborne troops. These, from the very nature of their activities, had to be dressed in a severely practical way; and so modern 'combat kit' was born.

Almost three hundred years have passed since the establishment of the regular standing army in Europe, and we have now reached the end of an era. But there are curious similarities where clothing is concerned. Now, as then, only bodyguards are dressed in a rich and colourful fashion, while the bulk of armies go to war, as they did at the end of the Thirty Years War, in an approximation of civilian dress. The colour may be different and drabber but, nonetheless, uniform in this 'push button' age differs little from the protective clothing of the worker, or sportsman. As far as parade, or off-duty uniforms are concerned, these, as usually happens, are based on the service dress of the early part of the century. But the present situation has some curious anomalies. The uniforms of the conservative capitalist countries, which are influenced by the United States, are looser and sloppier than those of the Socialist countries influenced by Russia. The muddled state of all but combat uniforms is best exemplified in present-day Germany, where the *Bundeswehr* of West Germany has been deliberately stripped of its traditional features and has been given instead a mixture of American and 'civil' uniform, while the *Nationale Volksarmee* of East Germany has, under Soviet guidance, had many of its traditional features restored, and still practises the *Parademarsch* from the era of Frederick the Great.

Bibliography

Anon. *Advice to the Officers of The British Army*, reprint, London, 1946
Anon. *New Regulations for the Prussian Infantry*, London, 1757
Anon. 'A Lieutenant-Colonel in the British Army', *The British Army*, London, 1899
Ashley, M. *Louis XIV and the greatness of France*, London, 1946
Brett-James, A. *Wellington at War, 1794–1815*, London, 1961
Brunon, J. *Grenadiers de Napoléon*, privately printed, 1955
Bryant, A. *The Age of Elegance, 1812–1822*, London, 1952
Carman, W. Y. *British Military Uniforms from Contemporary Pictures*, London, 1957
Carman, W. Y. *Indian Army Uniforms*, 2 vols., London, 1961, 1969
Cart, A. *Uniformes des Régiments Français de Louis XV à nos Jours*, Paris, 1945
Churchill, W. S. *Marlborough*, London, 1934
Cooper King, Lieutenant-Colonel, C. *The Story of The British Army*, London, 1897
Curtiss, J.S. *The Russian Army under Nicholas I, 1825–1855*, Durham N.C., 1965
Davenport, M. *The Book of Costume*, New York, 1962
Demeter, K. (tr. A. Malcolm) *The German Officer Corps*, London, 1965
Dodge, T. A. *Gustavus Adolphus*, 2 vols., Boston and New York, 1895
Droz, J. (tr. R. Baldick) *Europe between Revolutions, 1815–1848*, London, 1967
Esposito, Brigadier V. J. and Elting, Colonel J. R. *A Military History and Atlas of the Napoleonic Wars*, London, 1964
Fortescue, Hon. J. W. *A History of the British Army*, London, 1911
Fuller, Colonel J. F. C. *British Light Infantry in the Eighteenth Century*, London, 1925
Furneaux, R. *The Siege of Plevna*, London, 1958
Gayda, M and Krijitsky, A. *L'Armée Russe sous le Tsar Alexandre Ier*, Paris, 1955
Gernsheim, A. *Fashion and Reality*, London, 1963
Gleichen, Major-General Lord E. *A Guardsman's Memories*, London, 1932
Haswell Miller, A. E. and Dawnay, N. P. *Military Drawings and Paintings in The Collection of Her Majesty The Queen*, 2 vols., London, 1966, 1970
Hingley, R. *The Tsars*, London, 1968
Howard, M. *The Franco-Prussian War*, London, 1960
Huish, R. *Memoirs of George IV*, London, 1830
Jackson, Major D. *India's Army*, London, 1940
Kannik, P. (ed. W. Y. Carman) *Military Uniforms in Colour*, London, 1967
Knötel, R. *Uniformenkunde*, 18 vols., Rathenow, 1890–1921
Knötel-Sieg, *Handbuch der Uniformenkunde*, Hamburg, 1956

Lachouque, H. *Dix Siécles de Costume Militaire*, Paris, 1965

Lachouque, H. and Brown, A. S. K. *The Anatomy of Glory*, London, 1961

Laffont, R. *Histoire Universelle des Armées*, 4 vols., Paris, 1966

Laver, J. *Costume*, London, 1963

Laver, J. *British Military Uniforms*, London, 1948

Lawson, C. C. P. *A History of the Uniforms of the British Army*, 5 vols., London, 1940–1967

Lens, B. *The Grenadier's Exercise of The Granade, 1735*, reprint, London, 1967

Lethern, A. A. *The Development of the Mills Woven Cartridge Belt, 1877–1956*, London, 1956

McClellan, Major-General G. B. *The Armies of Europe*, Philadelphia, 1861

Macdonald, Captain R. J. *The History of the Dress of The Royal Regiment of Artillery, 1625–1897*, London, 1899

Mangerand, J. *Les Coiffures de L'Armée Française*, Paris, 1909

Mangerand, J. *L'Armée Française en 1845*, Paris, 1945

Martin, P. *Der Bunte Rock*, Stuttgart, 1963

Martin, P. *Die Preussische Armee unter Friedrich Wilhelm II und Friedrich Wilhelm III, 1786–1807*, Stuttgart, 1968

Merritt, Brigadier-General W. and others *The Armies of To-day*, London, 1893

Miles, Major-General N. A. *Military Europe*, New York, 1898

Mouillard, L. *Les Régiments sous Louis XV*, Paris, 1882

Nolan, Captain L. E. *Cavalry: its History and Tactics*, London, 1853

Norman, A. V. B. and Pottinger, D. *Warrior to Soldier*, London, 1966

Ogg, D. *Europe of the Ancien Régime*, London, 1965

Ollier, E. *Illustrated History of The Russo-Turkish War*, 2 vols., London, 1878

Ottenfeld, R. v. and Teuber, O. *Die Oesterreichische Armee, 1700–1867*, Vienna, 1895

Pajol, Lieutenant-Colonel Count *L'Armée Russe, 1854*, Paris, 1854

Peterson, H. *The Book of The Continental Soldier*, Harrisburg Pa., 1968

Quennevat, J. *Les Vrais Soldats de Napoléon*, Paris, 1968

Reynolds, P. W. *Military Costume of the Eighteenth and Nineteenth Centuries*, unpublished ms, c. 1891

Rousselot, L. *L'Armee Française, Ses Uniformes, Son Armement, Son Equipment*, current series of plates with descriptive text, Paris

Russell, F. *The French and Indian Wars*, New York, 1962

Thorburn, W. A. *French Army Regiments and Uniforms*, London, 1969

Todd, F. P. and Kredel, F. *Soldiers of The American Army, 1775–1914*, New York, 1941

Viskovatov, A. V. *Historical Description of the Uniforms and Armaments of the Russian Army*, 30 vols., St. Petersburg, 1844–1856

Waugh, N. *The Cut of Men's Clothes, 1600–1900*, London, 1964

Waugh, N. *The Cut of Women's Clothes, 1600–1930*, London, 1968

Whinyates, Colonel F. A. *From Coruna to Sevastopol*, London, 1893

Windham, W. and Townshend, Rt. Hon. Lord G. Viscount *A Plan of Discipline for the use of the Norfolk Militia*, London, 1759

Yule, Colonel H. and Burnell, A. C. *Hobson-Jobson, A Glossary of Colloquial Anglo-Indian Words and Phrases* . . . , new edition edited by William Crooke, London, 1968

Zweguintzow, W. *L'Armée Russe*, 2 vols., Paris, 1967, 1969

Because of the extensive reading necessitated of the following periodicals, especially those concerned with military history, references to individual articles have been omitted.

The Cavalry Journal

History To-day

The Journal of the Society for Army Historical Research

The Military Collector and Historian

The Navy and Army Illustrated

Punch

Carnets de la Sabretache

The Times

Zeitschrift für Heeres- und Uniformkunde

Index

Prussian, 142–3; Russian, 91, 112, 136–9
cuirassiers: trends in dress, equipment, 23,
    53, 57; Austrian, 83, 146–7, 177; French
    83, 108, 158, 167, 184, 197, 227; German,
    220; Prussian, 87, 90, 142–3, 184;
    Russian, 75, 90, 91, 112, 202–3
Culloden, battle of, 60
Cumberland, William Augustus, Duke of
    (d. 1765), 49, 56, 64, 68
Cumberland, Ernest Augustus, Duke of,
    later King of Hanover, 91, 125, 151–4
Custer, Colonel Armstrong, 219
cyphers see emblems
czapka see chapska

daggers, 60
Davy Crockett caps, 37
death's head emblems, 124, 192, 231
Decembrist Revolt, 1825, 136
Demi-Brigade, 9th, 82
Demi-Brigades, French, 79, 82
Demi-Brigades Légères, 79
demi-kaftans, 60, 181; see also tunics
Dettingen, battle of, 36
divisions, organisation of armies into, 43,
    109, 136
dolmans: origins, 57, 83; British, 95; French,
    105, 108, 163, 167, 197; Prussian, 142;
    see also coats, jackets
Don Cossacks *see* Cossacks
Dorsetshire Regiment, 1st, 215–6
doublets, 22, 26, 31, 180
Dragoon Guards, British, 94, 125, 184
Dragoon Guards, 6th (The Carabiniers), 177
dragoonka, 202, *see also* caps
dragoons: adoption of helmets, 60; dress,
    equipment, tactics in seventeenth century,
    20, 23, 31–2; in eighteenth century, 53;
    American, 169, 172; Austrian, 37, 86,
    124, 146–7, 177, 184, 196; British, 34, 94,
    125, 184; French, 32, 82, 83, 105, 108,
    158, 167, 184, 197, 227; German, 192,
    230; Prussian, 87, 90, 121, 142–3, 184;
    Russian, 48, 75, 90, 91, 112, 136–9, 184,
    202; Swedish, 20; *see also* cavalry, light
    dragoons
dress, military: arab influence on, 97–9;
    effect on civilian styles, 169; in
    seventeenth century, 20–5; influence of
    baroque art on, 45; influence of eastern
    traditions, 25–6, 31, 33; influence of
    French Revolution on, 96–9, 104;
    political implications, 133, 231–2;
    standardisation of national, 23–5, 30,
    44–5
drill, systems of, 19–20, 28, 40–1, 43, 64–6,
    70–1, 79, 95, 136, 138, 150, 162, 166–7,
    176
drummers, 23, 36
Duke of Brunswick-Oel's Corps, 124
Duke of Kingston's Light Horse, 60
Dumbarton's Regiment, 18
Dundas, Sir David, 71, 91, 95, 96
Dutch (Walloon) regiments in Austrian
    army, 37

ear covers, Prussian, 146
emblems, crests, national, regimental, and
    royal: origins, 30, 40, 48, 57; American
    (loyalist), 73; American (United States),
    172, 219–22; Austrian, 48, 83–6, 147,
    193–6; British, 48, 60–1, 71, 125, 177–80,
    207, 215–7; French, 48, 60, 82, 83–6,
    155, 197–200, 227; German, 188–92,
    230–1, Prussian, 48, 57, 142, 143;

Russian, 48, 75, 91, 112, 121, 138–9, 181,
    223–6
émigrés, French, 91–3, 95–6
engineer units, 43, 74, 138, 202
English Civil War, 20–2
epaulettes: origins, functions, 49;
    American, 74, 172, 219–22; Austrian,
    147; British, 155, 177–80; French, 166,
    167, 197, 226; German, 189; Russian,
    181–2
espontoons, 31, 67, 71, 91
esquavar see charivari
Evelyn, John, 33, 34
eye brows, blackening of, 57
Eylau, battle of, 109

feathers, feather plumes: as field signs, 22;
    as national, partisan emblems, 30–1, 133;
    American, 74, 172, 173, 219–22;
    Austrian, 86, 147–50, 196; British, 71,
    128, 154, 177; French, 105, 108, 167,
    169; German, 188–92; Italian, 176;
    Prussian, 45, 124, 143; Russian, 109
Fehrbellin, battle of, 34, 36
Feld Kappe, 193–6, 227–8 *see also* caps
feldgrau, 230–1
fez, 166, 176
Field Fusiliers, Prussian, 48
field signs, 22, 30, 147; *see also* emblems
fifes, 23
fire-arms, early equipment of infantry with,
    19–20; *see also* infantry, muskets,
    musketeers, rifles
firelock muskets, 28, 31, 32, 33, 36, 37, 40,
    43, 67, 68
flounders: American, 172, 219; French,
    105; Russian, 109, 112
flugel caps *see* caps, mirlitons
foot guards *see* guards regiments
Foot Guards, 1st Prussian, 142; 1st German,
    188
forage caps: adoption of, 82, 124; American,
    172; Austrian, 124; British, 124, 125,
    154–5, 177, 211; French, 163; German,
    124; Prussian, 124; Russian, 139; *see also*
    caps, *képis*
Forbes, Alexander, 200–2
Fort Duquesne, 64–6
Fort Ticondesoga, 66
Fra Diavolo's hats, 172; *see also* hats,
    American
France: army after reforms of Louvois,
    28–32; during eighteenth century, 43, 45,
    49, 57, 60, 61; during Napoleonic period,
    79–83, 104–8; in period after 1815, 133,
    155–8; in period of Louis Napoleon,
    159–63; in period 1870–1914, 196–200;
    in period since 1914, 226–7; contingent
    in support of American Revolution, 74;
    course of 1789 Revolution in, 77–9;
    creation of light infantry, 61; *émigrés,*
    91–3, 95, 96; formation of hussar
    regiments, 53, 56; influence on military
    dress of other states, 169–76
Franco-Prussian War, 183
francs-tireurs, French, 167–9
Franz Joseph, Emperor, 146, 192
Frederick II ('the Great'), King of Prussia,
    41, 44, 61, 71, 76, 87
Frederick William, Elector of Brandenburg,
    27, 34–6
Frederick William I, King of Prussia, 40–1;
    Frederick William II, 87; Frederick
    William III, 87, 121, 139–42; Frederick
    William IV, 142

Freikorps, Prussian, 61
French 56th Regiment, 82
frock-coats, 48, 87, 124, 125, 147–50, 155,
    166, 172, 180, 214, 216; *see also* coats,
    tunics
frogging, 26, 31, 49, 197; *see also* braiding
fusiliers: British, 154; French, 155; Polish,
    105; Prussian, 87–90, 142; Russian, 90,
    109–12; *see also* light infantry
fusils, officers', 67

Gage's Light Infantry, 67, 68
gaiters: origins, 31, 52; Austrian, 86–7, 124
    147; British, 71, 94, 180, 207; French,
    108, 158, 163, 166, 167, 169; Prussian,
    90, 121, 142; Russian, 90, 112
garance, 158, 227, *see also* trousers
Garde du Corps Regiment, Prussian, 142, 143
Garde-Grenadière, Prussian, 36
Garde Impériale, 1854, 167
Gardes du Corps, French, 155; Scots, 18
gardes mobiles, French, 167–9
Garibaldi fashions, 162, 172, 176, 177, 180,
    210
gas masks, 222
Gatling guns, 184
gauntlets *see* gloves
Gendarmes d'Élite d'Ordonnance, 104
general staffs: distinguishing uniforms, 121,
    167, 189, 189, 207, 216; Prussian concept
    of, 185
George IV, King of England, formerly
    Prince of Wales, 95, 125, 151
German states: employment of mercenaries
    from, 70, 73; unification, 146, 184–5;
    uniforms of 1848 revolutionaries, 133
Germany: army in period 1870–1914,
    184–92; in period since 1914, 228–32;
    see also Prussia
girdles, 90, 91, 105, 125
gloves, 23, 53, 90, 105, 124, 193, 219
gorgets: as officers' badge of rank, 30, 31,
    33, 49, 91, 167; embellishment with
    cyphers, 48; of pikemen, 23; trend
    towards abandonment, 67, 71, 154
greatcoats: Austrian, 176, 193–6, 227–8;
    British, 91, 125, 180, 211; French, 105,
    108, 158, 163, 167, 200; Italian, 176;
    Russian, 112, 138–9, 181–2, 202
Green (Scots) Brigade, 18, 23
grenades, introduction of, 28, 34
grenade pouches, 33, 34, 36; *see also*
    pouches
Grenadier Guards, British, 154–5, 177
grenadiers, grenadier regiments:
    introduction, development of, 28, 32–3,
    44; in period 1870–1914, 183; origin of
    caps, 23, 45, *see also* caps, helmets;
    Austrian, 37, 57, 124; British, 32–3, 45,
    94, 154; French, 32, 45, 82, 105–8, 155,
    167; German, 189; Prussian, 45, 87;
    Russian, 45, 90, 109–12
Grenadiers à Cheval, French, 105
grenz regiments, Austrian, 86, 147
Gribeauval, 43
grüngrau, 231
guards regiments: distinguished from 'line'
    regiments, 44; role in period 1870–1914,
    183–4; British, 71, 154; German, 192,
    230; Prussian, 142; Russian, 90–1, 203;
    see also Imperial Guard
Guards, 1st Russian, 223
guenille à Choiseul, 49; *see also* epaulettes
Gustavus Adolphus, King of Sweden, 18,
    19–20, 23

Gutta-Percha Talmas, 172
gymnasterka, 202, 223–6; *see also* shirts, tunics

habit-capote à la Polonaise, 166; *see also* coats, frock-coats
habit-veste, 83, 104, 105, 108; *see also* coats
haiduks, 56–7; *see also* caps
hair: powdering of, 44, 57, 75, 79, 91, 97, 109, 124; trends in length, 22, 31, 44, 60, 75, 79, 97, 105, 124, 169
halberds, 31, 34, 46
Haldane, Lord, 206
hammer hatchets, 33, 34
Handbook of the French Army, 227
Handbook of the German Army, 230
Hardee hats, 172, 219; *see also* hats, American
harquebusiers *see* horse, regiments of
hats: development of tricorne, 30, 45; in early seventeenth century, 22, 23; regulations on cocking of, 45, 97, 167; trend towards bicorne, 45, 82, worn by 1848 revolutionaries, 133, 147; American, 147, 172, 219–22; Austrian, 37, 83–6, 133, 193–6; British, 33, 45, 67–8, 71, 94–5, 125, 216–7; French, 82, 108, 167, 169; Italian, 176; Prussian, 36, 45, 61, 87; Russian, 75, 90, 91, 109; *see also* caps emblems, feathers, helmets *and under particular types of headwear*
haversacks *see* packs, soldiers'
Heavy Camel Regiment, 215
heavy cavalry: British, 94–5, 125, 133, 154, 177; French, 108, 197; Prussian, 121; *see also* cavalry, dragoons
helmets: *à chenille*, 86, 108, 112; *à la Tarleton*, 73, 82; adoption by dragoons, 60–1; in seventeenth century, 23, 31, 32, 34; trend towards spiked, 138–9, 143, 147, 154; American, 73, 173, 219–22; Austrian, 86, 124, 147, 196, 228; British, 68, 96, 125, 133, 154, 177, 207, 211, 214–7, 218, 222; French, 82, 108, 155, 158, 167, 200, 226–7; German, 188, 189–92, 230–1; Polish, 57; Prussian, 87, 121, 133, 142–3; Russian, 75, 112, 133, 138–9, 181, 223
Hepburn, Sir John, 18
Hesse Cassel *Jägers*, 70, 73
Highlanders, 93rd, 211
Holy Roman Empire *see* Austria, German States, Hungary, Italian States
Hompesch Hussars, 95
Honved, 147, 193–6
hoods, issue for winter wear, 71
horse artillery: Austrian, 196; French, 227; Prussian, 87; Russian, 223
horse grenadiers: British, 34; Russian, 139; *see also* dragoons, grenadiers
Horse Guards, British, 125
horse, regiments of: trends in dress, equipment, 23, 31–2, 53; British, 33–4; French, 32; Prussian, 184; Swedish, 20; *see also* cavalry *and under specialised types of mounted regiment*
Household Cavalry, British, 94, 125, 133, 143, 154, 177
Household Division, British, 125, 177
Howe, Lord, 66–7, 68
Hungarian regiments of Austrian Empire *see* Austria, Honved
Hungary: origins of hussars in, 25, 53; revolt of 1678, 36–7; revolt of 1848, 133, 146–7; uniforms of 1848 revolutionaries,

133, 147
hussars: origins 53–7; Austrian, 53, 56, 57, 86, 87, 124, 146–7, 184, 196; British, 56, 91, 95, 154–5, 177, 184; French, 56–7, 82, 83, 108, 158, 167, 184, 197–200; German, 192, 230; Prussian, 53, 57, 90, 121, 142–3; Russian, 53–4, 75, 90, 91, 112, 136–9, 184
Hussars, 11th British, 151
Hussars, 3rd German, 192

Imperial Guard, Napoleonic, 104–8
Imperial Guard, of Second French Empire, 197
Imperial Guard, Russian, 109, 139
India, British army in, 138
Indian Mutiny, 211
infantry: artillery used by, 20; in early seventeenth century, 23, 25; in eighteenth century, 38–53; in period 1870–1914, 183–4; strategic importance of fire power, 19–20, 40, 150, 206; trends in drilling, manoeuvring, 19–20, 28, 40–1, 43, 64–6, 70–1, 79, 95, 136–8, 150, 162, 166–7, 176, 206; American, 73, 74, 172–6, 219–22; Austrian, 37, 83–7, 124, 146, 147–50, 166–7, 193–6, 227–8; British, 32–3, 43, 66–7, 71, 94–7, 150–5, 177–81, 203–9, 211–7; French, 32, 43, 78–9, 79–82, 90, 105, 108, 155–8, 162, 163–9, 197–200, 226–7; German, 188–92, 230–1; Italian, 176; Prussian, 34–6, 40, 87–90, 121–4, 142–6; Russian, 44–5, 48, 74, 75–6, 109–21, 138–9, 202–3, 223–6; *see also* light infantry
Infantry Regiment, 28th French, 227
Iron Cross, Prussian, origins of, 121
iron ramrod, introduction of, 40
Italian states: Austrian influence on military dress, 133; campaign for unification, 162, 176
Italy, French influence on military dress, 176
Ivan IV ('the Terrible'), Tsar of Russia, 26

jackets: introduction of, 53, 57; American, 128, 169, 172, 173, 219–22; Austrian, 86–7, 147–50, 177, 227–8; British, 68, 71, 94, 95, 97, 154–5, 207, 214–7; French, 82, 105, 108, 155, 158, 163–9; German, 230; Polish, 105; Prussian, 90, 121, 142–3; Russian, 75, 91, 112–21, 223–6
Jägers regiments: absorption into British army, 95–6; Austrian and Tyrolean, 61, 124, 183, 193–6; German, 183, 188, 189, 230; Prussian, 61, 73, 87, 142, 143; Russian, 109, 112
James II, King of England, formerly Duke of York, 33
Jena, battle of, 87, 121
Jim Davis hats, 172; *see also* hats, American
joupans, 60; *see also* coats, jackets
jumpers, 211; *see also* tunics
justaucorps, 31, 32, 49; *see also* coats

kaftans, 25, 26, 31, 33, 36, 57, 60, 91, 121, 202
Kaiser Alexander Garde-Grenadière Regiment, 188
kalpaks, 56; *see also* caps
Kaputfrock, 87; *see also* coats
Kasketts, 61, 83–6, 87, 128, 163, 166, 172; *see also* helmets
képis, 133, 163, 166, 167, 172, 176, 180, 181, 193, 197, 202, 219, 226, 227–8

kettledrummers, 23
khaki, American, 222; British, 209, 210–7; French, 226–7; Russian, 222–3
Kiev Hussars, 11th, 139
Killicrankie, battle of, 28
kilts, 173, 211
King's German Legion, The, 124–5
King William's War, 63–4
King's American Dragoons, The, 73
Kitchener, Lord, 203–6
Kittel, 223; *see also* jackets
kiwers, 112, 132–3, 138, 202–3; *see also* caps, shakos
knapsacks *see* packs, soldiers'
knickerbockers, 200
Kollers, 230
Kolletts, 53, 75, 90, 91, 125, 142–3
Kossuth, Louis, 133, 146
kountouches, 57, 60
kurtkas, 75, 105, 108, 112, 125, 167; *see also* jackets

lacing *see* braiding
Lake George, battle of, 1755, 66
Lamarmora, General, 176
lancers: origins of dress, equipment, 57, 105; American, 173; Austrian, 86, 87, 124, 146–7, 196; British, 154, 177, 184; French, 105, 167; German, 230, 231; Polish, 121, 142–3; Russian, 75, 112, 136–9, 181
lances, 20, 25, 57, 60, 112, 184, 192
Landwehr: Austrian, 193–6, 227–8; Prussian, 121, 124, 142–3
lapels, lapel flaps: trends in, 48, 53; Austrian, 86–7; British, 49, 94, 125, 177; French, 83, 105, 108, 155; Prussian, 87–90; Russian, 112; *see also* braiding, coats
leggings, 31, 34, 67–8, 71, 222, 228; *see also* gaiters, puttees
legions, in army structure, 75, 158
Leopold of Anhalt-Dessau, Prince, 40
levée en masse, 121
Lexington, battle of, 70
Life Guards, British, 33, 33–4; 177; *see also* Household Cavalry
light artillery, American, 219
Light Brigade, charge of the, 155
light cavalry: origins, development, 53–7; Austrian, 53, 57, 61, 86; British, 56, 60–1, 125; French, 53, 56–7, 79, 197–200; Prussian, 53, 57, 61, 184; Russian, 53–6, 57–60, 112, 136–9; *see also* hussars, light dragoons
light column system, 163
light dragoons: origins, development, 56, 60–1; British, 94, 95, 125, 154, 177
Light Dragoons: 11th British, 126; 16th British, 71; 17th British, 71
light infantry: origins, development, 44, 61; British, 66–7, 71, 94, 207; Prussian, 87–90
Light Infantry, 80th (Gage's), 67, 68
light marching order, French, 163
Light Troops, British, 60–1
line regiments, distinguished from guards regiments, 44
litewkas, 124, 230; *see also* blouses, coats
Litzen see braiding
Lord Wentworth's Foot Guards, 32
Louis XIV, King of France, 27–8, 30, 34, 37
Louis Napoleon *see* Napoleon III
Louis-Philippe, King of France, 158
Louisburg, 64, 66, 68

Prepared by Brenda Hall, M.A., Registered Indexer of the Society of Indexers.

Säbeltasche für Husaren=Stabs=Officiere.

(Adjust. Vorschrift pag. 33.)